Meal Prep: 150 Quick and Easy Meal Prep Recipes

The Ultimate Meal Prepping Cookbook For Weight Loss and Clean Eating

Jeremy Stone

Elevate Publishing Limited

Table of contents

DINNER 113

SNACKS 151

Introduction

You have probably heard of a saying *"failing to prepare is preparing to fail"* and it can definitely apply to different aspects of our lives. Preparedness gives you the opportunity to be one step ahead in every challenge and your food and thereby health and wellbeing isn't the exception. Meal prepping is an effective and easy way to stay healthy and help you lose weight by having healthy choices available to you throughout the week. To find out more about meal prepping is about and what it entails, keep reading.

What is meal prepping?

If you're not really familiar with the term, meal prepping refers to planning and prepping your meals in advance for the entire week. This implies cooking items in a bulk and eating leftovers. If you have just rolled your eyes as soon as you read the word "leftover" you should bear in mind that practice of meal prepping is beneficial not only for your health but budget as well (more about that later).

Millions of people throughout the world have recognized the benefits of meal prepping and it became extremely popular in the United States as well. This practice of preparing foods for an entire week has become inseparable part of weight loss programs such as Weight Watchers or Ketogenic Diet. The reason is simple; meal prepping can help you stick with your diet plan and therefore achieve your weight loss goals!

Benefits of meal prepping

Meal prepping is popular due to the numerous benefits it offers. Are you thinking about doing the same? Well, if you're unsure then the following benefits will motivate you to start doing so!

- Saves time – This is the most important benefit of meal prepping. How many times have you wanted to start eating healthier foods, but you didn't have enough time to make meals yourself, so you ended up ordering a pizza? Yes, that happens to all of us. Meal prepping allows you to eat healthy meals throughout a week, without cooking every day after work.

- Less wasted food – Did you know that Americans waste about 40% of food and it's mostly in households and farms? If you take into account the cost of food you prepare, then add how much you waste on a weekly, monthly, and yearly basis, then you can safely conclude this is bad for your budget and for the environment as well. Meal prepping is all about portion control, choosing the right amount of ingredients, and eating all foods from the meal plan throughout the week.

- Healthier eating – in order to remain healthy one has to supply the body with a variety of vitamins, minerals, and other nutrients. For this, you have to eat different foods and, of course, they have to be healthy. Instead of munching on pizza and French fries every day, with meal prepping you can eat healthy foods that will deliver all those much-needed nutrients necessary for your overall health.

- Stress relief – you are familiar with this scenario; you're having a bad day at work and you come home only to change your clothes (sometimes not even that) and head to the kitchen to start cooking for your family. Stress from work coupled with exhaustion and frustration over what to cook can be too much. Don't you deserve some time to relax? Of course you do. That's why meal prepping is ideal for people who are on the go. When you're home from work you don't have to worry about what to cook because you have already prepared what to eat throughout a week. Now, you can just take your favorite book and read while sipping on some lemonade. Isn't that a better scenario?

- Avoids *"Mom, what's for dinner?"* questions – If you have kids, then you probably have to answer this question every single day. Sometimes you know the answer and say it and sometimes you don't. In the latter case, your child keeps asking what's for dinner until you figure it out. Let's face it: kids don't give up. When prepping meals for the week, you can just create a meal plan and post it onto a fridge. That way, your kids will always know what's for lunch or dinner, and you'll avoid your "favorite" question.

- **Saves money** – There is a popular belief that healthy eating habits are too expensive. But, that isn't necessarily correct. Do you go to the store every day to buy something to cook? And you still don't know what to prepare, so you buy a bunch of unhealthy items. This must be harmful for your budget. Meal prepping allows you to save money because planning meals prevents you from going to the store every day. Plus, shopping for this practice requires purchasing items in bulk, which is cheaper. If you're on a tight budget, or simply want to save money for something else, e.g. vacation, then meal planning is the perfect solution for you.

- **Easier shopping** – Meal prepping allows you to stay organized when it comes to shopping for groceries. You just have to know what to cook, plan ahead, and shop for ingredients. With a single trip to the supermarket, you can pick up everything you're going to need for that week or even a month.

- **More variety** – People are more likely to eat the same meals over and over again without the meal plan. The reason is simple: you like the meal, it's easy to prepare, and you make it whenever you can. But your body needs more diversity, as different food groups deliver different nutrients to your organism. When prepping meals, you get to introduce variety into your eating habits.

- **Multitask** – Are you a busy person with a hectic schedule? Meal prepping is ideal for you, and if you're about to ask *why,* then you should bear in mind that it will allow you to spend less time in the kitchen. This allows you to get organized better and accomplish more things at once.

- **More energy, less effort** – When you plan meals ahead, all you have to do is open the cooler, get a meal of your choice, and restore your energy levels. This will also boost your productivity.

Breakfast

Baked Sweet Potatoes and Tofu-Asparagus Scramble

Prep Time: 15 minutes; **Cook Time:** 30 minutes	

Serving Size: 201 g; **Serves:** 8; **Calories:** 144
Total Fat: 4 g **Saturated Fat:** 0.7 g; **Trans Fat:** 0 g
Protein: 6.5 g; **Net Carbs:** 17.6 g
Total Carbs: 22.6 g; **Dietary Fiber:** 5 g; **Sugars:** 8 g
Cholesterol: 0 mg; **Sodium:** 339 mg; **Potassium:** 626 mg;
Vitamin A: 34%; **Vitamin C:** 114%; **Calcium:** 10%; **Iron:** 27%

Ingredients:
For the baked sweet potato:
- 1 1/2 pounds sweet potato, cut into 1/2 -inch cubes (about 5-6 cups)
- 1 tablespoon olive oil
- 1/2 teaspoon salt
- 2 teaspoons chili powder

For the tofu scramble:
- 1 block extra firm tofu
- 2 cups asparagus, chopped
- 2 bell peppers, finely chopped
- 1/4 teaspoon pepper
- 1/2 teaspoon salt
- 1/2 red onion, finely chopped
- 1 teaspoon ground coriander
- 1 teaspoon cumin

For topping and serving (and/or):
- Avocado
- Cherry tomatoes
- Greek yogurt

Directions:
1. Preheat the oven to 425F.
2. Toss the sweet potatoes with the olive oil, salt, and chili powder.
3. Put the ingredients into a baking sheet. If the sweet potatoes won't fit in 1 baking sheet, use 2 pieces. Bake for 15 minutes; stir and bake for 15 to 20 minutes more or until the sweet potatoes are cooked through.
4. While the sweet potatoes are baking, mash the tofu using a potato masher until broken into small chunks.
5. Put the oil inside a large-sized nonstick pan and heat. When the oil is hot, add the bell peppers, onion, and asparagus; cook for about 5 minutes or more or until the veggies are soft.
6. Add the ground coriander, cumin, salt, pepper, and the tofu; cook for about 2 to 3 minutes or till the mixture is completely combined.
7. Divide the sweet potatoes and the tofu-asparagus scramble between 8 containers; store in the fridge for up to 4 days.

To serve: Take out needed servings. Put the content into a microwavable bowl; microwave for about 1 minute on MEDIUM or until heated through. Top with the suggested toppings.

Lentil and Zucchini Burritos

Prep Time: 30 minutes; **Cook Time:** 15 minutes		
Serving Size: 141 g; **Serves:** 6; **Calories:** 0303		
Total Fat: 14.4 g **Saturated Fat:** 7.2 g; **Trans Fat:** 0 g		
Protein: 18.8 g; **Net Carbs:** 16.2 g		
Total Carbs: 25.3 g; **Dietary Fiber:** 9.1 g; **Sugars:** 2.2 g		
Cholesterol: 152 mg; **Sodium:** 381 mg; **Potassium:** 416 mg;		
Vitamin A: 19; **Vitamin C:** 38%; **Calcium:** 26%; **Iron:** 17%		

Ingredients:

- 6 eggs
- 1 cup lentils, canned, drained and rinsed (I used brown)
- 1 cup zucchini, chopped
- 1/2 cup onion, chopped into small pieces (1/2 small onion)
- 1/2 tablespoon olive oil
- 1/2 teaspoon oregano
- 1/2 teaspoon salt
- 1/4 teaspoon pepper
- 1 bell pepper, chopped into small pieces
- 2 cups cheddar cheese, shredded
- 6 pieces (12-inch) tortillas

Directions:

1. Heat the oil in a frying pan on medium heat. Add the onion; cook for about 5 minutes or more or until translucent and soft.
2. Add the bell pepper and the zucchini; cook for about 5 minute or more or until cooked through and soft.
3. Meanwhile, beat the eggs with the oregano, salt, and pepper. Add the egg mix and the lentils into the pan; cook for about 3-4 minutes or till the eggs are cooked through.
4. Spread out about 1/2 cup of the filling into a tortilla and then sprinkle with about 1/3 cup of the cheddar cheese.
5. Roll the tortilla into a burrito; wrap with a plastic wrap until ready to serve. Repeat the process with the remaining filling, tortilla, and cheese.

To freeze: Individually wrap each burrito tightly with a plastic wrap; place Inside a large-sized ziplock bag. If storing for more than 1 to 2 weeks, individually wrap each burrito with aluminum foil before putting in a plastic bag.

To thaw: Transfer the burritos in the fridge; let thaw overnight. Alternatively, you can microwave them on a paper towel for about 30seconds each side. You can even crisp them in a frying pan or a George Foreman Grill

Stuffed Peppers

Prep Time: 10 minutes; Cook Time: 25 minutes	

Serving Size: 178 g; Serves: 8; Calories: 212	
Total Fat: 8.2 g Saturated Fat: 2.9 g; Trans Fat: 0 g	
Protein: 13.4 g; Net Carbs: 16.8 g	
Total Carbs: 21.4 g; Dietary Fiber: 4.6 g; Sugars: 4.3 g	
Cholesterol: 214 mg; Sodium: 405 mg; Potassium: 542 mg;	
Vitamin A: 61%; Vitamin C: 179%; Calcium: 09%; Iron: 15%	

Ingredients:
- 9 large eggs
- 4 large bell peppers, whatever color you like
- 1/4 teaspoon black pepper
- 1/3 cup cheese, shredded, plus more for topping if desired
- 1/2 cup spinach leaves, chopped
- 1/2 cup cooked quinoa
- 1/2 cup breakfast potatoes, fully cooked *
- 1 teaspoon salt
- 1/2 cup black beans

Directions:
1. Preheat the oven to 400F.
2. Cut the peppers lengthwise or widthwise into halves; remove the seeds. I suggest cutting widthwise so they will stand up better. Put in the baking sheet; bake for 5 minutes.
3. Crack the eggs inside a large-sized mixing bowl; beat using a fork.
4. Add the remaining ingredients; mix until well combined.
5. When baked, remove the peppers from the oven. Spoon the mixture into each pepper, evenly dividing the filling. Sprinkle the top with the cheese. Return to the oven; bake for about 20 minutes or till the eggs are set. Top with chopped herbs, if desired. Serve.

Notes: Store the stuffed peppers for up to 5 days in the fridge. When ready to serve, just reheat in the oven or in the microwave.

Sausage, Mushroom, and Spinach Casserole

Prep Time: 8 hours, 35 minutes; **Cook Time:** 1 hour, 20 minutes		

Serving Size: 127 g; **Serves:** 12; **Calories:** 229
Total Fat: 16.3 g **Saturated Fat:** 7 g; **Trans Fat:** 0 g
Protein: 13.7 g; **Net Carbs:** 5.3 g
Total Carbs: 6.8 g; **Dietary Fiber:** 1.5 g; **Sugars:** 2.3 g
Cholesterol: 183 mg; **Sodium:** 345 mg; **Potassium:** 272mg;
Vitamin A: 22%; **Vitamin C:** 45%; **Calcium:** 7%; **Iron:** 11%

Ingredients:

- 1 cup mushrooms, sliced
- 1 cup spinach, fresh
- 3/4 pound sausage, uncooked, casings removed
- 2 bell peppers, diced (any color you prefer; about 2 cups)
- 10 large eggs
- 1/2 medium yellow onion, diced
- 1/2 cup pepper jack cheese, shredded, divided
- 1/2 cup almond milk (or your preferred milk)
- 1 teaspoon minced garlic
- 1 teaspoon dried rosemary, optional, to give the sausage more flavor
- 4 slices whole-wheat bread, gluten free, day-old (or whole wheat, sourdough, white, etc.)
- Salt and fresh ground black pepper

Directions:

1. Put a large-sized skillet on medium heat. Grease with nonstick spray or drizzle with olive oil.
2. Put the sausage in the skillet; break up using a fork or a spatula. Stir in the rosemary; cook for about 6 to 7 minutes or till the sausages are browned.
3. Meanwhile, put another skillet on medium heat; grease with nonstick spray or drizzle with olive oil. If you're skillet is large enough to hold the sausages and the veggies, then you can add the veggies in the first skillet. Add the mushrooms, peppers, spinach, garlic, onion, and sprinkle of salt and pepper. Cook, stirring occasionally, for about 6-8 minutes or till the veggies are tender; set aside.
4. Generously grease a 13x9 baking pan. Break the bread into pieces; put in pan, spreading in an even layer.
5. Inside a large-sized bowl, whisk the eggs with the milk and 1/4 cup of the shredded cheese. Pour 1/2 of the egg mix over the bread layer in the baking dish. Top the bread with the sausages and the veggies. Pour the remaining egg mix over and then sprinkle with the remaining cheese; sprinkle with salt and pepper.
6. Cover the baking pan with an aluminum foil or plastic wrap; refrigerate for at least 2 hours or overnight or up to 24 hours. Let come to room temperature before baking.
7. Preheat the oven to 375F or 191C; remove the cover and bake for about 45-50 minutes or till the edges are crisp and the top is golden. The dish is ready when a toothpick come out clean when inserted in the center. Let cool for 10 minutes, then slice and serve. Serve with hot sauce, if desired.

Storing: This dish will keep for up to 5 days in the refrigerator. When ready to serve, just reheat in the microwave to your preference.

Freezing: You can prepare this dish up to layering the ingredients. Cover with a plastic wrap and then with aluminum foil; freeze for up to 3 months. When ready to bake, thaw in the fridge overnight and let come to room temperature. Bake according to instructions.

Notes: You can use ground beef, ground chicken, or ground turkey instead of sausages. For a vegetarian version, omit the meat and just add an extra cup of vegetables. You can also use smoked gouda, mozzarella, cheddar, or Swiss instead of pepper jack cheese.

Spinach, Mozzarella, and Egg Quesadillas

Prep Time: 10 minutes; **Cook Time:** 15 minutes			

Prep Time: 10 minutes; **Cook Time:** 15 minutes

Serving Size: 213 g; **Serves:** 5; **Calories:** 257

Total Fat: 14.8 g **Saturated Fat:** 5.9 g; **Trans Fat:** 0 g

Protein: 16.2 g; **Net Carbs:** 13.4 g

Total Carbs: 16.2 g; **Dietary Fiber:** 2.8 g; **Sugars:** 3.5 g

Cholesterol: 281 mg; **Sodium:** 470 mg; **Potassium:** 357 mg;

Vitamin A: 68%; **Vitamin C:** 63%; **Calcium:** 18%; **Iron:** 14%

Ingredients:

- 8 eggs
- 1 1/2 cup mozzarella cheese
- 1 red bell pepper
- 1/2 cup feta
- 1/2 red onion
- 1/4 cup milk
- 1/4 teaspoon pepper
- 1/4 teaspoon salt
- 2 teaspoons olive oil
- 4 handfuls spinach leaves
- 5 tortillas
- Spray oil

Directions:

1. Heat the olive oil Inside a large-sized nonstick pan on medium heat. Add the bell pepper and the onion; cook for about 4-5 minutes or till soft.
2. While cooking, whisk the eggs with the milk, salt, and pepper. Add the egg mix into the pan; cook, frequently stirring, until the eggs are almost cooked through.
3. Add the spinach and the feta; fold into the eggs, stirring, until the spinach is wilted and the eggs are cooked through. Remove the eggs from the heat.
4. Grease another large-sized nonstick pan with cooking spray; heat on medium.
5. Add the tortilla, then on 1/2 of the tortilla, spread about 1/2 of the egg mix and then top with about 1/3 cup of the mozzarella cheese. Fold the clear tortilla half over the topped part; cook for 2 minutes or till the bottom is golden brown. Flip the tortilla; cook for 1 minute or more or until the bottom is golden brown. Repeat the process with the remaining tortilla, filling, and cheese. Serve immediately.

Freezing: Put the quesadillas on a wire rack; let cool completely. Wrap with plastic wrap and store in a re-sealable container; refrigerate or freeze.

Reheating from fridge: Put the quesadillas on a nonstick frying pan; heat on medium heat until crisp. Alternatively, you can grill for them for about 2 to 3 minutes until crisp.

Reheating from freezer: Put the quesadillas on top of paper towel; microwave for about 30-60 seconds or until heated and then crisp in a frying pan or a grill.

Greek Spinach Quinoa Cheese Bowl

Prep Time: 10 minutes; **Cook Time:** 20 minutes		
Serving Size: 266 g; **Serves:** 6; **Calories:** 435		
Total Fat: 18.7 g **Saturated Fat:** 7.2 g; **Trans Fat:** 0 g		
Protein: 25 g; **Net Carbs:** 37.2 g		
Total Carbs: 42.5 g; **Dietary Fiber:** 5.3 g; **Sugars:** 4.1 g		
Cholesterol: 350 mg; **Sodium:** 624 mg; **Potassium:** 752 mg;		
Vitamin A: 65%; **Vitamin C:** 25%; **Calcium:** 24%; **Iron:** 29%		

Ingredients:

- ☐ 1 bag (5-ounce) baby spinach
- ☐ 1 cup feta cheese
- ☐ 1 pint cherry tomatoes, halved
- ☐ 2 cups quinoa, cooked
- ☐ 12 eggs
- ☐ 1/4 cup Greek yogurt, plain
- ☐ 1/2 teaspoon salt
- ☐ 1/2 teaspoon pepper
- ☐ 1 teaspoon onion powder
- ☐ 1 teaspoon olive oil
- ☐ 1 teaspoon granulated garlic

Directions:

1. Inside a large-sized bowl, whisk the eggs with the yogurt, granulated garlic, onion powder, salt, and pepper; set aside.
2. Heat the olive oil Inside a large-sized skillet. Add the spinach; cook for about 3 to 4 minutes or till slightly wilted.
3. Add the cherry tomatoes; cook for about 3 to 4 minutes or till soft.
4. Stir the egg mixture in the skillet; cook, stirring, for about 7 to 9 minutes or till set.
5. When set, stir in the quinoa and the feta cheese; cook until heated through. Serve hot.

Notes: Make this dish ahead of time. Store in the fridge or portion out and freeze. When ready to serve, heat in the microwave or in the stove.

Swiss Cheesy Quinoa, Mushroom, and Sundried Tomatoes Egg Muffin

Prep Time: 10 minutes; **Cook Time:** 30 minutes	
Serving Size: 58 g; **Serves:** 12; **Calories:** 127	
Total Fat: 5.6 g **Saturated Fat:** 2.4 g; **Trans Fat:** 0 g	
Protein: 7.7 g; **Net Carbs:** 10.2 g	
Total Carbs: 11.6 g; **Dietary Fiber:** 1.4 g; **Sugars:** 1.4 g	
Cholesterol: 90 mg; **Sodium:** 2147mg; **Potassium:** 219 mg;	
Vitamin A: 4%; **Vitamin C:** 2%; **Calcium:** 9%; **Iron:** 8%	

Ingredients:
- 6 eggs
- 1 cup mushrooms, sliced
- 1 cup quinoa, cooked
- 1 cup Swiss cheese, shredded (1/4 cup reserved for tops)
- 1/2 cup sundried tomatoes, drained and then chopped
- 1/2 onion
- 1/4 teaspoon pepper
- 1/4 teaspoon salt

Directions:
1. Preheat the oven to 350F.
2. Inside a large-sized bowl, whisk the eggs with the salt and the pepper. Stir in the remaining ingredients.
3. Line a standard-sized muffin pan with silicone muffin liners. Spoon the mixture into the muffin cups, dividing the mix evenly.
4. Sprinkle the tops with the reserved cheese and bake for about 20 to 25 minutes or till a knife come out clean when inserted in the center of the muffin.

Freezing: Wrap each muffin with plastic wrap and then store in a re-sealable container. When ready to serve; microwave for about 30 seconds to 1 minute, heating in increments to prevent burning, until heated.

Flavor Variations:
Broccoli and cheddar:
Replace the mushrooms, onions, and the sundried tomatoes with 1 1/2 cups small broccoli florets and replace the Swiss cheese with cheddar cheese.

Zucchini, feta, and dill:
Replace the mushrooms and the sundried tomatoes with 1 cup shredded zucchini (let it dry on a paper towel for 10 min first) and then replace 3/4 cup Swiss cheese with crumbled feta (sprinkle the tops with 1/4 cup cheddar or mozzarella cheese). Replace the salt and pepper with 1 teaspoon dried dill.

Baked Spinach, Artichoke, and Feta

Prep Time: 20 minutes; **Cook Time:** 32-25 minutes, plus 8-10 minutes standing

Serving Size: 148 g; **Serves:** 8; **Calories:** 132	
Total Fat: 7.5 g **Saturated Fat:** 3.2 g; **Trans Fat:** 0 g	
Protein: 11.9 g; **Net Carbs:** 3.5 g	
Total Carbs: 5.4 g; **Dietary Fiber:** 1.9 g; **Sugars:** 1.9 g	
Cholesterol: 195 mg; **Sodium:** 616 mg; **Potassium:** 408 mg;	
Vitamin A: 77%; **Vitamin C:** 30%; **Calcium:** 15%; **Iron:** 14%	

Ingredients:

- 8 large eggs
- 4 large egg whites
- 3/4 cup artichokes, chopped (from can), drained and then patted dry (about 126 g)
- 1 package (10-ounce) chopped spinach, fresh or frozen, thawed if frozen, all excess liquid squeezed out
- 1 tablespoon fresh dill, chopped
- 1/2 cup feta cheese, crumbled
- 1/2 cup scallions, finely chopped
- 1/3 cup red pepper, diced
- 1/4 cup fat-free milk
- 1/4 teaspoon ground pepper
- 2 tablespoons parmesan cheese, grated
- 1 clove garlic, minced
- 1 1/4 teaspoon kosher salt

Directions:

1. Preheat the oven to 375F. Grease a 13x9 baking dish with oil. Grease a casserole dish with nonstick cooking spray.
2. In a small-sized bowl, combine the artichoke, spinach, scallion, red pepper, dill, and garlic; pour into the casserole, spreading the mix evenly.
3. In another bowl, whisk the eggs with the egg whites, parmesan, milk, salt, and pepper. Mix in the feta and then pour the mix over the veggies; bake for about 32-35 minutes or till a knife come out clean when inserted in the center of the bake. Let the bake stand for about 8-10 minutes and then cut into 8 portions.

Notes: you can prepare the ingredients, assemble the casserole a day before, and have it ready to bake in the morning. You can reheat the bakes throughout the week.

Apple-Maple Breakfast Oats

Prep Time: 5 minutes; **Cook Time:** 25 minutes		

Serving Size: 169 g; **Serves:** 6; **Calories:** 118
Total Fat: 4.3 g **Saturated Fat:** 0 g; **Trans Fat:** 0 g
Protein: 2 g; **Net Carbs:** 15.9 g
Total Carbs: 18.7 g; **Dietary Fiber:** 2.8 g; **Sugars:** 9.4 g
Cholesterol: 0 mg; **Sodium:** 5 mg; **Potassium:** 126 mg;
Vitamin A: 0%; **Vitamin C:** 4%; **Calcium:** 2%; **Iron:** 5%

Ingredients:

- 1 cup steel cut oats
- 1 cup unsweetened applesauce
- 1 large apple, cut into small pieces
- 1 teaspoon ground cinnamon
- 1/2 teaspoon ground cardamom
- 2 teaspoons maple extract
- 3 cups water

After cooking:

- 1/3 cup chopped pecans
- 2 tablespoons maple syrup (or more to taste)

Directions:

1. In a medium pot, put all of the ingredients; stir to combine.
2. Bring the mixture to a boil. When boiling, reduce the heat, cover, and simmer, occasionally stirring, for about 20 to 35 minutes or till the oats are al dente.
3. If you want softer oatmeal, cook longer and, if needed, add cooking liquid.

Notes: If making ahead of time, cook the oats al dente since they will soften as they sit. You can keep this in the fridge for up to 4 days. When ready to serve, add additional liquid or milk, if desired; microwave at 80% for 1 minute, until heated.

Freezing: You can pour the oatmeal into silicone muffin liner lined muffin trays, freeze, and when frozen, put them in a ziplock bag and store in the fridge for up to 3 months. When ready to serve, thaw in the fridge and reheat.

Berry, Quinoa, Banana, and Oats Bake

Prep Time: 20 minutes; **Cook Time:** 60 minutes, plus 45-60 minutes cooling		
Serving Size: 152 g; Serves: 9; Calories: 250		
Total Fat: 14.9 g Saturated Fat: 11.8 g; Trans Fat: 0 g		
Protein: 5.2 g; Net Carbs: 22.7 g		
Total Carbs: 27.1 g; Dietary Fiber: 4.4 g; Sugars: 10.8 g		
Cholesterol: 41 mg; Sodium: 25 mg; Potassium: 400 mg;		
Vitamin A: 2%; Vitamin C: 18%; Calcium: 3%; Iron: 12%		

Ingredients:

- ☐ 3 bananas, medium, very ripe, sliced
- ☐ 2 large eggs
- ☐ 1 1/2 cup blueberries, washed and drained
- ☐ 1/2 cup raspberries, washed and drained
- ☐ 2 cups almond milk (or milk of choice)
- ☐ 1/2 cup steel cut oats, uncooked
- ☐ 1/2 cup quinoa, uncooked
- ☐ 1/2 teaspoon cinnamon
- ☐ 1 teaspoon pure vanilla extract
- ☐ 1-2 tablespoon maple syrup, skip if adding sweetened protein powder
- ☐ 1/4 cup unsweetened coconut flakes, toasted, optional
- ☐ 1 scoop protein powder, optional
- ☐ Cooking spray (I use Misto)
- ☐ Dash salt
- ☐ Non-fat Greek yogurt, for topping, optional

Directions:

1. Rinse the oats and the quinoa under running cold water about 3 times or until the water runs clear; drain well and set aside. Prepare the fruits and set aside.
2. If using, toast the coconut in a small-sized skillet over low to medium heat or in the oven at 375F until golden brown; carefully cooking or watching to prevent burning. Set aside.
3. In a medium-sized mixing bowl, whisk the eggs or the egg whites with the milk, salt, vanilla, cinnamon, and, if using, the maple syrup and protein powder; set aside.
4. Preheat the oven to 375F.
5. Grease an 8x8 baking dish with the cooking spray.
6. In an even single layer, lay the banana slices, raspberries, and the blueberries in the bottom of the baking dish.
7. With a spatula, spread the oats and the quinoa on top of the fruit layer. Top the oat and quinoa layer with remaining banana slices and berries.
8. Slowly pour the egg mix in the corner of the baking dish, making sure you do not disturb the set up. If you abruptly pour the liquid in the middle of the layers, the fruits may float on top. The fruits and the sweetness need to be evenly distributed.
9. If using, sprinkle the top with the toasted coconut and then bake, uncovered, for 60 minutes.
10. When baked, remove from the oven; let cool and set for about 45 to 60 minutes. Cut into 9 portions and serve hot, warm, or cold. If desired, top with a dollop of fat-free Greek yogurt.

Notes: If baking ahead of time, let cool and set completely, cover, and keep in the fridge for up to 5-6 days.

For a vegan version, use flax egg replacer instead of eggs.

Banana Zucchini Oatmeal Cups

Prep Time: 15 minutes; **Cook Time:** 22 minutes		

Serving Size: 108 g; **Serves:** 12; **Calories:** 174		
Total Fat: 7.2 g **Saturated Fat:** 2.7 g; **Trans Fat:** 0 g		
Protein: 5 g; **Net Carbs:** 20.1 g		
Total Carbs: 24.2 g; **Dietary Fiber:** 4.1 g; **Sugars:** 4.8 g		
Cholesterol: 0 mg; **Sodium:** 58 mg; **Potassium:** 468 mg;		
Vitamin A: 2%; **Vitamin C:** 14%; **Calcium:** 9%; **Iron:** 10%		

Ingredients:

- ☐ 3 over-ripe bananas, medium-large
- ☐ 3 cups oats, old-fashioned (use gluten-free, if necessary)
- ☐ 2 tablespoon ground flaxseed or chia seeds PLUS 6 tablespoon water (alternatively, you can use 2 eggs)
- ☐ 2 zucchini, small-medium, grated (don't squeeze water out)
- ☐ 1/4 teaspoon salt
- ☐ 1/4 cup pure maple syrup, optional for sweetness
- ☐ 1/4 cup almond butter (or peanut butter)
- ☐ 1/2 cup almond milk (any milk will work)
- ☐ 1 teaspoon vanilla extract
- ☐ 1 teaspoon cinnamon
- ☐ 1 tablespoon baking powder
- ☐ Cooking spray

Optional add-ins:
- ☐ 1/4 cup chocolate chips and/or walnuts

Directions:

1. Preheat the oven to 375F. Grease a muffin tin with the cooking spray or with a coconut oil. Alternatively, you can line with silicone muffin liners.
2. Put the flax and the water into a small-sized bowl; set aside until "gel".
3. Put the almond butter and the maple syrup into another small microwavable bowl; microwave for about 20-30 seconds and then stir to combine.
4. Put the bananas inside a large-sized bowl; mash using a fork. Add the zucchini, almond, milk, almond butter-maple syrup mix, vanilla, and flax; stir to combine.
5. Add the oats, the baking powder, salt, cinnamon, and choice of add ins; stir till just combined.
6. Spoon the mix into the prepared muffin cups, filling the muffins to the top; bake for about 22 to 25 minutes.

Notes: Let the oatmeal cups cool completely. Store in airtight containers and keep refrigerated or freeze. If you have any leftover batter, pour into a small-sized baking dish and make it into a breakfast bake.

Berry Quinoa Almond Breakfast

Prep Time: 5 minutes; Cook Time: 15 minutes		
Serving Size: 319 g; Serves: 4; Calories: 574		
Total Fat: 34.7 g Saturated Fat: 25.9 g; Trans Fat: 0 g		
Protein: 11 g; Net Carbs: 47.6 g		
Total Carbs: 59.2 g; Dietary Fiber: 11.6 g; Sugars: 20.2 g		
Cholesterol: 0 mg; Sodium: 21 mg; Potassium: 802 mg;		
Vitamin A: 0%; Vitamin C: 56%; Calcium: 9%; Iron:28%		

Ingredients:

- ☐ 1 cup quinoa
- ☐ 4 tablespoons almonds, sliced
- ☐ 4 cups mixed berries
- ☐ 2 tablespoons sugar-free maple syrup
- ☐ 2 cups almond milk (regular, not unsweetened)
- ☐ 1/4 teaspoon ground cardamom
- ☐ 1/2 teaspoon ground cinnamon

Directions:

1. In a medium-sized pot, combine the quinoa with the milk, cardamom, and cinnamon; bring the mixture to a boil. When boiling, reduce the heat; simmer for about 15 minutes or more or until the quinoa is cooked through.
2. When cooked, let the quinoa mix cool. Stir in the maple syrup and then divide between 4 containers. To assemble, top the quinoa with 1 cup of fruit and then sprinkle with 1 tablespoon almonds into microwavable containers that can hold the quinoa, fruits, and almonds.

Notes: Make these ahead of time and store in this breakfast in fridge. To reheat, just add a little almond milk, stir, and then microwave at 80% until slightly heated.

28

Baked Apple Cinnamon Oatmeal

Prep Time: 8 minutes; **Cook Time:** 40 minutes	
Serving Size: 175 g; **Serves:** 8; **Calories:** 315	
Total Fat: 15.3 g **Saturated Fat:** 10.5 g; **Trans Fat:** 0 g	
Protein: 0 g; **Net Carbs:** 32.8 g	
Total Carbs: 40.6 g; **Dietary Fiber:** 7.8 g; **Sugars:** 9.2 g	
Cholesterol: 70 mg; **Sodium:** 37 mg; **Potassium:** 419 mg;	
Vitamin A: 2%; **Vitamin C:** 8%; **Calcium:** 7%; **Iron:** 17%	

Ingredients:

- ☐ 3 3/4 cups rolled oats (use gluten free, if necessary)
- ☐ 2 medium apples, peeled, cored and diced into 1/4 inch pieces
- ☐ 3 large eggs, room temperature
- ☐ 3/4 cup unsweetened applesauce
- ☐ 1/4 teaspoon allspice
- ☐ 1/3 cup sugar-free maple syrup
- ☐ 1 teaspoon pure vanilla extract
- ☐ 1 teaspoon ground flax seeds
- ☐ 1 teaspoon baking powder
- ☐ 1 tablespoon ground cinnamon
- ☐ 1 1/2 cups almond milk (or any other milk of your choice)
- ☐ 1/2 cup berries, fresh or frozen (I used blackberries and blueberries), optional

Serving options (and/or):
- ☐ Maple syrup
- ☐ Milk of choice
- ☐ Mixed fruit
- ☐ Nuts
- ☐ Toasted coconut

Directions:

1. Preheat the oven to 350F. Lightly grease a 13x9 baking pan or casserole; set aside.
2. Inside a large-sized bowl, whisk the eggs with the mil until combined. Add the applesauce, vanilla, maple syrup, allspice, cinnamon, and baking powder. Stir in the oats and then fold in the chunks of apple.
3. Evenly spread the batter into the prepared pan and then top with your choice of berries; bake for about 35-40 minutes or till the center is no longer jiggly and the top is golden.
4. When baked, remove from the oven. If desired, top with extra maple syrup and berries. Toasted walnuts and pecans is a great topping as well.

Notes: Make ahead of time, store in a covered container, and keep in the fridge for up to 3 days. Prepare on a Sunday and you have a quick breakfast for the weekdays.

Banana Strawberry Oatmeal Bake

Prep Time: 15 minutes; **Cook Time:** 35-40 minutes, plus 5 minutes standing

Serving Size: 193 g; **Serves:** 8; **Calories:** 246	
Total Fat: 5.8 g **Saturated Fat:** 1.9 g; **Trans Fat:** 0 g	
Protein: 10.1 g; **Net Carbs:** 34.7 g	
Total Carbs: 40.8 g; **Dietary Fiber:** 6.1 g; **Sugars:** 8.4 g	
Cholesterol: 48 mg; **Sodium:** 209 mg; **Potassium:** 390 mg;	
Vitamin A: 2%; **Vitamin C:** 29%; **Calcium:** 17%; **Iron:** 12%	

Ingredients:

- ☐ 4 cups oats, old-fashioned
- ☐ 3 cups milk (any choice)
- ☐ 2 eggs
- ☐ 2 teaspoons vanilla extract
- ☐ 1 1/2 cups strawberries, chopped plus more for serving
- ☐ 1 cup ripe banana, mashed (about 3 medium)
- ☐ 1 teaspoon baking powder
- ☐ 1 teaspoon cinnamon
- ☐ 1/2 teaspoon salt
- ☐ 1/4 cup sugar-free maple syrup

Directions:

1. Preheat the oven to 350F. Lightly grease a 13x9-inch baking dish.
2. Inside a large-sized bowl, whisk the mashed banana with the milk, eggs, vanilla, maple syrup, salt, cinnamon, and baking powder. Stir the oats into the mix and then the strawberries until combined.
3. Carefully pour the mix into the baking dish; bake for about 35 to 40 minutes or till the oatmeal is set and a toothpick comes out mostly clean than wet when inserted in the center.
4. Remove from the oven and let stand for 5 minutes. Top with extra strawberries, if desired. Serve.

Notes: Make ahead of time and store in the fridge for up to 3 days. To reheat, just put a serving size into a microwavable bowl. Pour a little milk in and microwave until hot, breaking the oatmeal using a spoon as needed. Serve with desired topping.

Zucchini Apple Oat Waffles

Prep Time: 15 minutes; **Cook Time:** 2-3 minutes per waffle		
Serving Size: 114 g; **Serves:** 4; **Calories:** 242		
Total Fat: 17.5 g **Saturated Fat:** 5.2 g; **Trans Fat:** 0 g		
Protein: 8.9 g; **Net Carbs:** 11.5 g		
Total Carbs: 15.2 g; **Dietary Fiber:** 3.7 g; **Sugars:** 4.1 g		
Cholesterol: 78 mg; **Sodium:** 342 mg; **Potassium:** 415 mg;		
Vitamin A: 6%; **Vitamin C:** 4%; **Calcium:** 18%; **Iron:** 9%		

Ingredients:

- 3 eggs
- 2 teaspoons baking powder
- 1/2 teaspoon salt
- 1/2 teaspoon nutmeg
- 1/2 teaspoon baking soda
- 1/2 cup zucchini, shredded
- 1/2 cup apple, shredded
- 1 teaspoon cinnamon
- 1 cup oats, old-fashioned
- 1 1/2 cups low fat buttermilk
- 1 1/2 cups almond flour
- 4 tablespoons butter, melted

Directions:

1. Inside a large-sized bowl, whisk the oats with the flour, baking soda, baking powder, cinnamon, salt, and nutmeg.
2. Add the buttermilk, eggs, and melted butter; whisk until the mixture is well combined.
3. Stir in the apple and the zucchini.
4. Cook the batter in a Belgian waffle maker until golden and crisp. Serve immediately with butter and maple syrup or honey, or with poached egg. I love to serve mine with honey and freshly sliced apples.

Notes: The batter can be made a night before; just store in the fridge. You can also freeze a batch. When ready to serve, just heat in the toaster.

Crispy Sweet Potato Waffles

Prep Time: 20 minutes; **Cook Time:** 10 minutes

Serving Size: 166 g; **Serves:** 4; **Calories:** 366		
Total Fat: 25.1 g **Saturated Fat:** 3.4 g; **Trans Fat:** 0 g		
Protein: 8.7 g; **Net Carbs:** 0 g		
Total Carbs: 29.9 g; **Dietary Fiber:** 4.1 g; **Sugars:** 6.4 g		
Cholesterol: 45 mg; **Sodium:** 672 mg; **Potassium:** 587 mg;		
Vitamin A: 113%; **Vitamin C:** 6%; **Calcium:** 24%; **Iron:** 13%		

Ingredients:

- 1 cup sweet potato puree (about 2 1/2 cups of 1/2-inch cubes sweet potatoes)
- 1 egg
- 1 teaspoon salt
- 1/3 cup cornmeal
- 1/4 cup oil
- 2 teaspoons baking powder
- 3/4 cup almond flour
- 3/4 cup milk

Directions:

1. Steam the sweet potato cubes for about 10 minutes or till soft; using a hand mixer, blend or mash until smooth.
2. Combine the sweet potato puree with the egg, milk, and oil; mix until well combined.
3. In another bowl, combine the flour with the baking powder, cornmeal, and salt. Add the wet ingredients into the dry ingredients; mix until just combined.
4. Cook the batter into a greased waffle maker for about 3 to 4 minutes or till cooked through. Serve immediately or, if not serving right away, let cool completely.

Freezing: When the waffles are completely cooled, individually wrap in plastic bags or plastic wraps. Put the individual portions inside a large-sized ziplock freezer bag. When ready to serve, put the frozen waffles into the toaster; toast until heated through and crisp.

Notes: Vegetable or coconut oil makes the waffles crispy. You can substitute the oil with applesauce but the waffles will not crisp. Be careful when cooking to prevent them from burning.

Topping suggestions:

- Avocado, pepitas, and corn (with sea salt)
- Almond butter, shredded coconut, and hemp seeds
- Yogurt, almonds, berries, and cinnamon
- Poached egg

Breakfast Eggs and Bacon Burritos

Prep Time: 5 minutes; **Cook Time:** 10 minutes

Serving Size: 176 g; **Serves:** 4; **Calories:** 279
Total Fat: 16 g **Saturated Fat:** 4.4 g; **Trans Fat:** 0.2 g
Protein: 17.7 g; **Net Carbs:** 13.4 g
Total Carbs: 16.3 g; **Dietary Fiber:** 2.9 g; **Sugars:** 4.3 g
Cholesterol: 335 mg; **Sodium:** 406 mg; **Potassium:** 317 mg;
Vitamin A: 27%; **Vitamin C:** 66%; **Calcium:** 9%; **Iron:** 14%

Ingredients:

- ☐ 8 eggs, large
- ☐ 4 piece bacon, thick-cut, cooked until crispy
- ☐ 4 Multi Grain with Flax flatbreads (I used Flatout Flatbreads)
- ☐ 1 tablespoon garlic, minced
- ☐ 1 tablespoon extra-virgin olive oil
- ☐ 1 red pepper, finely minced
- ☐ 1/2 red onion, finely minced
- ☐ Salt and pepper, to taste
- ☐ Splash milk

Directions:

1. Put the olive oil and the minced garlic into a medium-sized saucepan. Turn the heat to medium high; cook until the oil is heated.
2. Inside a large-sized bowl, whisk the eggs with a splash of milk; set aside.
3. Add the onion and the red pepper into the saucepan; sauté for a couple of minutes or till the onions start to become translucent.
4. Add the egg mix into the saucepan; sauté for about 3 to 5 minutes or till cooked.
5. Put 1/4 of the egg mix and 1 piece of cooked bacon on top of the bread. Sprinkle with cheese. Wrap tightly and enjoy.

Notes: Make this ahead of time and you have a quick protein-packed delicious burritos for breakfast.

7-Ingredient Waffles

Prep Time: 15 minutes; **Cook Time:** 15 minutes	

Serving Size: 99 g; **Serves:** 6; **Calories:** 268
Total Fat: 23.4 g **Saturated Fat:** 2.4 g; **Trans Fat:** 0 g
Protein: 7 g; **Net Carbs:** 8.2 g
Total Carbs: 13.6 g; **Dietary Fiber:** 5.4 g; **Sugars:** 1.2 g
Cholesterol: 0 mg; **Sodium:** 78 mg; **Potassium:** 194 mg;
Vitamin A: 0%; **Vitamin C:** 0%; **Calcium:** 19%; **Iron:** 9%

Ingredients:
For the waffles:

- Heaping 1/2 cup gluten free rolled oats
- 1/4 cup sugar-free maple syrup
- 1/4 cup olive, canola or melted coconut oil
- 1 3/4 cups almond flour
- 1 1/4 cup unsweetened almond milk + 1 teaspoon white or apple cider vinegar
- 1 1/2 teaspoon baking powder
- Pinch sea salt

Optional add-ins:

- 1 tablespoon flax seed meal
- 1 teaspoon vanilla extract
- 1/2 teaspoon cinnamon
- 1/4 cup bananas, chopped (or other fresh fruit)
- 1/4 cup chocolate chips, dairy-free

Directions:
1. In a small-sized mixing bowl, combine the almond milk with the vinegar; let sit for a couple of minutes to activate or curdle. Add the olive oil and the agave nectar or the maple syrup; whisk to combine and set aside.
2. Put all the dry ingredients inside a large-sized mixing bowl; whisk until well combined. Add the wet ingredients into the dry ingredients mix; mix until well incorporated. Test the batter for flavor and sweetness. If desired, add more vanilla extract or sweetener or agave. Let the batter stand for 5 minutes while you preheat your waffle iron. I set my waffle iron to 4 for crispy waffles. Adjust heat to your preference.
3. When the waffle iron is ready, generously coat with non-stick spray. Pour about 1/2 cup batter into the waffle iron; cook according to the manufacturer's instructions. Transfer into a baking rack in a 200F oven to keep warm. Do not stack the waffles. Keep them in a single layer instead to retain the crispiness.
4. Serve immediately with your desired toppings, such as maple syrup or fresh berry-cherry compote.

Notes: Make ahead of time and store in a freezer bag for up to a couple of months. When ready to serve, reheat in the toaster. I split mine in half and then heat them in the toaster. Alternatively, you can heat them in a 400F oven until warmed through and golden brown.

Walnut Apricot Bars

Prep Time: 15 minutes; Cook Time: 0 minutes

Serving Size: 51 g; **Serves**: 6; **Calories**: 171	
Total Fat: 12.7 g **Saturated Fat**: 0.7 g; **Trans Fat**: 0 g	
Protein: 5.6 g; **Net Carbs**: 9.4 g	
Total Carbs: 12.1 g; **Dietary Fiber**: 2.7 g; **Sugars**: 8.6 g	
Cholesterol: 0 mg; **Sodium**: 1 mg; **Potassium**: 188 mg;	
Vitamin A: 6%; **Vitamin C**: 14%; **Calcium**: 2%; **Iron**: 16%	

Ingredients:
- ☐ 1 cup walnuts
- ☐ 1 lemon, zested
- ☐ 1 tablespoon chia seeds
- ☐ 1 tablespoon hemp seeds
- ☐ 1 tablespoon lemon juice
- ☐ 1/2 cup dried apricot
- ☐ 1/4 cup goji berries
- ☐ 4 dates, pits removed, softened in water for 10 mins

Directions:
1. Soak the dates in warm water for about 10 minutes or till softened a bit; drain the water.
2. Put all the ingredients into a food processor; process until almost smooth, but not completely.
3. Pour the mixture into a baking tray; freeze for about 10-15 minutes or till set.
4. Cut into bars and store in the fridge.

Apple Pecan Hemp Hearts Granola

Prep Time: 5 minutes; **Cook Time:** 35 minutes	
Serving Size: 72 g; **Serves:** 10; **Calories:** 284	
Total Fat: 20.7 g **Saturated Fat:** 6.3 g; **Trans Fat:** 0 g	
Protein: 5.7 g; **Net Carbs:** 17.6 g	
Total Carbs: 23.3 g; **Dietary Fiber:** 5.7 g; **Sugars:** 2.8 g	
Cholesterol: 0 mg; **Sodium:** 5 mg; **Potassium:** 190 mg;	
Vitamin A: 0%; **Vitamin C:** 1%; **Calcium:** 3%; **Iron:** 9%	

Ingredients:
- 3 cups rolled oats (gluten-free if necessary)
- 1/4 cup coconut oil, melted
- 1/3 cup sugar-free maple syrup
- 1/2 cup unsweetened dried apple rings, chopped
- 1/2 cup unsweetened applesauce
- 1/2 cup hemp seeds
- 1 teaspoon vanilla extract
- 1 teaspoon cinnamon
- 1 1/2 cups pecans, chopped
- 1 egg white, whipped, optional

Directions:
1. Preheat the oven to 350F.
2. Inside a large-sized bowl, combine the oats with the hemp hearts, pecans, and cinnamon.
3. Add the applesauce, coconut oil, vanilla extract, honey, and egg white; stir until the well combined and the oat is well coated.
4. Line a baking sheet with a silicone mat or parchment paper. Spread the granola into the baking sheet; bake for 15 minutes.
5. Remove the baking sheet from the oven. Flip the granola as well as you can. Return the baking sheet into the oven; bake for 15 to 20 minutes more.
6. Remove the baking sheet from the oven; let the granola cool completely inside the baking sheet. When cool, add the dried apple rings.

Notes: Store the granola into airtight container and keep for up to 2 weeks.

Baked Almond Dark Chocolate Oatmeal

Prep Time: 10 minutes; **Cook Time:** 35 minutes

Serving Size: 139 g; **Serves:** 6; **Calories:** 241		
Total Fat: 12.9 g **Saturated Fat:** 5.1 g; **Trans Fat:** 0 g		
Protein: 6.6 g; **Net Carbs:** 22 g		
Total Carbs: 26.7 g; **Dietary Fiber:** 4.7 g; **Sugars:** 6.2 g		
Cholesterol: 31 mg; **Sodium:** 68 mg; **Potassium:** 269 mg;		
Vitamin A: 1%; **Vitamin C:** 2%; **Calcium:** 17%; **Iron:** 11%		

Ingredients:

- ☐ 1 1/2 ounces dark chocolate, 70%, roughly chopped OR 1/4 cup chocolate chips
- ☐ 1 1/2 tablespoons coconut oil, melted and slightly cooled
- ☐ 1 3/4 cup unsweetened almond milk
- ☐ 1 3/4 cups rolled oats (gluten free, if desired)
- ☐ 1 large egg
- ☐ 1 teaspoon baking powder
- ☐ 1 teaspoon cinnamon
- ☐ 1/2 cup ripe banana, mashed (about 1 large ripe banana)
- ☐ 1/2 cup salted almonds, roughly chopped
- ☐ 1/4 teaspoon almond extract
- ☐ 2 teaspoons vanilla extract
- ☐ Coarse sea salt, for sprinkling on top

For sprinkling on top:
- ☐ Chopped salted almonds
- ☐ Banana slices

Directions:

1. Preheat the oven to 350F. Grease a 9-inch baking dish and 9-inch skillet with non-stick cooking spray or oil.
2. Inside a large-sized bowl, whisk the oats with the baking powder, chopped almonds, and the cinnamon.
3. In another bowl, mix the mashed banana with the egg, almond milk, coconut oil, almond extract, and vanilla until well combined.
4. Add the wet ingredients into the dry ingredients; mix to combine. Pour the mix into the prepared dish or skillet; smooth the top. Sprinkle the chocolate chunks or chips ove the top; baker for about 32 to 37 minutes or till the edges start to turn slightly golden brown. If desired, top with bananas, sprinkle with sea salt, and chopped almonds before baking. Serve warm with almond milk.

Notes: Divide into 6 individual containers and store in the refrigerator. When ready to serve, add 1-2 tablespoons milk and reheat in the microwave. For a vegan version, use 1 flax egg (1 tablespoon flax seed meal mixed with 3 tablespoons water) instead of egg.

Sausage and Kale Waffle Stratta

Prep Time: 30 minutes; **Cook Time:** 45 minutes-1 hour, 10 minutes sitting

Serving Size: 237 g; **Serves:** 6; **Calories:** 525	

Total Fat: 41.4g **Saturated Fat:** 10.8 g; **Trans Fat:** 0 g
Protein: 31.2 g; **Net Carbs:** 0 g
Total Carbs: 9.3 g; **Dietary Fiber:** 3.3 g; **Sugars:** 1.5 g
Cholesterol: 421 mg; **Sodium:** 961 mg; **Potassium:** 640 mg;
Vitamin A: 113%; **Vitamin C:** 68%; **Calcium:** 16%; **Iron:** 22%

Ingredients:

- 1 pound breakfast sausage, ground, pork, turkey or meat alternative
- 8 large eggs
- 6 almond flour waffles, toasted
- 3 cups kale, stems removed, roughly chopped
- 1/4 cup unsweetened almond milk, non-dairy (or regular milk)
- 1 tablespoon olive oil or butter, for greasing the pan
- Cheese, crumbled or grated, optional
- Red pepper flakes, optional
- Sea salt and pepper, to taste

Directions:

1. Preheat the oven to 350F if baking right away.
2. Lightly grease an 8x8-inch glass baking pan or a casserole dish with olive oil or butter or your choice.
3. Heat a skillet over medium-high heat. Add the ground sausage; cook until lightly browned. Remove from the skillet and then set aside.
4. Add the kale in the same skillet; quickly wilt; remove from the skillet and set aside.
5. In a bowl, whisk the eggs with the milk and a season of salt and pepper to taste; set aside.
6. Dice the toasted waffles into 1-2 inch square pieces. Layer 1/2 of the waffle squared into the bottom of the prepared pan. Add 1/2 of the browned sausage and then 1/2 of the wilted kale. If using cheese, sprinkle 1/2 of the cheese over the top.
7. Layer the remaining waffle squares, sausage, and the kale. Pour the egg mix over the top. Sprinkle with the remaining cheese, if using, and season with salt and pepper to taste. Sprinkle with the red pepper flakes, if desired.
8. If desired, let the mixture sit overnight to allow the waffles to absorb the egg mix. But you can bake right away.
9. Bake for about 45 minutes to 1 hour or until the eggs are set and the strata is firm and a knife come out clean when inserted in the middle. Bake for 5 to 10 minutes more, if needed. When baked, let sit for 10 minutes before cutting or scooping into portions.

Savory Sweet Potato, Turkey Sausage, and Egg Bowl

Prep Time: 10 minutes; Cook Time: 20 minutes	

Serving Size: 451 g; Serves: 4; Calories: 746
Total Fat: 58.1 g Saturated Fat: 32.3 g; Trans Fat: 0 g
Protein: 21.2 g; Net Carbs: 27.9 g
Total Carbs: 39.7 g; Dietary Fiber: 11.8 g; Sugars: 5.6 g
Cholesterol: 211 mg; Sodium: 544 mg; Potassium: 1575 mg;
Vitamin A: 300%; Vitamin C: 270%; Calcium: 27%; Iron: 21%

Ingredients:

- [ ] 1 avocado, sliced
- [ ] 1 cup red onion, chopped
- [ ] 2 cups sweet potatoes, cooked, cubed
- [ ] 2 red pepper, chopped
- [ ] 4 eggs
- [ ] 4 tablespoons hot sauce, optional
- [ ] 8 cups greens
- [ ] 8 ounces turkey sausage, nitrate-free {equivalent to 1 sausage patty}
- [ ] 8 tablespoons coconut oil or extra virgin olive oil
- [ ] Salt and pepper, to taste

Directions:

1. Heat 1 tablespoon coconut or extra-virgin olive oil in a medium-large-sized pan on the stove. Add the sweet potato cubes; sauté for about 10 minutes or till the edges start to golden. Remove from the pan and set aside.
2. In the same pan, add the turkey sausages and cook until brown. Remove from the pan and set aside.
3. In the same pan, add the onion, red pepper, and the greens; sauté for 3 minutes.
4. In a different pan, fry about 1-2 eggs with 1 tablespoon oil until over easy or until cooked to your desired doneness.
5. Divide the veggies, greens, sweet potato cubes, and turkey sausages between 4 bowls. Top each serve with the fried eggs. Season with salt and pepper and, if desired, serve with hot sauce.

Notes: You can cook a large batch of sweet potato cubes and turkey sausages at the start of the week; store in the fridge. When ready to serve, just cook the onion, red pepper, and greens, and then fry eggs while you reheat the sweet potato cubes and the turkey sausage. Meal will be ready in 5-10 minutes. This will be good for up to 1 week.

Breakfast Harvest Cookies

Prep Time: 10 minutes; **Cook Time:** 20 minutes	

Serving Size: 39 g; Serves: 12-16; Calories: 61	
Total Fat: 2 g Saturated Fat: 1.7 g; Trans Fat: 0 g	
Protein: 0.7 g; Net Carbs: 10 g	
Total Carbs: 11.8 g; Dietary Fiber: 1.8 g; Sugars: 7.6 g	
Cholesterol: 0 mg; Sodium: 107 mg; Potassium: 152 mg;	
Vitamin A: 32%; Vitamin C: 3%; Calcium: 1%; Iron: 6%	

Ingredients:

- 1 cup banana, mashed
- 1 teaspoon baking soda
- 1/2 cup pumpkin puree
- 1/2 cup raisins
- 1/2 cup unsweetened coconut, shredded
- 1/3 cup coconut flour
- 1/4 teaspoon ginger
- 2 teaspoons apple cider vinegar
- 2 teaspoons cinnamon
- 4 Medjool dates, soft

Directions:

1. Preheat the oven to 350F. Line a baking sheet with parchment paper or silpat.
2. Put the mashed banana, dates, and the pumpkin puree into a blender or a food processor; blend or process until the dates are mixed well with the purees.
3. Add the flour, baking soda, ginger, cinnamon, and vinegar; blend or process again until the mixture is a thick batter.
4. Gently fold in the raisins and the shredded coconut. By heaping tablespoons, scoop the batter into the prepared baking sheet. With your hands, flatten them into cookie shapes. Bake for about 20-25 minutes or till the center of the cookies are not too soft to touch and he edges are golden. Let them cool in pan for about 15 minutes in the baking sheet since they will very soft when baked.
5. With a spatula, transfer then onto wire racks and let cool completely.
6. Serve immediately or store in the fridge for up to 7 days.

Notes: It's preferred to use a silpat for these cookies since they have longer baking time. This will prevent the bottoms from burning. If you don't have a silpat, carefully watch the bottom of the cookies. If needed, reduce the temperature of the oven and bake for a longer time.

Nutty Fruity Baked Oatmeal

Prep Time: 20 minutes; **Cook Time:** 20 minutes	

Serving Size: 106 g; **Serves:** 8; **Calories:** 189

Total Fat: 8 g **Saturated Fat:** 3.1 g; **Trans Fat:** 0 g

Protein: 6 g; **Net Carbs:** 23.6 g

Total Carbs: 28 g; **Dietary Fiber:** 4.4 g; **Sugars:** 8.3 g

Cholesterol: 35 mg; **Sodium:** 83 mg; **Potassium:** 274 mg;

Vitamin A: 3%; **Vitamin C:** 1%; **Calcium:** 11%; **Iron:** 8%

Ingredients:

- ☐ 2 cups oats, old-fashioned
- ☐ 1/4 cup nuts, chopped (walnuts, almonds, pecans)
- ☐ 1/3 cup dried fruit (raisins, cranberries, cherries)
- ☐ 1/2 cup unsweetened applesauce
- ☐ 1/2 cup packed brown sugar (1/2 tablespoon molasses + 1/2 cup low carb sweetener)
- ☐ 1 teaspoon baking powder
- ☐ 1 large egg
- ☐ 1 1/2 cups 2% milk
- ☐ 2 tablespoons butter, melted

Directions:

1. Preheat the oven to 375F.
2. Stir the oats with the brown sugar, dried fruits, nuts, and the baking powder in a bowl.
3. In another bowl, whisk the milk with the egg, butter, and applesauce. Stir the milk mix into the oat mixture until well combined.
4. Grease a 7x11-inch baking dish with nonstick spray. Pour the batter into the dish; level the top and then bake for 20 minutes.
5. When baked, let cool and then cut into serving portions.

Notes: Make ahead of time, wrap each serve with a plastic wrap and then put them in a freezer bag; store in the freezer. When ready to serve, remove the wrap, microwave for about 45 seconds until warm and gooey.

Breakfast Burritos

Prep Time: 15 minutes; **Cook Time:** 30 minutes

Serving Size: 146 g; **Serves:** 12-14; **Calories:** 300

Total Fat: 20.1 g **Saturated Fat:** 6.9 g; **Trans Fat:** 0 g

Protein: 17.2 g; **Net Carbs:** 11 g

Total Carbs: 12.8g; **Dietary Fiber:** 1.8 g; **Sugars:** 1.6 g

Cholesterol: 226 mg; **Sodium:** 510 mg; **Potassium:** 263 mg;

Vitamin A: 7%; **Vitamin C:** 14%; **Calcium:** 12%; **Iron:** 10%

Ingredients:

- 1 pound turkey sausage
- 1 green or red sweet pepper, chopped
- 1 small onion, chopped
- 1 tablespoon olive oil
- 1/2 teaspoon pepper
- 1/2 teaspoon salt
- 12 large eggs
- 1-2 tablespoon cheese per serving, shredded
- 12-14 tortillas, medium-sized
- 1/2 cup 2% milk, optional
- Salsa, optional

Directions:

1. Line a baking sheet with wax paper.
2. Heat the olive oil inside a large-sized skillet on medium heat. Add the turkey, onion, and pepper; cook, breaking the sausage into tiny pieces and sauté until completely cooked and browned. Set aside.
3. Inside a large-sized bowl, whisk the eggs with the milk and seasoning of the salt and pepper until combined.
4. Over medium heat, heat a large-sized nonstick frying pan. Add 1 tablespoon butter and let melt. When the butter is melted, add the eggs; scramble until cooked.
5. Warm the tortilla in the microwave according to directions on the package.
6. Layer 1/2 cup scrambled eggs, 1/2 cup sausage mix, about 1 to 2 tablespoon cheese, and a bit of salsa on a warm tortilla; fold into a burrito.

Freezing: Place each burrito into the prepared baking sheet; flash freeze in the freezer for at least 1 hour. Individually wrap each burrito with foil, put them in a freezer bag, and keep in the freezer.

When ready to serve, remove the foil, wrap each burrito with paper towel, and then microwave for about 60 seconds, or until warmed through.

Cheesy Bacon and Eggs Oat Muffins

Prep Time: 20 minutes; **Cook Time:** 15-20 minutes	

Serving Size: 61 g; **Serves:** 12; **Calories:** 129

Total Fat: 8.9 g **Saturated Fat:** 2.3 g; **Trans Fat:** 0 g

Protein: 8.4 g; **Net Carbs:** 3.7 g

Total Carbs: 5.2 g; **Dietary Fiber:** 1.5 g; **Sugars:** 1.2 g

Cholesterol: 103 mg; **Sodium:** 298 mg; **Potassium:** 283 mg;

Vitamin A: 8%; **Vitamin C:** 11%; **Calcium:** 13%; **Iron:** 7%

Ingredients:
- 6 large eggs
- 1 cup almond flour
- 1/4 cup Canadian bacon, chopped
- 1/3 cup oats, old-fashioned
- 1/2 teaspoon salt
- 1/2 cup red pepper, chopped
- 1/2 cup cheddar cheese, shredded
- 1 tablespoon baking powder
- 1/4 cup fresh parsley, chopped
- 1/4 cup unsweetened applesauce
- 1/4 teaspoon cinnamon
- 1/4 teaspoon pepper

Directions:
1. Preheat the oven to 375F.
2. Inside a large-sized bowl, whisk the eggs with the applesauce until well combined.
3. In a different bowl, combine the flour with the baking powder, oats, cinnamon, and season with salt and pepper. Add the flour mix into the egg mix; stir till just combined.
4. Mix in the cheese, the bacon, parsley, and the pepper.
5. Grease a 12-muffin pan with nonstick spray. Pour the batter into the muffin cups and bake for about 15-20 minutes or till baked through; The muffin tops should be set and a toothpick should come out clean when inserted in the muffin. Put the muffin pan on a wire rack and let cool for 5 minutes. Remove from the muffin cups and let cool completely on the wire rack.

Notes: When completely cool, individually wrap each muffin with plastic wrap, put them in a freezer bag, and store in the freezer.

When ready to serve, remove the plastic wraps, individually wrap each muffin with paper towel, and then microwave for about 30 to 45 minutes until heated through.

Maple, Pecan, and Sour Cherry Granola Bars

Prep Time: 40 minutes; **Cook Time:** 45-55 minutes, plus 30 minutes cooling		
Serving Size: 61 g; **Serves:** 16; **Calories:** 252		
Total Fat: 18.8 g **Saturated Fat:** 5.3 g; **Trans Fat:** 0 g		
Protein: 7.9 g; **Net Carbs:** 13.3 g		
Total Carbs: 20.5 g; **Dietary Fiber:** 7.2 g; **Sugars:** 1.5 g		
Cholesterol: 0 mg; **Sodium:** 81 mg; **Potassium:** 287 mg;		
Vitamin A: 1%; **Vitamin C:** 2%; **Calcium:** 4%; **Iron:** 19%		

Ingredients:
- 2 cups oats, old-fashioned
- 1/3 cup light brown sugar (mix 1 tsp molasses + 1/3 cup low carb sweetener)
- 1/2 teaspoon kosher salt
- 1/2 cup wheat germ
- 1/2 cup golden flaxseed
- 1/2 cup almonds, sliced
- 1 large egg white, beaten
- 1 cup unsweetened coconut shavings
- 1 cup pumpkin seeds (pepitas)
- 1 cup pecans, chopped
- 1 cup dried sour cherries
- 1 1/2 teaspoons vanilla extract
- 3 tablespoons virgin coconut oil
- 3/4 cup sugar-free maple syrup

Directions:
1. Preheat the oven to 375F.
2. In a rimmed baking sheet, toss the oats with the pecans, coconut, pumpkin seeds, almonds, and flaxseeds. Toast in the oven, occasionally stirring, for about 10 to 15 minutes or till slightly golden.
3. Reduce the temperature of the oven to 325F; transfer the mix inside a large-sized bowl, stir in the cherries and the wheat germ.
4. Mix the maple syrup with the coconut oil, brown sugar substitute, salt, and vanilla in a small-sized saucepan; bring to a boil and cook for about 4 minutes, occasionally stirring, until the sugar is dissolved. Let cool for 15 minutes and then whisk the egg white in.
5. Pour the maple syrup mix over the oat mix; stir until well coated.
6. Line a different baking sheet with rim with parchment paper. Scrape the oat mix and bake for about 45 to 55 minutes or till deep golden brown. Let cool for 30 minutes and then cut into bars.

Notes: Make these bars ahead and store in airtight containers for up to 3 weeks.

Toasted Coconut Pumpkin Bread

Prep Time: 30 minutes; **Cook Time:** 50-60 minutes, plus 30 minutes or so cooling

Serving Size: 78 g; Serves: 10; Calories: 219		
Total Fat: 13 g Saturated Fat: 10 g; Trans Fat: 0 g		
Protein: 4.2 g; Net Carbs: 23.4 g		
Total Carbs: 27.4 g; Dietary Fiber: 4 g; Sugars: 3.3 g		
Cholesterol: 37 mg; Sodium: 250 mg; Potassium: 236 mg;		
Vitamin A: 77%; Vitamin C: 2%; Calcium: 7%; Iron: 11%		

Ingredients:

- ☐ 1 1/4 cups all-purpose flour
- ☐ 1 cup (packed) light brown sugar (mix 1 tablespoon molasses + 1 cup low carb sweetener)
- ☐ 1 cup pure pumpkin, canned
- ☐ 1 tablespoon granulated sugar (equal amount Swerve sweetener)
- ☐ 1 teaspoon ground cinnamon
- ☐ 1 teaspoon ground ginger
- ☐ 1 teaspoon kosher salt
- ☐ 1/2 cup virgin coconut oil, warmed, slightly cooled
- ☐ 1/2 cup whole-wheat flour
- ☐ 1/4 teaspoon ground allspice
- ☐ 1/4 teaspoon ground nutmeg
- ☐ 1/8 teaspoon ground cloves
- ☐ 2 large eggs, room temperature
- ☐ 2 tablespoons raw pumpkin seeds (pepitas)
- ☐ 2 tablespoons unsweetened coconut flakes
- ☐ 2 teaspoons baking powder
- ☐ Nonstick vegetable oil spray

Directions:

1. Preheat the oven to 350F. Lightly grease a 4 1/2 x 8 1/2 loaf pan with nonstick spray and then line with parchment paper, leaving a 2-inch overhang on all sides.
2. Whisk the all-purpose flour with the wheat flour, the baking powder, ginger, cinnamon, allspice, salt, nutmeg, and cloves inside a large-sized bowl.
3. Whisk the eggs with the brown sugar substitute, pumpkin, and oil in another large-sized bowl until smooth.
4. Mix the wet ingredients into the dry ingredients mix. Scrape the batter into the prepared pan, smooth the top, and then sprinkle with the coconut, pumpkin seeds, and the granulated sugar substitute.
5. Bake the bread for about 50 to 60 minutes or till golden brown or a toothpick come out clean when inserted in the center.
6. Transfer the pan on a wire rack and let cool in pan for 30 minutes. Turn the bread out on the wire rack; let cool completely.

Notes: You can bake this bread ahead of time. Tightly wrap and keep for 3 days at room temperature.

Cashew, Sesame, and Flaxseed Bars

Prep Time: 20 minutes; **Cook Time:** 25-30 minutes

Serving Size: 29 g; **Serves:** 12; **Calories:** 152		
Total Fat: 12.3 g **Saturated Fat:** 30 g; **Trans Fat:** 0 g		
Protein: 4.2 g; **Net Carbs:** 6.9 g		
Total Carbs: 10.3 g; **Dietary Fiber:** 3.4 g; **Sugars:** 0.9 g		
Cholesterol: 0 mg; **Sodium:** 151 mg; **Potassium:** 156 mg;		
Vitamin A: 0%; **Vitamin C:** 0%; **Calcium:** 5%; **Iron:** 15%		

Ingredients:
- 6 tablespoons raw sesame seeds
- 5 tablespoons flaxseed
- 3/4 teaspoon kosher salt
- 1/4 teaspoon ground cardamom
- 1/4 cup wheat bran
- 1/2 cup pure maple syrup
- 1 tablespoon coconut oil
- 1 1/2 cups cashews
- Nonstick vegetable oil spray

Directions:
1. Preheat the oven to 350F. Grease an 8x8 baking pan with vegetable oil spray and then line with parchment paper, leaving an overhang on all the sides.
2. In another rimmed baking sheet, put the cashews, flaxseed, and the sesame seeds without mixing them; toast in the oven, occasionally stirring, but not mixing, for about 10-12 minutes or till golden brown. Let cool; set aside 1 tablespoon flaxseed and 2 tablespoons sesame seeds.
3. Process the cashews and the remaining seeds with the wheat bran, cinnamon, and salt in a food processor until the mix is mostly finely chopped; transfer into a medium-sized bowl.
4. Mix the maple syrup with the coconut oil in a small-sized saucepan; bring to a boil, stirring, for 1 minute. Pour in the cashew mix; stir until well coated.
5. Wet hands and firmly press the mix into the prepared pan. Top with the reserved 1 tablespoon flaxseed and 2 tablespoons sesame seeds; press to adhere. Bake for about 25 to 30 minutes or till golden brown; let cool and then cut into bars.

Notes: Make these bars ahead of time and store in airtight containers for about 2 weeks at room temperature.

Savory Cornbread

Prep Time: 20 minutes; **Cook Time:** 25-30 minutes		

Serving Size: 112 g; **Serves:** 8; **Calories:** 265			
Total Fat: 15.6 g **Saturated Fat:** 4.5 g; **Trans Fat:** 0 g			
Protein: 8.9 g; **Net Carbs:** 21.7 g			
Total Carbs: 25.2 g; **Dietary Fiber:** 3.5 g; **Sugars:** 6.2 g			
Cholesterol: 84 mg; **Sodium:** 513 mg; **Potassium:** 459 mg;			
Vitamin A: 6%; **Vitamin C:** 1%; **Calcium:** 19%; **Iron:** 10%			

Ingredients:

- 1 1/3 cups almond flour
- 1 1/3 cups cornmeal
- 1 cup buttermilk
- 1 tablespoon baking powder
- 1 teaspoon kosher salt
- 1/2 cup whole milk
- 2 tablespoons sugar (equal amount Swerve sweetener)
- 3 large eggs, beaten to blend
- 3 tablespoons unsalted butter, melted, cooled, plus more for baking dish
- 3/4 teaspoon baking soda

Directions:

1. Preheat the oven to 350F. Butter an 8x8-inch baking dish.
2. Whisk the flour with the cornmeal, baking powder, sugar substitute, baking soda, and salt inside a large-sized bowl.
3. In a medium-sized bowl, whisk the eggs with the milk and the buttermilk.
4. Whisk the egg mix into the dry ingredients mix until just combined; the batter will be slightly lumpy. Mix in 3 tablespoons of butter.
5. Scrape the batter into the prepared baking dish; bake for about 25 to 30 minutes or till a toothpick come out clean when inserted in the center.
6. Serve with fruit compote, jam, honey, and maple syrup.

Notes: Make this dish ahead of time; just wrap tightly and freeze.

This unsweetened cornbread is already delicious as is. If you want to sweeten, just drizzle a bit of maple syrup, molasses, or honey over the top of the bread as soon as it comes out of the oven. The sweeteners will sink into the bread as it cools, making the cornbread even more moist.

Zucchini-Oat Bread

Prep Time: 30 minutes; **Cook Time:** 70-80 minutes	

Serving Size: 92 g; **Serves:** 16; **Calories:** 329
Total Fat: 38.3 g **Saturated Fat:** 6 g; **Trans Fat:** 0 g
Protein: 9.8 g; **Net Carbs:** 15.2 g
Total Carbs: 25 g; **Dietary Fiber:** 9.8 g; **Sugars:** 2.8 g
Cholesterol: 56 mg; **Sodium:** 501 mg; **Potassium:** 413 mg;
Vitamin A: 3%; **Vitamin C:** 11%; **Calcium:** 11%; **Iron:** 11%

Ingredients:
- ☐ 3 large eggs
- ☐ 3 cups almond flour
- ☐ 3 1/2 cups zucchini, coarsely grated (from about 1 lb. zucchini)
- ☐ 1/4 teaspoon freshly grated nutmeg
- ☐ 1/2 teaspoon baking powder
- ☐ 1/2 cup (packed) light brown sugar (1/2 tablespoon molasses + 1/2 cup sweetener)
- ☐ 1 teaspoon ground cinnamon
- ☐ 1 teaspoon baking soda
- ☐ 1 tablespoon vanilla extract
- ☐ 1 cup vegetable oil
- ☐ 1 1/4 cups old-fashioned rolled oats, divided
- ☐ 1 1/4 cups granulated sugar (equal amount Swerve sweetener)
- ☐ 1 1/2 teaspoons kosher salt
- ☐ 3 tablespoons raw sugar (equal amount Swerve sweetener)
- ☐ 1 cup walnuts, optional
- ☐ Non-stick vegetable oil spray

Directions:
1. Preheat the oven to 350F. Grease to pieces 4 1/2 x 8 1/2-inch loaf pans with nonstick spray and then line with parchment paper, leaving a generous overhang on the long sides.
2. If using walnuts, spread them in a rimmed baking sheet; toast for about 8-10 minutes until fragrant or until slightly darkened. Let cool and then coarsely chop.
3. Inside a large-sized bowl, whisk the eggs with the brown sugar substitute, granulated sugar substitute, and vanilla until smooth.
4. In a different large-sized bowl, whisk the flour with the baking powder, baking soda, cinnamon, salt, and nutmeg just to combine.
5. Make a well in the center of the dry ingredients mix. Add the egg mix and with a fork, slowly incorporate with the dry ingredients; the batter will look dry.
6. Fold the zucchini, the walnuts, and 1 cup of the oats into the batter. Scrape the batter into the prepared pans.
7. In a small sized bowl, toss the remaining oats with the raw sugar substitute; sprinkle the oat-sugar mix over the batter; bake for about 70 to 80 minutes or till a tester come out clean when inserted in the center.
8. Transfer the pans onto wire rack; let the bread cool for 30 minutes in pan. Turn the bread out onto the wire racks and then let cool completely.

Notes: You can bake these ahead of time, wrap tightly, and store for about 4 days at room temperature.

48

Cherry-Almond Granola Bars

Prep Time: 15 minutes; **Cook Time:** 25 minutes		
Serving Size: 30 g; **Serves:** 24; **Calories:** 111		
Total Fat: 5.8 g **Saturated Fat:** 3 g; **Trans Fat:** 0 g		
Protein: 2.1 g; **Net Carbs:** 12.8 g		
Total Carbs: 15 g; **Dietary Fiber:** 2.2 g; **Sugars:** 6.4 g		
Cholesterol: 0 mg; **Sodium:** 99 mg; **Potassium:** 84 mg;		
Vitamin A: 0%; **Vitamin C:** 1%; **Calcium:** 1%; **Iron:** 6%		

Ingredients:
- 3/4 cup unsweetened coconut, finely shredded (about 3 ounce)
- 3/4 cup raw almonds, whole
- 3/4 cup dried tart cherries, coarsely chopped (about 4 ounce)
- 2 tablespoons flaxseeds, toasted
- 2 1/4 cups oats, old-fashioned
- 1/4 cup coconut oil, plus more
- 1/2 cup sunflower seeds, shelled, unsalted, roasted (about 3 ounce)
- 1/2 cup honey
- 1/2 cup (packed) light brown sugar (mix 1/2 tablespoon molasses + 1/2 cup sweetener)
- 1 teaspoon kosher salt

Directions:
1. Preheat the oven to 400F.
2. Ina large-sized, heavy rimmed baking sheet, mix the oats with the almonds; bake for about 10 minutes, stirring once, until just golden. Transfer the baking sheet on a wire rack and let cool on the baking sheet.
3. Reduce the temperature of the oven to 325F.
4. Meanwhile, brush a 9x13x2-inch glass or metal baking dish with coconut oil and then line with parchment paper, leaving a generous overhang over the long sides. Brush the parchment paper with oil.
5. Generously brush a large-sized bowl with oil. Put the oat mix, coconut, cherries, flaxseeds, and sunflower seeds into the bowl.
6. Mix 1/4 cup of oil with the light brown sugar substitute, salt, and honey in a medium-sized, heavy, deep saucepan; bring to a boil; boil for 1 minute, stirring to dissolve the sugar. As soon as the sugar is dissolved, pour over the oat mix and with a heat-safe spatula, stir to evenly coat. Transfer the mix into the prepared pan; lightly press to even and then smooth the top. Bake for 10 minutes; turn the pan and continue baking for another 15 minutes or till the granola is golden brown and the edges are slightly darker.
7. Transfer the pan onto a wire rack; let the granola cool completely in pan. Hold the paper overhang and lift the granola from the pan. Cut into 24 bars.

Notes: Make these bars ahead of time and store in airtight containers for up to 4 days at room temperature.

Better Oat Granola with Coconut, Nuts, and Sesame Seeds

Prep Time: 20 minutes; **Cook Time:** 40-45 minutes

Serving Size: 82 g; **Serves:** 12; **Calories:** 324
Total Fat: 19.2 g **Saturated Fat:** 5.2 g; **Trans Fat:** 0 g
Protein: 6.9 g; **Net Carbs:** 29.8 g
Total Carbs: 35 g; **Dietary Fiber:** 5.2 g; **Sugars:** 1.8 g
Cholesterol: 0 mg; **Sodium:** 423 mg; **Potassium:** 253 mg;
Vitamin A: 0%; **Vitamin C:** 2%; **Calcium:** 6%; **Iron:** 19%

Ingredients:

- 3 cups oats, old-fashioned
- 2 tablespoons (packed) light brown sugar (1/8 tablespoon molasses + 1/8 cup low carb sweetener)
- 1/4 cup sesame seeds
- 1/4 cup olive oil or warmed coconut oil
- 1/2 teaspoon ground cinnamon
- 1/2 cup agave syrup
- 1 large egg white, lightly beaten
- 1 cup dried cherries or cranberries
- 1 1/2 teaspoons kosher salt
- 1 1/2 cups nuts, chopped (such as almonds, pecans, pistachios, or walnuts)
- 1 1/2 cups coconut shavings

Directions:

1. Preheat the oven to 300F.
2. Inside a large-sized bowl, toss the egg whites with the oats, coconut shavings, nuts, oil, agave syrup, brown sugar substitute, sesame seeds, cinnamon, and salt. Spread the mix into a rimmed baking sheet; bake for about 40 to 45 minutes, stirring every 10 minutes, until golden brown. When baked, let cool in the baking sheet. The mix will become crispier as it cools. Mix in the cherries.
3. Serve over low-fat yogurt or layer in a glass with yogurt and fresh fruits.

Notes: Make this granola ahead of time, store in airtight containers for up to 2 weeks at room temperature.

You can use honey or maple syrup for a different sweetness. If you want chocolate chips, add them at the end.

Pistachio-Prune Oat Bars

Prep Time: 20 minutes; **Cook Time:** 20-25 minutes	

Serving Size: 51 g; **Serves:** 12; **Calories:** 166
Total Fat: 5.9 g **Saturated Fat:** 2.4 g; **Trans Fat:** 0 g
Protein: 3.4 g; **Net Carbs:** 24 g
Total Carbs: 28.3 g; **Dietary Fiber:** 4.3 g; **Sugars:** 14 g
Cholesterol: 0 mg; **Sodium:** 182 mg; **Potassium:** 318 mg;
Vitamin A: 2%; **Vitamin C:** 2%; **Calcium:** 5%; **Iron:** 6%

Ingredients:
- ☐ 1 1/2 cups oats, old-fashioned
- ☐ 1 cup dried figs, chopped
- ☐ 1 cup prunes, chopped
- ☐ 1 tablespoon orange juice, fresh
- ☐ 1/2 teaspoon orange zest, finely grated
- ☐ 1/2 vanilla bean, split lengthwise
- ☐ 2 tablespoons coconut oil
- ☐ 3 tablespoons plus 1 cup pistachios
- ☐ 3/4teaspoon kosher salt
- ☐ Nonstick vegetable oil spray

Directions:
1. Preheat the oven to 200F. Lightly grease an 8x8-inch baking pan with vegetable oil spray and then line with parchment paper, leaving a generous overhang on all sides.
2. Inside a large-sized skillet, heat the coconut oil on medium heat. Add the oats, cook, stirring frequently, for about 4 minutes or till golden brown. Transfer to a plate and let cool.
3. Meanwhile, put 3 tablespoons pistachios into a food processor, process until finely ground and then transfer into a small-sized bowl.
4. Scrape the vanilla bean seeds into the food processor. Add the prunes, figs, 1/2 cup pistachios, orange juice, orange zest, and 2 tablespoons water; process till smooth. Transfer the mix into a medium-sized bowl.
5. Coarsely chop the remaining 1/2 cup pistachios; add into the medium-sized bowl. Add the oats; mix well. Firmly press the mix into the prepared baking pan and then sprinkle with the ground pistachios, pressing to adhere. Bake for about 20-25 minutes or till no longer sticky; let cool and then cut into bars.

Notes: Make these bars ahead of time and store in airtight containers for up to 2 weeks at room temperature.

Cheesy Carrot, Corn, and Peas Muffins

Prep Time: 15 minutes; **Cook Time:** 18-20 minutes, plus 10 minutes cooling

Serving Size: 164 g; **Serves:** 12; **Calories:** 145		

Serving Size: 164 g; **Serves:** 12; **Calories:** 145

Total Fat: 8.4 g **Saturated Fat:** 4 g; **Trans Fat:** 0 g

Protein: 12.9 g; **Net Carbs:** 4.1 g

Total Carbs: 5 g; **Dietary Fiber:** 0.9 g; **Sugars:** 1.6 g

Cholesterol: 139 mg; **Sodium:** 231 mg; **Potassium:** 119 mg;

Vitamin A: 54%; **Vitamin C:** 11%; **Calcium:** 4%; **Iron:** 5%

Ingredients:

- 1 1/2 cups carrots, shredded (about 4 medium carrots, peeled and trimmed)
- 1/2 cup frozen corn
- 1/2 cup frozen peas
- 1/2 cup orange bell peppers, small-diced
- 12 tablespoons mozzarella cheese, shredded divided
- 8 large eggs
- Salt and pepper, to taste

Directions:

1. Preheat the oven to 375F. Generously grease a nonstick 12-cup regular-sized muffin pan with cooking spray. Spray the sides and the base; run your finger over the sides to liberally coat. Make sure the muffin cups are generously coated with oil or you chisel off stuck food. Set aside.
2. Inside a large-sized bowl, toss the carrots with the peas, corn, peppers until combined. You can mix and match your favorite veggies.
3. Loosely pile about 3tablespoon of the veggie mix into each muffin cup; fill each cup about 2/3-3/4 full, evenly distributing the filling the mix between the cups until all the filling is gone. Set the pan aside.
4. In a 2-cup glass measuring cup, crack the eggs lightly beat using a whisk. The measuring cup will make pouring easier. Season the egg with salt and pepper to taste and whisk to combine. pour about 2 to 3 tablespoons of the egg mix into each cup, distributing evenly. The cups will be 3/4 full.
5. Top each cup with a generous pinch of cheese, about 1 tablespoon each; bake for about 18 to 20 minutes or till the muffins are set, cooked through, and lightly golden.
6. The muffins will puff in the oven, but they sink when cooling. Transfer the muffin pan onto a wire rack; let the muffins cool in the muffin pan for about 10 minutes. Run a knife around the edges of the muffin and then with a small spoon, pop the muffins out from the muffin pan.

Notes: Make ahead of time. Store in airtight containers and keep in the fridge for up to 7 days. When ready to serve; gently reheat in the microwave or serve cold.

52

Vegetarian Make-Ahead Freezer Breakfast Sandwiches

Prep Time: 30 minutes; **Cook Time:** 20-25 minutes		

Serving Size: 124 g; **Serves:** 12; **Calories:** 271		
Total Fat: 12.2 g **Saturated Fat:** 4.8 g; **Trans Fat:** 0 g		
Protein: 14.3 g; **Net Carbs:** 23.9 g		
Total Carbs: 25.9 g; **Dietary Fiber:** 2 g; **Sugars:** 2.5 g		
Cholesterol: 181 mg; **Sodium:** 480 mg; **Potassium:** 205 mg;		
Vitamin A: 6%; **Vitamin C:** 2%; **Calcium:** 17%; **Iron:** 18%		

Ingredients:
- 12 eggs
- 12 sausage patties
- 12 whole-wheat English muffins
- 3/4 cup cheddar cheese, shredded

Directions:
1. Preheat the oven to 350F. Grease a regular muffin tin with nonstick cooking spray or coat with coconut oil.
2. Crack 1 egg into each muffin cup; bake for about 20-25 minutes or till the eggs are set. Let the eggs cool to room temperature; this will prevent the English muffins from becoming soggy.
3. Slice the English muffins into bottom and top halves. Place 1 sausage patty onto each muffin bottom halves, sprinkle with a pinch of cheese, top with egg, and then with the muffin tops.

Freezing: Wrap each muffin tightly with saran wrap, put them in a freezer bag, and freeze for up to 3 months.

Reheating: When ready to serve, take out needed muffin from the freer bag, keep the saran wrap on and put in a microwavable plate; microwave for 30 seconds, turn, and microwave for another 30 seconds. Remove the wrap and check for doneness. The muffins may need 15-20 seconds more in the microwave.

Gluten-Free Carrot Cake Breakfast Cookies

Prep Time: 20 minutes; **Cook Time:** 8-10 minutes		

Prep Time: 20 minutes; **Cook Time:** 8-10 minutes

Serving Size: 71 g; **Serves:** 12; **Calories:** 211

Total Fat: 11.7 g **Saturated Fat:** 5.8 g; **Trans Fat:** 0 g

Protein: 4.3 g; **Net Carbs:** 20 g

Total Carbs: 25.1 g; **Dietary Fiber:** 5.1 g; **Sugars:** 4.8 g

Cholesterol: 0 mg; **Sodium:** 158 mg; **Potassium:** 203 mg;

Vitamin A: 31%; **Vitamin C:** 2%; **Calcium:** 3%; **Iron:** 11%

Ingredients:

- 2 cups oats, old fashioned, gluten-free certified
- 1/4 cup honey
- 1/4 cup ground flaxseed meal, gluten-free
- 1/4 cup coconut oil, melted
- 1/4 cup almond milk (or any kind)
- 1/2 teaspoons salt
- 1/2 teaspoon baking soda
- 1/2 cup unsweetened applesauce
- 1/2 cup pecans, gluten-free, finely chopped
- 1/2 cup banana, very ripe, mashed (about 1 large banana)
- 1 teaspoon cinnamon
- 1 cup carrots, finely grated (about 2 large carrots)
- 1 1/4 cups oat flour (blended from 1-1/2 cups old fashioned oats, gluten-free certified)
- 2 tablespoons maple syrup

Directions:

1. Preheat the oven to 350F. Line a baking sheet with parchment paper or silpat; set aside.
2. Inside a large-sized bowl, mix the oats with the flaxseed meal, oat flour, baking soda, cinnamon, and salt until combined.
3. In another bowl, mix the mashed bananas with the honey, applesauce, milk, coconut oil, and maple syrup until combined.
4. Add the wet ingredients into the dry ingredients; mix. Add the grated carrots and the chopped pecans; mix until combined.
5. With an ice cream scooper, scoop about 1/4 cup-worth batter into the prepared baking sheet. Wet hands with water and the press the batter down to flatten slightly into cookies. Bake for about 8-10 minutes or till golden brown.

Notes: Make these cookies ahead of time, store in airtight containers and keep for up to 3-4 days in the refrigerator. Alternatively, you can individually wrap them with plastic wrap, put in a freezer bag, and freeze. When ready to serve, remove the plastic wrap, wrap in paper towel, and microwave for about 20 to 30 seconds to thaw.

Ham and Cheese Waffle Sandwiches

Prep Time: 15 minutes; Cook Time: 4-5 minutes
Serving Size: 80 g; Serves: 8; Calories: 234
Total Fat: 15.2 g Saturated Fat: 4.7 g; Trans Fat: 0 g
Protein: 12 g; Net Carbs: 12.2 g
Total Carbs: 14.2 g; Dietary Fiber: 2 g; Sugars: 11 g
Cholesterol: 109 mg; Sodium: 534 mg; Potassium: 199 mg;
Vitamin A: 5%; Vitamin C: 1%; Calcium: 16%; Iron: 7%

Ingredients:
- 8 waffle
- 4 1/2 ounces deli ham, sliced
- 4 slices cheddar cheese, sharp, sliced

Directions:
1. Top each 4 waffles with 1 slice cheese and 2 slices ham. Top each with the remaining waffles, making waffle sandwiches.
2. Place the waffle sandwiches into a baking sheet; broil for about 4 to 5 minutes or till the cheese is melted and the outside is crispy.

Freezing: Individually wrap each waffle sandwich with plastic wrap, put in freezer bags, label, and freeze. When ready to serve, remove the plastic wraps, place into a baking sheet, and broil for about 4 to 5 minutes or till the cheese is melted and the outside is crispy

Freezer Waffles

Prep Time: 10 minutes; **Cook Time:** 20 minutes	

Serving Size: 121 g; **Serves:** 8; **Calories:** 358
Total Fat: 31.2 g **Saturated Fat:** 5.5 g; **Trans Fat:** 0 g
Protein: 7.2 g; **Net Carbs:** 12.6 g
Total Carbs: 15.3 g; **Dietary Fiber:** 2.7 g; **Sugars:** 3.8 g
Cholesterol: 44 mg; **Sodium:** 442 mg; **Potassium:** 288 mg;
Vitamin A: 1%; **Vitamin C:** 1%; **Calcium:** 15%; **Iron:** 5%

Ingredients:

- 1 1/2 cups almond flour
- 1 1/2 cups buttermilk
- 1 1/2-2 teaspoon cinnamon (optional)
- 1 teaspoon baking powder
- 1 teaspoon salt
- 1 teaspoon vanilla
- 1/2 cup cornstarch
- 1/2 cups milk
- 1/2 teaspoon baking soda
- 2 eggs, separated
- 2 tablespoons granulated sugar (equal amount Swerve sweetener)
- 3/4 cups vegetable oil

Directions:

1. Preheat the waffle iron.
2. Inside a large-sized bowl, mix the flour with the cornstarch, baking powder, baking soda, and the cinnamon; set aside.
3. In a medium-sized bowl, combine the milk with the buttermilk, egg yolks, and the vegetable oil; set aside.
4. In another medium-sized bowl, with an electric mixer, beat the egg whites until soft peaks form. Add the vanilla and the sugar; continue beating until stiff peaks form.
5. Pour the milk mix into the dry ingredients; whisking until just mixed. Fold in the egg whites until just combined.
6. Pour the batter into the preheated waffle iron; cook to your desired crispness. The amount of batter needed will depend on your waffle iron.
7. Remove the waffles, separate into sections, and let cool while cooking the rest of the batter.

Notes: When the waffles are cool, put into gallon-sized freezer bag and freeze. When ready to serve, remove needed serving from the freezer; cook in a toaster oven or toaster to your desired crispness.

Ham and Vegetable Strata

Prep Time: 15 minutes; Cook Time: 60-70 minutes
Serving Size: 186 g; Serves: 8; Calories: 301
Total Fat: 16.1 g Saturated Fat: 6.5 g; Trans Fat: 0 g
Protein: 19 g; Net Carbs: 17.2 g
Total Carbs: 18.9 g; Dietary Fiber: 1.7 g; Sugars: 4.7 g
Cholesterol: 220 mg; Sodium: 824 mg; Potassium: 320 mg;
Vitamin A: 11%; Vitamin C: 18%; Calcium: 23%; Iron: 11%

Ingredients:
- 8 large eggs, beaten
- 2 cups skim milk
- 1/4 teaspoon pepper
- 1/4 pound mild cheddar cheese, shredded
- 1/2 pound boneless ham, diced
- 1 teaspoon dry mustard powder
- 1 cup frozen green and red peppers and onion strips (or broccoli, if desired)
- 1 bag (6-ounce) seasoned croutons

Directions:
1. Preheat the oven to 350F.
2. Grease a 9x13-inch casserole dish with cooking spray.
3. Inside a large-sized bowl, whisk the milk with the eggs and the mustard powder. Add the frozen veggies, ham, croutons, and pepper; mix until every crouton is saturated.
4. Pour the mix into the prepared casserole dish and then top with the shredded cheese; bake for about 60-70 minutes or till the center is cooked through and the top is golden brown.

Freezing: When making ahead of time, assemble the dish, cover the dish with a plastic wrap and then with an aluminum foil, and freeze. When ready to cook, transfer into the fridge and let thaw overnight. Remove the plastic wrap and the foil; bake as directed.

Bagel Bombs

Prep Time: 45 minutes; **Cook Time:** 25 minutes	

Serving Size: 492 g; **Serves:** 8; **Calories:** 387
Total Fat: 24.1 g **Saturated Fat:** 8 g; **Trans Fat:** 0 g
Protein: 14.8g; **Net Carbs:** 25.3 g
Total Carbs: 27.5 g; **Dietary Fiber:** 2.2 g; **Sugars:** 2.6 g
Cholesterol: 27 mg; **Sodium:** 691 mg; **Potassium:** 181 mg;
Vitamin A: 3%; **Vitamin C:** 1%; **Calcium:** 13%; **Iron:** 10%

Ingredients:
- 1 pound pizza dough, refrigerated
- 1 tablespoon honey
- 10 egg whites (or 5 whole eggs)
- 12 cups water
- 4-8 ounces shredded cheese
- 6 ounces diced ham
- Everything bagel seasoning, to taste
- Salt and pepper, to taste

For the everything bagel seasoning:
- 1/4 cup sesame seeds
- 3 tablespoons dried onion flakes
- 3 tablespoons dried garlic flakes
- 2 tablespoons coarse sea salt
- 1/4 cup poppy seeds

Directions:
1. Toss all the bagel seasoning ingredients until well mixed. Alternatively, put everything in a container with a tight lid; shake until well mixed.
2. Divide the pizza dough into 8 even portions and then roll into balls. Cover with kitchen towel and let rise for 20 minutes.
3. Meanwhile, scramble the eggs in a nonstick pan on medium heat, seasoning with salt and pepper to taste; set aside and let cool.
4. Preheat the oven to 425F. Line a nonstick baking sheet with parchment paper.
5. With your palm, gently flatten the dough balls. Top with 1/8 of the eggs, the diced ham, and the shredded cheddar cheese. Pull the sides of the dough up around the filling; pinch to seal. Pull up the perpendicular sides of the dough and then pinch. Continue the process until the filling is completely covered and the dough is sealed. With the seam-side down, put into the prepared baking sheet and cover with the kitchen towel; let sit for 15 minutes. Repeat the process with the remaining dough and filling.
6. Fill a large-sized pot with 12 cups water; bring to a boil. Mix in 1 tablespoon of honey into the boiling water.
7. Put 4 of the bagel bundles into the boiling water; boil for 1 minute, turning once, halfway through boiling. With a slotted spoon, remove from the boiling water and transfer into the prepared baking sheet. Repeat the process for the 4 remaining bagels.
8. Sprinkle with the bagel seasoning and bake for about 25 to 30 minutes or till cooked through and golden brown. You can serve these bagels warm or let cool to room temperature.

Notes: When bagels are completely cool, individually wrap with plastic wrap, put in freezer bag, and freeze. When ready to serve, remove plastic wrap, wrap with paper towel, and microwave on HIGH for about 1 minutes and 15 seconds or until warmed through.

Breakfast Spinach and White Beans Cheese Quesadilla

Prep Time: 20 minutes; **Cook Time:** 6 minutes per quesadilla		

Serving Size: 154 g; **Serves:** 8; **Calories:** 300			
Total Fat: 9.3 g **Saturated Fat:** 2.9 g; **Trans Fat:** 0 g			
Protein: 21.7 g; **Net Carbs:** 26.4 g			
Total Carbs: 33.8 g; **Dietary Fiber:** 7.4 g; **Sugars:** 1.7 g			
Cholesterol: 191 mg; **Sodium:** 379 mg; **Potassium:** 871 mg;			
Vitamin A: 41%; **Vitamin C:** 9%; **Calcium:** 24%; **Iron:** 31%			

Ingredients:

- ☐ 8 medium whole-wheat tortillas
- ☐ 8 large eggs
- ☐ 5 cups fresh spinach, roughly chopped
- ☐ 1/2 teaspoon kosher salt
- ☐ 1/2 teaspoon garlic powder
- ☐ 1/2 teaspoon black pepper
- ☐ 1 tablespoon milk
- ☐ 1 tablespoon extra-virgin olive oil, plus additional for cooking the quesadillas
- ☐ 1 can (10-ounce) white beans, rinsed and then drained
- ☐ 1 1/2 cups cheese, freshly grated, such as cheddar, mozzarella, Swiss, or any similar melty, cheesy

Directions:

1. Inside a large-sized bowl, whisk the eggs with the milk, pepper, garlic powder, and the salt; set aside.
2. Put 1 tablespoon olive oil inside a large-sized nonstick skillet; heat on medium heat until shimmering. Add the spinach; cook for about 1 minute, stirring often, or until starting to wilt.
3. Add the beans and then carefully pour in the eggs; cook for about 3 minutes, occasionally stirring, or until the eggs are just set. Taste, and if desired, season with more salt and pepper; remove from the heat.
4. Sprinkle each tortilla with 1/8 of the shredded cheese, leaving a small border all around the edge. Spoon 1/8 of the egg mix over the cheese and then fold the tortilla into half. Repeat the process with the remaining tortillas, cheese, and filling.
5. Carefully wipe clean the skillet where you cooked the eggs; lightly coat with the olive oil and heat on medium heat. Carefully put a quesadilla into the pan; cook for 3 minutes, carefully flip, and cook the other side for 3 minutes more or until both sides are golden and the cheese is melted. Cut into triangles. Serve warm.

Freezing: Assemble the quesadillas as directed above. Individually wrap each with plastic wrap. Arrange in a baking sheet in a single layer or in a flat surface that will fir your freezer. Flash freeze until the quesadillas are firm. Transfer them into a freezer bag or in an airtight container; store in the freezer for up to 2 months.

Cooking: Remove the plastic wrap; microwave for about 2-3 minutes or till heated through. Alternatively, thaw them in the fridge overnight and cook in the skillet as directed above.

Simple Oatmeal Cups

Prep Time: 20 minutes; **Cook Time:** 2-3 minutes	

Serving Size: 80 g; **Serves:** 24; **Calories:** 78
Total Fat: 2.3 g **Saturated Fat:** 1.2 g; **Trans Fat:** 0 g
Protein: 2.7 g; **Net Carbs:** 10.9 g
Total Carbs: 12.4 g; **Dietary Fiber:** 1.5 g; **Sugars:** 3.4 g
Cholesterol: 3 mg; **Sodium:** 27 mg; **Potassium:** 78 mg;
Vitamin A: 01%; **Vitamin C:** 7%; **Calcium:** 5%; **Iron:** 3%

Ingredients:

- ☐ 3 cups oats, gluten free
- ☐ 3 cups milk, your preferred choice
- ☐ 1/4 cup brown or demerara sugar, or to taste (mix 1/4 tablespoon molasses + 1/4 cup low carb sweetener)
- ☐ 1 cup assorted chopped fruit, nuts, chocolate chips, or other toppings
- ☐ 3 cups water
- ☐ Pinch salt

Directions:

1. Inside a large-sized saucepan, combine the oats with the milk, water, and sugar substitute; bring to a boil. Reduce the heat to medium; cook for about 2-3 minutes or to desired consistency; set aside and let cool slightly.
2. Grease 2 pieces 12-cup muffin tins with cooking spray; set the toppings in bowls.
3. Divide the cooked oatmeal between the muffin cups; top each with your desired toppings. Cover the muffin tins with plastic wrap and the freeze in the freezer for a couple of hours or until frozen.
4. When frozen, loosen with a small spatula or a butter knife and then pop out from the muffin cups. Wrap each with plastic wrap or sandwich bags.
5. When ready to serve, take our needed servings from the freezer day or a night before serving day. Microwave for about 1-2 minutes or till warm. If desired, stir in a little more milk.

Buttermilk Whole-Wheat Pancakes

Prep Time: 20 minutes; **Cook Time:** 6 minutes per pancake	
Serving Size: 124 g; **Serves:** 6; **Calories:** 226	
Total Fat: 9.8 g **Saturated Fat:** 4.8 g; **Trans Fat:** 0 g	
Protein: 7 g; **Net Carbs:** 30.4 g	
Total Carbs: 35 g; **Dietary Fiber:** 4.6 g; **Sugars:** 3.1 g	
Cholesterol: 49 mg; **Sodium:** 422 mg; **Potassium:** 274 mg;	
Vitamin A: 5%; **Vitamin C:** 1%; **Calcium:** 14%; **Iron:** 10%	

Ingredients:
- ☐ 3/4 cup whole-wheat flour
- ☐ 3/4 cup sugar-free maple syrup
- ☐ 3/4 cup all-purpose flour
- ☐ 3 tablespoons sugar (equal amount Swerve sweetener)
- ☐ 3 tablespoons butter
- ☐ 1/2 teaspoon salt
- ☐ 1/2 teaspoon baking soda
- ☐ 1 tablespoon vegetable oil
- ☐ 1 large egg white
- ☐ 1 large egg
- ☐ 1 1/2 teaspoons baking powder
- ☐ 1 1/2 cups low-fat buttermilk
- ☐ Cooking spray

Directions:
1. Inside a large-sized bowl, whisk the flours, baking powder, sugar substitute, baking soda, and the salt until combined.
2. In another bowl, whisk the buttermilk with the egg, egg white, and the oil until combined.
3. Add the buttermilk mix into the flour mix, stirring until just most.
4. Over medium heat, heat a nonstick skillet or nonstick griddle coated with cooking spray.
5. Spoon about 1/4 cup of the batter onto the griddle; cook until the top bubbles and the edges look cooked, flip and cook until the bottom of the pancake is set. Serve with syrup and with butter. If serving immediately, keep the cooked pancakes warm in a 200F oven while cooking the rest of the batter.

Freezing: If making ahead of time, let cool completely after cooking. Line a cookie sheet with parchment paper. Put the pancaked into the cookie sheet, placing the pancakes without touching each other. Cover with parchment paper and put another layer of pancakes. Place into the freezer and freeze until solid. When frozen, transfer into a gallon-sized freezer bag, label, and keep in the freezer. When ready to serve, reheat on toaster, microwave, or oven.

Biscuit-Crusted Sausage-Egg Pie

Prep Time: 30 minutes; **Cook Time:** 25 minutes	

Serving Size: 207 g; **Serves:** 4; **Calories:** 505

Total Fat: 37.7 g **Saturated Fat:** 12.3 g; **Trans Fat:** 0 g

Protein: 20.9 g; **Net Carbs:** 18.1 g

Total Carbs: 20.4 g; **Dietary Fiber:** 2.3 g; **Sugars:** 3.4 g

Cholesterol: 261 mg; **Sodium:** 875 mg; **Potassium:** 306 mg;

Vitamin A: 8%; **Vitamin C:** 5%; **Calcium:** 16%; **Iron:** 17%

Ingredients:

- ☐ 4 pieces biscuit dough, refrigerated such as Pillsbury
- ☐ 2 ounces feta cheese, crumbled
- ☐ 2 large eggs, plus 2 large egg yolks
- ☐ 1/4 cup Kalamata olives, sliced
- ☐ 1/2 tablespoon fresh oregano, chopped
- ☐ 1/2 pound pork sausage, breakfast
- ☐ 1/2 cup milk
- ☐ 1 red onion, thinly sliced
- ☐ 1 1/2 teaspoons extra-virgin olive oil
- ☐ Salt and pepper

Directions:

1. Preheat the oven to 375F.
2. Put 1 tablespoon olive oil Inside a large-sized skillet; heat on medium-high heat. Add the sausage and the oregano; cook for about 5 minutes, breaking the sausage, until juts browned. Drain excess grease and let cool.
3. Grease a 9-inch pie pan with the remaining 1/2 teaspoon olive oil. Place 1 piece of biscuit dough inside a large-sized re-sealable plastic bag, with a rolling pin, roll into a 1/8-inch thick disk. Transfer the dough disk into the prepared pie pan. Repeat the process with the remaining dough pieces; pinch together in pan to form a crust.
4. Inside a large-sized bowl, combine the sausage with the feta, onion, and olives. Spread the mix evenly over the crust.
5. In a medium-sized bowl, beat the eggs with the egg yolks, the milk, 1/8 teaspoon salt, and 1/8 teaspoon pepper.
6. Pour the egg mix over the sausage mix; bake for about 25 minutes or till set. Let cool for 10 minutes and serve.

Freezing: Wrap the baked pie with foil and then freeze. When ready to serve, thaw in the fridge, tent with foil, then heat in a 350F degree oven for about 15 minutes.

Baked Cinnamon Apple Oatmeal with Raisins, Walnuts, and Flax Seeds

Prep Time: 10 minutes; **Cook Time:** 20 minutes		
Serving Size: 80 g; **Serves:** 20; **Calories:** 308		
Total Fat: 24.5 g **Saturated Fat:** 3.1 g; **Trans Fat:** 0 g		
Protein: 11.1 g; **Net Carbs:** 12.1 g		
Total Carbs: 17.1 g; **Dietary Fiber:** 5 g; **Sugars:** 3.5 g		
Cholesterol: 23 mg; **Sodium:** 120 mg; **Potassium:** 304 mg;		
Vitamin A: 2%; **Vitamin C:** 2%; **Calcium:** 6%; **Iron:** 12%		

Ingredients:

- 1 apple, cored and diced (peeled or unpeeled is fine)
- 1 cup milk
- 1 teaspoon baking powder
- 1 teaspoon cinnamon
- 1/4 cup butter (1/2 stick), melted
- 1/4 cup ground flaxseed (or substitute more oats)
- 1/4 cup raisins
- 11/2 cup walnuts, chopped
- 2 3/4cups oats (quick or rolled)
- 2 eggs
- 2/3 cup brown sugar (mix 2 tsp molasses + 2/3 cup low carb sweetener)
- 3/4 teaspoon salt

Directions:

1. Preheat the oven to 350F. Grease an 8x8-inch metal or a glass baking dish.
2. Inside a large-sized bowl, whisk the oats with the brown sugar substitute, flaxseed, baking powder, salt, and cinnamon.
3. In another bowl, whisk the milk with the eggs and the melted butter.
4. Pour the wet ingredients into the dry ingredients; stir until well combined. Gently stir in the apples, raisins, and walnuts.
5. Pour the batter into the prepared baking dish; bake for about 20-25 minutes or till a toothpick come out clean when inserted in the center. Serve with warm milk, and, if desired, a little brown sugar substitute on top.

Freezing: Assemble the dish, but do not bake. Tightly wrap the casserole dish with a few layers of plastic wrap and then with 1 layer of foil; freeze.

When ready to bake, transfer in the fridge and let thaw for 24 hours; bake according to directions. Alternatively, you can defrost in the microwave and then bake as directed.

If baking from frozen, cover the oatmeal with foil; bake longer until the middle is cooked through, about 1 1/2 times longer than original baking time.

Baked Pumpkin Blueberry French Toast

Prep Time: 25 minutes; **Cook Time:** 30-35 minutes		
Serving Size: 87 g; **Serves:** 26; **Calories:** 157		
Total Fat: 8.5 g **Saturated Fat:** 4.2 g; **Trans Fat:** 0 g		
Protein: 5.3 g; **Net Carbs:** 0 g		
Total Carbs: 18.4 g; **Dietary Fiber:** 2.7 g; **Sugars:** 3.6 g		
Cholesterol: 66 mg; **Sodium:** 240 mg; **Potassium:** 110 mg;		
Vitamin A: 27%; **Vitamin C:** 4%; **Calcium:** 6%; **Iron:** 7%		

Ingredients:

- 8 eggs
- 2 loaves French baguette, cut into 1" slices (not too crusty - 24 slices)
- 2 teaspoons vanilla extract
- 2-3 cups blueberries, fresh or frozen
- 3/4 cup brown sugar, firmly pack (mix 3/4 tablespoon molasses + 3/4 cup sweetener)
- 3/4 cup pumpkin puree
- 2 1/2 cups milk
- 1/4 teaspoon salt
- 1/4 cup sugar-free maple syrup
- 1/4 cup butter
- 1 1/2 teaspoon ground cinnamon

For crumble topping (optional):

- 1/2 cup almond flour
- 1 teaspoon cinnamon
- 1 stick cold butter, cut into pieces
- 1/2 cup brown sugar, firmly packed (mix 1/2 tablespoon molasses + 1/2 cup low carb sweetener)
- 1/4 teaspoon salt

Directions:

1. If using crumble topping, mix until well combined and store in an airtight container right until before baking.
2. Preheat the oven to 375F. Grease a 9x13-inch baking pan; set aside.
3. Arrange the bread into the prepared baking pan.
4. Inside a large-sized bowl, whisk the eggs with the milk, brown sugar substitute, pumpkin, cinnamon, vanilla, and salt.
5. Pour the egg mix over the bread layer; toss to completely coat. Cover and refrigerate overnight.
6. Just before baking, sprinkle with berries, and, if using, the crumble topping.
7. If not using crumble topping, heat the butter and the maple syrup in a microwave or in a small-sized saucepan on medium heat until melted; drizzle over the berries.
8. Bake about 30-35 minutes or till set. When baked, dust with powdered sugar, if desired. Drizzle with maple syrup.

Freezing: Assemble the dish, including topping with crumble or drizzling with maple syrup mix, but do not bake.

When ready to bake, transfer to the fridge and thaw overnight; bake as directed. You may need to bake longer if the prepared dish is partially frozen. If the dish begins to get too brown, cover with foil.

Baked Oatmeal Brownie

Prep Time: 10 minutes; **Cook Time:** 20 minutes

Serving Size: 100 g; **Serves:** 8; **Calories:** 204		
Total Fat: 8.4 g **Saturated Fat:** 4.3 g; **Trans Fat:** 0 g		
Protein: 7.4 g; **Net Carbs:** 21.7 g		
Total Carbs: 27.8 g; **Dietary Fiber:** 6.1 g; **Sugars:** 2.9 g		
Cholesterol: 43 mg; **Sodium:** 252 mg; **Potassium:** 402 mg;		
Vitamin A: 49%; **Vitamin C:** 1%; **Calcium:** 12%; **Iron:** 18%		

Ingredients:

- 2 3/4 cups oatmeal (quick or rolled oats work)
- 1/4 cup ground flaxseed (or more oats)
- 1/4 cup cocoa powder
- 1/3-1/2 cup honey or brown sugar (mix 1 teaspoon molasses + 1/3 cup sweetener or mix 1/2 tablespoon molasses + 1/2 cup sweetener)
- 1/2cup pumpkin puree
- 1/2 teaspoon cinnamon
- 1 cup milk
- 2 eggs
- 2 tablespoons coconut oil or butter, melted
- 2 teaspoons baking powder
- 2 teaspoons vanilla
- 3/4 teaspoon salt
- 1/4-1/2 cup dark chocolate chips, optional

Directions:

1. Preheat the oven to 350F. Grease a 9x13-inch pan; set aside.
2. Inside a large-sized bowl, whisk all the dry ingredients together until combined.
3. In another bowl, whisk the eggs with the milk, vanilla, pumpkin puree, coconut oil, and honey.
4. Pour the wet ingredients into the dry ingredients; mix well. If using, stir in the chocolate chips.
5. Pour the batter into the prepared baking pan; bake for about 20 minutes or till a toothpick come out clean when inserted in the center.
6. Serve with warm milk on top.

Freezing: Prepare the dish, but skip baking. Tightly wrap with a few layers of plastic wrap and then with 1 foil; put in the back of the freezer for up to 3 months.

When ready to bake, transfer in the fridge and let thaw for 24 hours; bake according to directions. Alternatively, you can defrost in a microwave and then bake.

Sneaky Chocolate Waffles

Prep Time: 20 minutes; **Cook Time:** 3 1/2 minutes per batch	

Prep Time: 20 minutes; **Cook Time:** 3 1/2 minutes per batch

Serving Size: 78 g; **Serves:** 12; **Calories:** 142

Total Fat: 8.6 g **Saturated Fat:** 5.1 g; **Trans Fat:** 0 g

Protein: 4.8 g; **Net Carbs:** 12.5 g

Total Carbs: 15.1 g; **Dietary Fiber:** 2.6 g; **Sugars:** 2.4 g

Cholesterol: 30 mg; **Sodium:** 133 mg; **Potassium:** 319 mg;

Vitamin A: 1%; **Vitamin C:** 3%; **Calcium:** 12%; **Iron:** 8%

Ingredients:

- 1 cup whole-wheat flour
- 1/2 cup almond flour
- 1 teaspoon vanilla
- 1 tablespoon baking powder
- 1 cup zucchini, pureed in food processor (pureed pumpkin would work here)
- 1 3/4 cup milk
- 1 1/2 teaspoon cinnamon
- 1/2 cup cocoa powder, sifted
- 1/2 teaspoon baking soda
- 1/4 cup brown sugar (mix 1/4 tablespoon molasses + 1/4 cup sweetener)
- 1/4 cup coconut oil or butter, melted
- 1/4 teaspoon salt
- 2 eggs
- 1 cup chocolate chips, optional

Directions:

1. Inside a large-sized bowl, whisk all the dry ingredients until combined.
2. In another bowl, whisk the brown sugar with the melted coconut oil. Whisk in the milk, egg, and the pureed zucchini.
3. Add the wet ingredients into the dry ingredients; whisk until just combined, making sure not to over mix. Stir in the chocolate chips, if using.
4. Pour about 1/4 cup batter per batter and cook in your waffle iron according to manufacturer's directions. I cooked mine about 3 1/2 minutes per batch.

Freezing: Let the waffles cool completely. Put the waffles into a parchment-lined baking sheet. Flash freeze for about 2 hours until frozen. When frozen, transfer into a freezer bag, label, and freeze. When ready to serve, just reheat in the oven, toaster, or microwave.

Easy Casserole Muffins

Prep Time: 20 minutes; **Cook Time:** 15-18 minutes	
Serving Size: 76 g; **Serves:** 12; **Calories:** 128	
Total Fat: 7.5 g **Saturated Fat:** 3.4 g; **Trans Fat:** 0 g	
Protein: 9.2 g; **Net Carbs:** 5 g	
Total Carbs: 5.8 g; **Dietary Fiber:** 0.8 g; **Sugars:** 1.8 g	
Cholesterol: 125 mg; **Sodium:** 245 mg; **Potassium:** 109 mg;	
Vitamin A: 5%; **Vitamin C:** 1%; **Calcium:** 12%; **Iron:** 6%	

Ingredients:
- 8 eggs
- 3-4 slices deli ham (use preservative-free)
- 3-4 pieces whole-wheat bread, torn into small pieces (enough to fill muffin tins almost to top)
- 2 teaspoons ground mustard
- 1 teaspoon ground pepper (or more or less to taste)
- 1 cup milk
- 1 cup cheddar cheese, shredded
- Dried parsley

Directions:
1. Preheat the oven to 400F. Grease muffins tins well.
2. Put the bread pieces into each muffin cups, filling them about 2/3 full. Divide the ham between each muffin cup, topping on top of the bread layer, and evenly sprinkle the cheese over.
3. Whisk the eggs with the milk, pepper, and ground mustard; pour the egg mix into each muffin cup. Sprinkle with a bit of dried parsley and bake for about 15-18 minutes or till the top is golden brown and the middle is cooked through.

Notes: If making ahead of time, individually wrap with plastic wrap, put in a freezer bag, and freeze. When ready to serve, microwave for about 1 minute, turning once through heating.

Pumpkin Almond Pancakes

Prep Time: 10 minutes; **Cook Time:** 20 minutes	

Serving Size: 78 g; **Serves:** 10-12; **Calories:** 140
Total Fat: 10.8 g **Saturated Fat:** 2.2 g; **Trans Fat:** 0 g
Protein: 5.7 g; **Net Carbs:** 5.1 g
Total Carbs: 7.8 g; **Dietary Fiber:** 2.7 g; **Sugars:** 2.9 g
Cholesterol: 34 mg; **Sodium:** 91 mg; **Potassium:** 341 mg;
Vitamin A: 33%; **Vitamin C:** 1%; **Calcium:** 17%; **Iron:** 6%

Ingredients:

- 2 cups almond flour
- 1/4 teaspoon salt
- 1/2 cup pumpkin puree (canned pumpkin)
- 1 teaspoon vanilla
- 1 teaspoon cinnamon
- 2 cups milk
- 2 eggs
- 2 tablespoons brown sugar (or 12 drops liquid stevia)
- 4 teaspoons baking powder
- 4 teaspoons butter or coconut oil, melted, plus more for greasing skillet
- Pinch nutmeg

Directions:

1. Inside a large-sized bowl, whisk the dry ingredients until combined.
2. In another bowl, whisk the wet ingredients until combined.
3. Pour the wet ingredients into the dry ingredients; whisk until just smooth, careful not to over mix.
4. Let the batter rest for about 5 minutes.
5. Cook the batter in batches. Butter the skillet and heat over medium temperature. Pour batter into pan, cook until bubbles form on the top. Flip and cook until golden brown.
6. Serve warm with maple syrup and butter.

Freezing: Lay the pancakes individually into a cookie sheet. After 30 minutes, stack the in a freezable container. When ready to serve, pop them into the toaster or microwave for 20-second intervals until heated through.

Ham and Cheese Crescent Rolls

Prep Time: 10 minutes; **Cook Time:** 15 minutes

Serving Size: 259 g; **Serves:** 8; **Calories:** 453	
Total Fat: 24 g **Saturated Fat:** 13.5 g; **Trans Fat:** 0 g	
Protein: 23.3 g; **Net Carbs:** 20.5 g	
Total Carbs: 38 g; **Dietary Fiber:** 2.8 g; **Sugars:** 1.1 g	
Cholesterol: 103 mg; **Sodium:** 1023 mg; **Potassium:** 195 mg;	
Vitamin A: 9%; **Vitamin C:** 3%; **Calcium:** 7%; **Iron:** 14%	

Ingredients:
For the dough:
- 4 cups flour
- 2 eggs, beaten
- 2 1/2 teaspoons yeast
- 1/2 cup sugar
- 1 teaspoon salt
- 1 stick butter, softened
- 1 cup milk

For the filling:
- 1 pound deli ham, more or less
- 16 ounces mozzarella cheese, more or less (or a large bag of shredded)
- 5 tablespoons butter, melted

Directions:
1. Put the dough ingredients into the bread machine according to the manufacturer's instructions.
2. After the dough cycle is complete, divide the dough into 2 portions, making a mound. Flour a clean surface and a rolling pin very well.
3. Roll 1 mound into a 1/2-inch thick piece, about the size of a large-sized pizza. Brush the dough with melted butter. With a pizza cutter, cut into pie-shaped pieces, cutting in a straight line like you would cut a pizza.
4. Add about 2 pieces ham and then 1 piece cheese into each slice. Starting at the large end, roll up the dough. With the end side in the bottom, put the rolled dough into a greased baking dish. Repeat the process with the remaining slice and repeat the process with the remaining dough mound.
5. Bake at 350F for about 20-25 minutes or till the rolls are golden brown; brush the rolls with melted butter, let cool, and serve.

Freezing: When the rolls are baked, let them cool completely and put into airtight bags or containers. When ready to serve, warm then in the oven or in the microwave.

Lunch

Chicken Chili

Prep Time: 20 minutes; **Cook Time:** 10-12 hours	

Serving Size: 372 g; **Serves:** 8; **Calories:** 564	
Total Fat: 6.5 g **Saturated Fat:** 1.6 g; **Trans Fat:** 0 g	
Protein: 44 g; **Net Carbs:** 62.5 g	
Total Carbs: 87.6 g; **Dietary Fiber:** 25.1 g; **Sugars:** 7.1 g	
Cholesterol: 50 mg; **Sodium:** 286 mg; **Potassium:** 2130 mg;	
Vitamin A: 30%; **Vitamin C:** 48%; **Calcium:** 19%; **Iron:** 61%	

Ingredients:
- ☐ 15-ounce canned cannellini beans, drained and rinsed
- ☐ 15-ounce canned black beans, drained and rinsed
- ☐ 14 1/2-ounce canned petite diced tomatoes, undrained
- ☐ 14 1/2-ounce canned diced tomatoes with green chilies, undrained
- ☐ 1 pound boneless, skinless chicken breasts, cut into 1-inch pieces
- ☐ 1 tablespoon paprika
- ☐ 1/4 teaspoon crushed red pepper
- ☐ 12/3 cup frozen corn
- ☐ 1 medium yellow onion, chopped
- ☐ 1 cup frozen medley of green and red peppers and onion strips
- ☐ 1 1/2 teaspoons oregano
- ☐ 2 teaspoons ground cumin
- ☐ 3 teaspoons chili powder
- ☐ 4 cloves garlic, minced

Directions:
1. Put the beans, corn, onions, pepper medley, and the tomatoes in a 1-gallon plastic freezer bag. Add the garlic and then the seasonings. Add the chicken.
2. Remove as much air as you can from the bag, seal, and lay flat in the freezer.

To cook: Place the bag in the refrigerator; let thaw overnight. Put all the contents into a slow cooker; cook for about 10-12 hours on LOW or until the chicken is tender.

Tamale Pie

Prep Time: 30 minutes; **Cook Time:** 30 minutes		
Serving Size: 280 g; **Serves:** 8; **Calories:** 311		
Total Fat: 13.3 g **Saturated Fat:** 4.3 g; **Trans Fat:** 0 g		
Protein: 31.5 g; **Net Carbs:** 12.1 g		
Total Carbs: 19.8 g; **Dietary Fiber:** 7.7 g; **Sugars:** 9.4 g		
Cholesterol: 51 mg; **Sodium:** 451 mg; **Potassium:** 578 mg;		
Vitamin A: 86%; **Vitamin C:** 22%; **Calcium:** 13%; **Iron:** 61%		

Ingredients:

- 4 ounces canned diced green chilies
- 3/4 pound ground beef, extra-lean
- 3/4 cup Mexican blend cheese, shredded
- 3 cups water
- 2 tablespoons olive oil
- 2 tablespoons grated lime zest
- 2 scallions, chopped
- 2 cloves garlic, minced
- 15-ounce can diced tomatoes
- 1/2 onion, chopped
- 1 teaspoon paprika
- 1 teaspoon dried oregano
- 1 teaspoon cumin
- 1 teaspoon coriander
- 1 cup sliced black olives
- 1 cup corn kernels
- 1 cup coarse cornmeal
- Salt and freshly ground black pepper

Directions:

1. Preheat the oven to 350F. Grease a 7x11-inch baking dish with cooking spray; set aside.
2. Inside a large-sized skillet, heat the olive oil on medium-high heat. Add the onion; sprinkle with a bit of salt and pepper; cook, frequently stirring, until the onions are soft. Stir in the coriander, cumin, garlic, and oregano; cook for 1 minute more.
3. Add the beef; cook, frequently stirring, until browned. Stir in the scallions and the lime zest; cook for 1 minute. Add the tomatoes, olives, and chilies; stir to combined and cook until heated through. Reduce the heat to low.
4. Meanwhile, in a medium-sized saucepan, bring the water to boil. Add the cornmeal and then season with salt and pepper. Continually whisk until the mix begins to thicken. Add the corn and the paprika; continue whisking until the cornmeal is thick, similar to oatmeal in consistency. Stir in the cheese and remove from the heat.
5. Spoon the beef mix into the prepared baking dish; spread evenly. Pour the cornmeal mix over the beef mix; spreading evenly to cover the beef layer.
6. Bake for about 30 minutes or till the cornbread topping is set; transfer the baking dish on a wire rack and let cool completely.

Freezing: Individually store the portions in freezable and microwavable containers and then freeze. If serving for a crowd, cover the baking dish with plastic wrap and then cover with heavy-duty aluminum foil.

Reheating: When ready to serve, transfer to the fridge and let thaw overnight. Reheat individual servings in a microwave for 3 minutes at 60 percent power or until heated through. Alternatively, preheat the oven to 350F. Remove the foil and the plastic from the baking dish, recover with foil, and bake for about 30 minutes or till heated through.

Bacon and Cheese Quiche

Prep Time: 20 minutes; **Cook Time:** 30-40 minutes, plus 5-10 minutes cooling	

Serving Size: 103 g; **Serves:** 8; **Calories:** 349	
Total Fat: 27.4 g **Saturated Fat:** 12.8 g; **Trans Fat:** 0 g	
Protein: 15.7 g; **Net Carbs:** 9.9 g	
Total Carbs: 9.9 g; **Dietary Fiber:** 0 g; **Sugars:** 2.1 g	
Cholesterol: 185 mg; **Sodium:** 910 mg; **Potassium:** 176 mg;	
Vitamin A: 9%; **Vitamin C:** 0%; **Calcium:** 20%; **Iron:** 7%	

Ingredients:
- 6-12 slices bacon, cooked and then crumbled
- 6 eggs
- 1/4 teaspoon freshly ground black pepper
- 1/2 teaspoon kosher salt
- 1 prepared pie crust, store-bought is fine
- 1 cup heavy cream
- 1 1/2 cups Mexican blend cheese, shredded, or any other cheese you like

Directions:
1. Preheat the oven to 425F.
2. In a bowl, whisk the eggs with the cream, salt, and the pepper.
3. Put the piecrust into a round 9-inch pan or in a deep pie plate dish. Using a fork, prick the crust several times. Sprinkle the bacon across the bottom of the piecrust and then cover the bacon with the cheese. Pour the egg mix over the cheese.
4. Bake for about 15 minutes. Reduce the heat to 300F and bake for another 30-40 minutes or till the quiche is lightly browned and puffy. Let the pie cool for about 5 to 10 minutes and serve.

Freezing: Let the quiche cool completely. Tightly cover with foil and then freeze until ready to serve. When ready to serve, transfer in the fridge let thaw completely. Warm in the oven with the foil cover on or slice into individual servings and warm in the microwave.

Alternatively, after cooling completely, you can cut the quiche into individual servings and store them in Ziploc bags or airtight containers; when ready to serve, just warm in the microwave.

Taco Sweet Potato and Spinach Egg Bake

Prep Time: 20 minutes; **Cook Time:** 50 minutes, plus 10 minutes cooling

Serving Size: 100 g; **Serves:** 9; **Calories:** 152		
Total Fat: 8.8 g Saturated Fat: 5.2 g; Trans Fat: 0 g		
Protein: 6.9 g; **Net Carbs:** 10.1 g		
Total Carbs: 12.2 g; Dietary Fiber: 2.1 g; Sugars: 1 g		
Cholesterol: 131 mg; **Sodium:** 357 mg; **Potassium:** 438 mg;		
Vitamin A: 18%; **Vitamin C:** 15%; **Calcium:** 8%; **Iron:** 7%		

Ingredients:

- 6 large eggs OR 3 large eggs PLUS 1 cup egg whites
- 3 small sweet potatoes, coarsely grated (12 ounces)
- 2 handfuls baby spinach
- 1/4 cup cilantro, chopped, optional
- 1/2 teaspoon taco seasoning, all natural
- 1/2 cup full-fat white cheddar cheese, shredded (or any you prefer)
- 1/2 cup almond milk (or any you prefer)
- 1 teaspoon salt
- 1 teaspoon black pepper, ground
- 1 tablespoon jalapeno, seeded & minced (for kid friendly I used 1/2 tablespoon)
- 1 small garlic clove, crushed
- Cooking spray

Directions:

1. Preheat the oven to 350F. Line an 8x8-inch baking dish with parchment paper and then grease with cooking spray.
2. Inside a large-sized bowl, whisk the eggs with the taco seasoning, salt, and pepper for 30 seconds.
3. Add the milk, cilantro, cheese, jalapeno pepper, and garlic; whisk to combine.
4. Add the spinach and the sweet potatoes; mix to combine.
5. Transfer the mix into the prepared baking dish; bake for 50 minutes. Remove from the oven; let cool for 10 minutes and cut into servings. Serve hot, warm, or cold.

Notes: Store these bakes in airtight containers for up to 1 week in the fridge or freeze for up to 3 to 4 months.

Prep Time: 10 minutes; **Cook Time:** 10 minutes		

Serving Size: 154 g; **Serves:** 4; **Calories:** 342
Total Fat: 16.4 g **Saturated Fat:** 8.3 g; **Trans Fat:** 0 g
Protein: 21.4 g; **Net Carbs:** 24.5 g
Total Carbs: 26.9 g; **Dietary Fiber:** 2.4 g; **Sugars:** 2.4 g
Cholesterol: 185 mg; **Sodium:** 834 mg; **Potassium:** 221 mg;
Vitamin A: 9%; **Vitamin C:** 4%; **Calcium:** 32%; **Iron:** 19%

Ingredients:

- ☐ 4 slices sharp cheddar cheese
- ☐ 4 slices black forest ham, or cooked bacon
- ☐ 4 English muffins, or mini croissants
- ☐ 3 large eggs
- ☐ 1 tablespoon water
- ☐ Butter, for greasing pan
- ☐ Salt and pepper, to taste

Directions:

1. Heat a small-sized skillet on medium heat.
2. Meanwhile, whisk the eggs with the water, a pinch of salt, and a pinch of pepper until combined and frothy.
3. When the skillet is hot, grease the bottom with a thin coat of butter. Pour just enough egg mix to cover the pan; cook for 1 minute or until the egg is almost cooked through. Flip and then cook for 15 seconds more. Remove the egg crepe and transfer into a plate. Repeat the process with the remaining egg mix.
4. Slice the bread into halves. Put 1 slice ham or bacon, 1 slice cheddar cheese, 1 egg crepe into each bread half and top with the other bread half.

Notes: Put the sandwiches into individual Ziploc plastic bag and freeze for up to 6 weeks. When ready to serve, line a microwavable plate with paper tower; microwave each individual sandwich for 1 minute or until the sandwich is hot and the cheese is melted.

76

Chicken and Bean Cheesy Taquitos

Prep Time: 10 minutes; **Cook Time:** 50 minutes		
Serving Size: 128 g; **Serves:** 12; **Calories:** 286		
Total Fat: 8.9 g **Saturated Fat:** 3.4 g; **Trans Fat:** 0 g		
Protein: 29.1 g; **Net Carbs:** 17.3 g		
Total Carbs: 21.4 g; **Dietary Fiber:** 4.1 g; **Sugars:** 1.1 g		
Cholesterol: 74 mg; **Sodium:** 235 mg; **Potassium:** 445 mg;		
Vitamin A: 2%; **Vitamin C:** 2%; **Calcium:** 12%; **Iron:** 11%		

Ingredients:

For the chicken:

- 1 pounds chicken breasts or thighs, boneless, skinless
- 1 teaspoon olive oil or olive oil spray
- 1/2 teaspoon chili powder
- 1/4 teaspoon coarse sea salt
- 1/4 teaspoon cumin
- 1/4 teaspoon garlic powder
- 1/4 teaspoon onion powder

For the taquitos:

- 12 corn tortillas
- 1 pound chicken, shredded (about 3 cups)
- 1 cup pinto beans, mashed or refried (about 1 can 15-ounce)
- 1 cup Mexican blend cheese, shredded
- Olive oil spray (or teaspoon of olive oil)

Directions:

For the chicken:

1. Preheat the oven to 350F.
2. In a small-sized bowl, mix the chili powder, onion powder, cumin, sea salt, and garlic powder.
3. Put the chicken into a baking sheet; coat with olive oil or spray with olive oil spray. Sprinkle the chicken top with the seasoning; bake for about 25-30 minutes or till fully cooked. With a knife and fork, shred the chicken meat. If needed, season with more salt.

For the taquitos:

1. Preheat the oven to 350F.
2. Grease a large-sized baking sheet the olive oil spray or grease with olive oil.
3. Heat the corn tortillas for about 30 seconds in the microwave or on a hot griddle or until pliable and soft.
4. Spoon about 1 tablespoon or more beans and shredded cheese in the center of the tortilla and then top with about 2 tablespoon shredded chicken; tightly roll and secure with a toothpick. With the seam side down, put the rolled tortillas into a baking sheet. Repeat the process with the remaining tortillas, beans, cheese, and chicken.
5. Spray or lightly brush the top of the taquitos with olive oil and then sprinkle with a little sea salt. Bake in the oven for 15-20 minutes or till the edges of the taquitos are browned.
6. Serve topped with cheese, chopped greens, your favorite salsa or dipping sauce, and sour cream.

Notes: To reduce the amount of time preparing the taquitos, you can use store-brought rotisserie chicken and shred it instead of baking your own.

Freezing: Let the taquitos cool completely. Put them in a baking sheet, arranging in a single layer, and freeze. When frozen, put the taquitos into freezer bag and keep in the freezer until ready to serve. When ready to serve, remove from the freezer bag; bake in a 350F oven for about 10-15 minutes or till hot.

Crunchy 4-Ingredient Parmesan Chicken Nuggets

Prep Time: 30 minutes; **Cook Time:** 25 minutes	
Serving Size: 147 g; **Serves:** 4; **Calories:** 338	
Total Fat: 10.9 g **Saturated Fat:** 3.3 g; **Trans Fat:** 0 g	
Protein: 38 g; **Net Carbs:** 18.4 g	
Total Carbs: 19.6 g; **Dietary Fiber:** 1.2 g; **Sugars:** 1.7 g	
Cholesterol: 105 mg; **Sodium:** 923 mg; **Potassium:** 329 mg;	
Vitamin A: 2%; **Vitamin C:** 0%; **Calcium:** 11%; **Iron:** 15%	

Ingredients:
- ☐ 1 pound ground chicken (450 grams), mix of dark and white meats
- ☐ 1/4 cup parmesan cheese, finely grated
- ☐ 1 cup breadcrumbs
- ☐ 1 teaspoon kosher salt

Directions:
1. In a medium-sized bowl, mix the breadcrumbs, parmesan cheese, and pinch of salt.
2. In a different bowl, mix the ground chicken well with 1 teaspoon salt.
3. With a tablespoon measure or with your hands, scoop about 1 tablespoon of the meat mix and put in the center of the breadcrumb mix. With your fingertips, scoop the breadcrumb mix from around the meat and sprinkle on top. The breadcrumbs make the meat mix less sticky. Press gently down to flatten into 1/2-inch thickness, making sure not to flatten too much or they will cook dry. Lightly toss it a bit with more breadcrumbs until well and evenly coated; you may gently press down with just enough pressure to adhere the breadcrumbs. Repeat the process until all the ground meat is used. This recipe makes enough for 24 nuggets.
4. Preheat the oven to 375F or 190C. Put the nuggets into a baking sheet lined with parchment paper or on a wire rack set on a baking sheet; bake for 25 minutes.
5. Serve with a mixed equal parts spicy brown mustard and honey, simple steamed veggies, and baked sweet potato fries for a complete meal.

Freezing: You can prepare the nuggets ahead of time. In a single layer, lay the nuggets into the baking sheet lined with parchment paper; flash freeze for about 1-2 hours or until firm. When firm, transfer into a freezer bag or freezable container and freeze for up to 3 months.

When ready to serve, bake the nuggets as directed for 30 minutes.

79

Turkey, White Bean, and Spinach Stuffed Bell Peppers

Prep Time: 10 minutes; **Cook Time:** 1 hour	
Serving Size: 234 g; **Serves:** 6; **Calories:** 641	
Total Fat: 13.5 g Saturated Fat: 4.4 g; Trans Fat: 0 g	
Protein: 47.9 g; Net Carbs: 31.8 g	
Total Carbs: 41.8 g; Dietary Fiber: 10 g; Sugars: 5.2 g	
Cholesterol: 34 mg; Sodium: 256 mg; Potassium: 941 mg;	
Vitamin A: 55%; **Vitamin C:** 139%; **Calcium:** 11%; **Iron:** 21%	

Ingredients:

- 6 green peppers, or red bell, medium to large
- 1 pound ground turkey breast, extra lean
- 1 can (15 ounces) great northern beans
- 1 cups brown rice, cooked
- 4 ounces burrata cheese, sliced (or fresh mozzarella)
- 3 cups fresh spinach, organic
- 2 teaspoons olive oil
- 1/2 cup fresh basil leaves
- 1 tablespoon Italian seasoning
- 1 tablespoon dried oregano
- 1 medium yellow onion, diced
- 6 cloves garlic
- 1 1/2 cups chunky tomato sauce, divided
- Freshly ground salt and black pepper, to taste

Directions:

1. Put the tomato sauce, basil, and garlic cloves into a food processor or blender; process or blend on HIGH for 1 to 2 minutes or till smooth. Set aside.
2. Preheat the oven to 350F.
3. Put the olive oil into a 10-inch skillet or frying pan; hat on medium-high heat. add the onions and the turkey; cook, breaking up the meat while stirring, for about 6-8 minutes or till the turkey is no longer pink and cooked. Stir the tomato sauce in. Stir in the Italian seasoning, oregano, and spinach; reduce heat to medium low and simmer, uncovered, for about 10 to 15 minutes; stirring every couple of minutes. Expect the spinach to break down as it cooks.
4. Meanwhile, cut the tops of the peppers; remove the seeds and the ribs. Put each pepper next to each other in a greased 2-quart baking dish.
5. When the turkey is simmered and cooked, stir in the rice and the beans. Taste, and if needed, adjust the salt, pepper, and seasoning.
6. Fill each pepper with the turkey mix. Add 1 spoonful of tomato sauce on top of the turkey filling and then sprinkle with the burrata cheese. Cover the dish with foil; bake for 30 minutes. Remove the foil and bake for additional 10 to 15 minutes or till the peppers are tender.

Notes: You use quinoa instead of brown rice, if preferred. You can also buy and use pre-cooked brown rice.

You can prepare the peppers ahead of time up to covering with foil; just store them in the fridge until ready to bake.

When baked, let the stuffed peppers cool completely, and store in the freezer. Just reheat when ready to serve.

Ancho Chili Pork, Tomatoes, and Hominy Stew

Prep Time: 30 minutes; **Cook Time:** 40 minutes		

Serving Size: 484 g; **Serves:** 6; **Calories:** 343

Total Fat: 8.9 g **Saturated Fat:** 2.1 g; **Trans Fat:** 0 g

Protein: 35.5 g; **Net Carbs:** 22.7 g

Total Carbs: 29.5 g; **Dietary Fiber:** 6.8 g; **Sugars:** 7.4 g

Cholesterol: 83 mg; **Sodium:** 886 mg; **Potassium:** 923 mg;

Vitamin A: 47%; **Vitamin C:** 74%; **Calcium:** 6%; **Iron:** 20%

Ingredients:

- ☐ 1 1/2 cups green bell pepper, chopped
- ☐ 1 1/2 pounds pork tenderloin, trimmed and then cut into 1/2-inch pieces
- ☐ 1 1/2 teaspoons smoked paprika
- ☐ 1 can (14.5-ounce) fire-roasted diced tomatoes, undrained
- ☐ 1 can (28-ounce) hominy, drained
- ☐ 1 tablespoon garlic, minced
- ☐ 1 tablespoon olive oil, divided
- ☐ 1 teaspoon ground cumin
- ☐ 1/2 teaspoon salt
- ☐ 2 1/2 cups chicken broth, fat-free, lower-sodium
- ☐ 2 cups onion, chopped
- ☐ 2 tablespoons ancho chili powder
- ☐ 2 teaspoons dried oregano

Directions:

1. Combine the chili powder, dried oregano, smoked paprika, ground cumin, and salt Inside a large-sized bowl; set aside 1 1/2 teaspoons of the spice mix.
2. Put the pork into the bowl; toss well to coat with the spice mix.
3. Put 2 teaspoons olive oil Inside a large-sized Dutch oven; heat on medium-high heat. Add the pork into the pan; cook for about 5 minutes, occasionally stirring, or until browned. Remove the pork from the pan and set aside.
4. In the same pan, add the remaining 1 teaspoon olive oil. Add the bell pepper, onion, and garlic; sauté for about 5 minutes, occasionally stirring, until tender.
5. Return the pork into the pan. Add the reserved spice mixture, the broth, tomatoes, and hominy; bring the mix to a boil. Partially cover and reduce the heat to a simmer; cook, simmering, for 25 minutes.

Notes: Double a batch and make ahead of time; just freeze for up to 2 months.

Sausage, Grilled Pepper, and Onion Calzones

Prep Time: 1 hour, 30 minutes; **Cook Time:** 15 minutes, pus 5 minutes standing

Serving Size: 245 g; **Serves:** 8; **Calories:** 405
Total Fat: 27.2 g **Saturated Fat:** 9 g; **Trans Fat:** 0 g
Protein: 18.8 g; **Net Carbs:** 18.1 g
Total Carbs: 20.8 g; **Dietary Fiber:** 2.7 g; **Sugars:** 3.8 g
Cholesterol: 57 mg; **Sodium:** 872 mg; **Potassium:** 264 mg;
Vitamin A: 21%; **Vitamin C:** 75%; **Calcium:** 5%; **Iron:** 14%

Ingredients:
- ☐ 1 portion pizza dough, preferably homemade
- ☐ 1 3/4 cups PLUS 3 tablespoons pizza sauce, New York-Style, divided
- ☐ 1 pound hot Italian turkey sausage links
- ☐ 1 red bell pepper, quartered
- ☐ 1 Vidalia, or other sweet onion, cut into 1/2-inch-thick slices (about 14 ounces)
- ☐ 1 yellow bell pepper, quartered
- ☐ 5 ounces mozzarella cheese, part-skim, shredded
- ☐ Cooking spray

Directions:
1. Remove the pizza dough from the fridge and let stand for 1 hour at room temperature.
2. Preheat the grill to medium-high heat.
3. Coat the bell pepper and the onion slices with cooking spray.
4. Coat the grill rack with cooking spray. Put the sausages and the veggies on a grill rack. Grill the veggies for about 4 minutes per side or until browned. Grill the sausages for 8 minutes, occasionally turning, until all sides are browned.
5. When cooked, remove the veggies and the sausages from the grill; let cool slightly.
6. Cut the onion slices into halves. Cut the bell peppers into 1/2-inch strips. Cut the sausages diagonally into thin slices.
7. Preheat the oven to 500F.
8. Lightly flour a clean work surface. Put the dough and then divide into 4 equal portions. Roll each portion into a 5x9-inch rectangle. Leaving a 1/4-inch border on each dough rectangle, spread pizza sauce over; arrange the sausage slices over 1/2 of each rectangle and then evenly top the sausage with the bell peppers and the onions. Spread the topping layers with about 1/3 cup of cheese. Fold the un-topped half of the rectangle over the topped half, covering the filling; with a fork, press the edges to seal.
9. Put the calzones into a cooking spray coated baking sheet. Coat the top of the calzones with the cooking spray; bake for about 15 minutes or till golden brown.
10. Remove from the oven and let stand for 5 minutes. Serve with the remaining pizza sauce.

Freezing: If making ahead of time, let cool completely. Individually wrap each calzone with plastic wrap tightly. Put in a freezer and freeze. When ready to serve, transfer into the fridge and then let thaw for a few hours. Microwave in 1 minute intervals on HIGH until heated through, about2 to 3 minutes or heat in a toaster oven at 300F.

Chicken, Cilantro, Cream Cheese, and Pepper Jack Cheese Taquitos

Prep Time: 20 minutes; **Cook Time:** 15 minutes	
Serving Size: 125 g; **Serves:** 15; **Calories:** 303	
Total Fat: 11.9 g **Saturated Fat:** 5.8 g; **Trans Fat:** 0 g	
Protein: 17.8 g; **Net Carbs:** 27 g	
Total Carbs: 33.9 g; **Dietary Fiber:** 6.9 g; **Sugars:** 5.3 g	
Cholesterol: 53 mg; **Sodium:** 179 mg; **Potassium:** 423 mg;	
Vitamin A: 68%; **Vitamin C:** 7%; **Calcium:** 14%; **Iron:** 11%	

Ingredients:

- 8 ounces cream cheese
- 3 cups roasted chicken breast, shredded (or roast beef)
- 1 can (6 ounces) green chilies (or 1/2 cup green salsa verde)
- 1 teaspoon onion powder
- 1/4 teaspoon garlic powder
- 2 tablespoons lime juice
- 3/4 teaspoon cumin
- 4 tablespoons cilantro, chopped
- 1 1/2 teaspoon chili powder
- 1 1/2 cups pepper-jack cheese, shredded
- Cooking spray
- Fine sea salt
- Small-sized corn or flour tortillas

Directions:

1. Melt thee cream cheese until melty and soft.
2. Put all the spices, lime juice, cilantro, chicken, green chilies, and cheese inside a large-sized bowl; mix well until blended well.
3. Heat the tortillas until pliable and soft.
4. Add about 2 tablespoons of the chicken mix into each tortilla; roll the tortillas, and, with the seam side down, put them in a cookie sheet lined with parchment paper or foil. Spray with a bit of olive oil spray and then sprinkle with a bit of salt; bake at a 425F oven for 15 minutes.

Freezing: If making ahead of time, arrange the rolls in the cookie sheet without touching each other. Flash freeze in the freezer until frozen. Transfer into a gallon-sized freezer bag, label, and keep in the freezer.

When ready to eat, take out needed serving and put in a cookie sheet lined with foil or parchment paper. Spray lightly with olive oil and then sprinkle with a bit of salt; bake at 425F for about 15 to 20 minutes or till crispy.

Chicken Enchiladas

Prep Time: 20 minutes; **Cook Time:** until heated through	

Serving Size: 264 g; **Serves:** 6; **Calories:** 631

Total Fat: 22.7 g **Saturated Fat:** 12.5 g; **Trans Fat:** 0 g

Protein: 51.3 g; **Net Carbs:** 45.5 g

Total Carbs: 72.1 g; **Dietary Fiber:** 26.6 g; **Sugars:** 0.9 g

Cholesterol: 125 mg; **Sodium:** 415 mg; **Potassium:** 1414 mg;

Vitamin A: 17%; **Vitamin C:** 35%; **Calcium:** 80%; **Iron:** 158%

Ingredients:
- ☐ 6 flour tortillas, burrito size
- ☐ 4 cups chicken, cooked, shredded
- ☐ 3 cups Monterey Jack cheese, shredded
- ☐ 2 cans (10 ounces) enchilada sauce
- ☐ 1 jalapeño pepper, diced, optional

Directions:
1. Put the chicken and 2 cups of the cheese into a bowl; toss together.
2. Divide the chicken-cheese mix between 6 tortillas. Fold the ends or the sides in; roll tightly and then with the seam side down, put into a 9x11-inch baking dish.
3. Preheat the oven to 375F.
4. Pour 2 cans of enchilada sauce over the tortillas and then top with the remaining 1 cup shredded cheese; bake, uncovered, until heated through and the cheese is melted.
5. Serve with salsa, sour cream, and cilantro.

Notes: You can assemble these enchiladas in the baking dish ahead of time. After assembling, cover with foil and store in the fridge.

You can bake a pan of these enchiladas, store in a Ziploc container, and freeze. Just reheat and take one each day.

Cheesy Ham Sliders

Prep Time: 40 minutes; **Cook Time:** 20 minutes	
Serving Size: 111 g; **Serves:** 15-20; **Calories:** 301	
Total Fat: 14.8 g **Saturated Fat:** 7.6 g; **Trans Fat:** 0 g	
Protein: 16.2 g; **Net Carbs:** 22.1 g	
Total Carbs: 27 g; **Dietary Fiber:** 4.9 g; **Sugars:** 3.9 g	
Cholesterol: 46 mg; **Sodium:** 739 mg; **Potassium:** 253 mg;	
Vitamin A: 6%; **Vitamin C:** 2%; **Calcium:** 19%; **Iron:** 10%	

Ingredients:

- ☐ 1 pound deli ham, more or less
- ☐ 7 ounces Swiss cheese slices
- ☐ 15-20 mini wheat rolls
- ☐ 1/3 cup brown sugar (mix 1 teaspoon molasses + 1/3 cup sweetener)
- ☐ 1/2 cup butter
- ☐ 1 tablespoon Worcestershire
- ☐ 1 tablespoon poppy seeds
- ☐ 1 tablespoon mustard

Directions:

1. Preheat the oven to 350F.
2. Sandwich folded 1-2 slices ham and 1/2 slice cheese between each roll. Put the sandwiches side by side into a 9x13-inch baking dish or whatever size you have.
3. In a medium-sized saucepan, mix the butter with the Worcestershire sauce, mustard, brown sugar substitute, and poppy seeds; bring the mix to a boil over medium-high heat; when boiling reduce the heat. Lightly drizzle each sandwich with the sauce.
4. Cover the baking dish with foil and then bake for about 20 minutes.

Freezing: You can assemble these sandwiches ahead of time up to lightly drizzling with the sauce. Cover the baking dish tightly with plastic wrap and/or with foil and freeze. When ready to serve, just let thaw completely and bake according to directions.

You can bake a bunch of these sandwiches, freeze them individually, and just reheat when ready to serve

86

Cheesy Bean Burritos

Prep Time: 20 minutes; **Cook Time:** 0 minutes	
Serving Size: 165 g; **Serves:** 8; **Calories:** 222	
Total Fat: 6.8 g **Saturated Fat:** 3.6 g; **Trans Fat:** 0 g	
Protein: 11.3 g; **Net Carbs:** 22 g	
Total Carbs: 29.8 g; **Dietary Fiber:** 7.8 g; **Sugars:** 1.1 g	
Cholesterol: 24 mg; **Sodium:** 438 mg; **Potassium:** 381 mg;	
Vitamin A: 3%; **Vitamin C:** 13%; **Calcium:** 16%; **Iron:** 13%	

Ingredients:

- ☐ 8 tortillas, burrito size, about 8 1/2-inch across
- ☐ 4 ounces mild cheddar cheese, freshly grated (about 1 cup)
- ☐ 2 cans (16 ounces) refried beans
- ☐ 1 medium sweet yellow onion, diced

Directions:

1. Cut 8 pieces 12x12-inch pieces of foil and wax paper.
2. Top each tortilla with 1/3 cup of refried beans, 2 tablespoons cheddar cheese, and 2 tablespoons onions.
3. Wrap each burrito tortilla around each filling. Wrap each burrito with a wax paper and then with a foil.

Freezing: Put the wrapped burritos into a gallon-sized plastic freezer bag. Freeze for up to 3 months.

When ready to serve, take our needed serving. Remove the foil and the wax paper cover from each burrito. Wrap each with paper towel. Microwave each for about 2 minutes or till the filling is heated through.

Lasagna Roll-Ups

Prep Time: 40 minutes; **Cook Time:** 35 minutes, plus 5 minutes standing

Serving Size: 180 g; **Serves:** 24; **Calories:** 315

Total Fat: 7.3 g **Saturated Fat:** 2.9 g **Trans Fat:** 0 g

Protein: 18.7 g; **Net Carbs:** 41.4 g

Total Carbs: 43.1 g; **Dietary Fiber:** 1.7 g; **Sugars:** 5.7 g

Cholesterol: 56 mg; **Sodium:** 385 mg; **Potassium:** 302 mg;

Vitamin A: 9%; **Vitamin C:** 3%; **Calcium:** 11%; **Iron:** 23%

Ingredients:

- 1 pound ground beef or turkey
- 1 egg
- 1 1/2 cups Parmesan cheese, grated
- 1 tablespoon Italian seasoning
- 1 teaspoon onion powder
- 1/4 teaspoon pepper
- 1/4 teaspoon salt
- 15 ounces ricotta cheese
- 2 cloves garlic, minced (or 2 teaspoons garlic powder)
- 2 tablespoons parsley flakes
- 24 lasagna noodles, uncooked
- 3 cups Mozzarella cheese, shredded
- 6 cups pasta sauce, your favorite (red sauce)
- Salt and Pepper, to taste

Directions:

1. In a skillet, brown the meat with the onion powder, garlic, salt, pepper, and Italian seasoning; drain when browned. Add 4 cups of the pasta sauce; cook until heated through.
2. Meanwhile, stir the ricotta cheese with the egg, 2 cups mozzarella cheese, egg, 1 cup parmesan cheese, parsley, salt, and pepper.
3. Cook the lasagna noodles according to the directions on the package. Add a little olive oil to the water to prevent them from sticking after draining. Drain the cooked lasagna noodles and then line on a wax paper sheet.
4. Spread the cheese mix over the noodles. You can use the same spatula you use to frost cakes.
5. Spread the meat-sauce mix evenly over the noodles.
6. Spread 1/2 cup pasta sauce in a 9x13-inch baking dish; this dish makes 2 pans.
7. Roll the noodles and with the seam side down, put them into the prepared baking dish.
8. Cover the noodles with 1/2 cup pasta sauce, sprinkle with 1/2 cup mozzarella cheese, 1/4 cup Parmesan cheese, and with parsley flakes.
9. Cover the baking dish with foil, making sure the foil is not touching the cheese; bake at 375F for 35 minutes. Let sit for 5 minutes and serve.

Freezing: You can freeze the meal before baking. Cover the baking dish with foil, sealing well; label and then freeze.

Chicken Poblano Soup

Prep Time: 20 minutes; **Cook Time:** 30 minutes	
Serving Size: 308 g; **Serves:** 5; **Calories:** 187	
Total Fat: 6.7 g **Saturated Fat:** 1.8 g; **Trans Fat:** 0 g	
Protein: 25 g; **Net Carbs:** 4.4 g	
Total Carbs: 5.7 g; **Dietary Fiber:** 1.1 g; **Sugars:** 2.3 g	
Cholesterol: 62 mg; **Sodium:** 683 mg; **Potassium:** 465 mg;	
Vitamin A: 10%; **Vitamin C:** 70%; **Calcium:** 4%; **Iron:** 13%	

Ingredients:
- ☐ 4 cups chicken broth or stock
- ☐ 3/4 cups onion, dice
- ☐ 2 1/2 cups boneless chicken breasts, diced
- ☐ 1/4 cups lime juice
- ☐ 1/4 cups fresh cilantro, chopped
- ☐ 1/2 tablespoons chili powder
- ☐ 1/2 cups poblano pepper, seeded and diced
- ☐ 1 tablespoon cumin

Directions:
1. Inside a large-sized stockpot, combine the chicken broth with the onion, poblano peppers, chili powder, and cumin; bring to a boil.
2. Add the chicken, lime juice, and cilantro; reduce the heat to a simmer. Cover and cook for 30 minutes.

Freezing: Let cool completely. Divide the soup into indicated number of serving into quart freezer bags, label and freeze.

When ready to serve, just microwave for about 1-2 minutes or till heated.

Homemade Hot Pockets

Prep Time: 2 hours; **Cook Time:** 15 minutes	

Serving Size: 198 g; **Serves:** 8; **Calories:** 448

Total Fat: 17.5 g **Saturated Fat:** 7.1 g; **Trans Fat:** 0 g

Protein: 21.1 g; **Net Carbs:** 47.9 g

Total Carbs: 50.6 g; **Dietary Fiber:** 2.7 g; **Sugars:** 0 g

Cholesterol: 49 mg; **Sodium:** 1155 mg; **Potassium:** 254 mg;

Vitamin A: 4%; **Vitamin C:** 3%; **Calcium:** 18%; **Iron:** 21%

Ingredients:
- 4 cups flour
- 1 1/2 cups cheddar cheese
- 1 1/2 cups mozzarella cheese
- 1 1/2 cups warm water
- 1 1/2 tablespoon yeast
- 1 1/2 teaspoon salt
- 2 1/2 cups ham or pepperoni, chopped
- 3 tablespoons olive oil
- Pizza sauce (for the pizza hot pockets)

Directions:
1. Put the flour, yeast, and salt into a food processor with the blade attachment; pulse until well mixed. Add the olive oil, pulsing in.
2. Turn the motor of the food processor on. With the motor running, pour in the warm water; let the machine run until the dough pulls away from the edges and forms a ball.
3. Put the dough into a greased bowl and then cover; let rise until the size is doubled.
4. Take out a handful of dough; roll into a small circle, about the size of your hand.
5. Add some meat and cheese into the dough circle; fold to make a half circle. Seal the edges and put into an ungreased cookie sheet. Repeat the process with the remaining dough, meat, and cheese.
6. Preheat the oven to 450F. Bake the pockets for about 12 to 15 minutes.

Freezing: Let cool completely. Individually wrap each pocket with plastic wrap, put into a freezer bag, and freeze.

When ready to serve, remove the plastic wrap, cover each pocket with paper towel, and microwave for about 1 1/2 minutes until thawed. Remove the towel, and then microwave again for about 30-60 seconds.

Chicken Salsa Pockets

Prep Time: 30 minutes; **Cook Time:** 10-15 minutes			

Serving Size: 104 g; **Serves:** 10 **Calories:** 236	
Total Fat: 9.2 g **Saturated Fat:** 4.2 g; **Trans Fat:** 0 g	
Protein: 12.2 g; **Net Carbs:** 24.4 g	
Total Carbs: 25.7 g; **Dietary Fiber:** 1.3 g; **Sugars:** 1 g	
Cholesterol: 29 mg; **Sodium:** 427 mg; **Potassium:** 139 mg;	
Vitamin A: 4%; **Vitamin C:** 0%; **Calcium:** 13%; **Iron:** 11%	

Ingredients:

For the dough:

- ☐ 1 1/4 cup unbleached flour
- ☐ 1 1/4 cup whole-wheat flour
- ☐ 1 cup warm water (105-115F)
- ☐ 1 tablespoon active dry yeast
- ☐ 1 teaspoon salt
- ☐ 1 teaspoon sugar
- ☐ 2 tablespoons olive oil

For the filling:

- ☐ 1-2 cups chicken, baked and then chopped
- ☐ 1 1/2 cups cheese, shredded
- ☐ 1/2 cup salsa

Directions:

1. Mix the yeast with the warm water until dissolved. Add the sugar, oil, salt, and the flour; mix well and then put the dough on a floured working surface. Knead for about 3 to 5 minutes or till the dough is soft.
2. Divide the dough into 10 portions. Roll each portion into balls and then with a rolling pin, flatten the balls into circles. Put a spoonful salsa into each dough circle and sprinkle with chicken and cheese; fold over and then tightly seal.
3. Put into a greased cookie sheet and bake at 500F for about 10-15 minutes or till browned.

Freezing: Let cool completely and store in an airtight freezer bag for up to 2 to 3 months.

When ready to serve, take out needed serving from the freezer. Individually microwave for about 2 minutes or till heated thoroughly. Alternatively, you can warm in a 350F oven for about 20 minutes or till heated through.

Shrimp and Cheese Tortillas

Prep Time: 15 minutes; **Cook Time:** 15 minutes		
Serving Size: 221 g; **Serves:** 12; **Calories:** 387		
Total Fat: 15.5 g **Saturated Fat:** 8.8 g; **Trans Fat:** 0 g		
Protein: 45.4 g; **Net Carbs:** 13 g		
Total Carbs: 14.7 g; **Dietary Fiber:** 1.7 g; **Sugars:** 1.3 g		
Cholesterol: 367 mg; **Sodium:** 703 mg; **Potassium:** 361 mg;		
Vitamin A: 16%; **Vitamin C:** 5%; **Calcium:** 42%; **Iron:** 5%		

Ingredients:
- 2 bags (2 pound each) frozen raw shrimp (31-40 per pound), thawed and then tails removed
- 12 pieces (10-inch) flour tortillas
- 1 pound gouda cheese, shredded
- 1 tablespoon garlic, finely chopped
- 1 lemon, halved
- 2 tablespoons butter
- 3 chipotle chilies in adobo sauce, plus 1 tablespoon adobo sauce
- Salt and pepper, to taste

Directions:
1. Inside a large-sized, deep skillet, melt the butter on medium-high heat.
2. Add the shrimp, garlic, 1/2 teaspoon pepper, and 1/2 teaspoon salt. Increase the heat to thigh; cook, stirring frequently, for about 4 minutes or till the shrimps are just opaque. Squeeze the lemon halves over the shrimps; remove from heat and set aside.
3. In a small-sized bowl, mash the chipotles with the adobo sauce until paste. Spread a thin layer of the paste on each tortilla. Cover 1/2 of each tortilla with a single layer shrimp; sprinkle with the cheese and then fold the other half over the filling.
4. Working in batches, cook 2 quesadillas; place them on the skillet with the cheese side down Inside a large-sized nonstick skillet and cook on medium-high heat for about 2 minutes per side, or until golden. Cut the quesadillas into wedges.

Freezing: You can assemble the quesadillas ahead of time. Individually wrap with foil and then stack 4 pieces into 1 gallon freezer bags; seal, label, and freeze.

When ready to serve, let thaw for 2 hours are room temperature and cook as directed.

Mini Italian Burgers

Prep Time: 8 minutes; Cook Time: 12 minutes	

Serving Size: 259 g; Serves: 4; Calories: 552
Total Fat: 21.4 g Saturated Fat: 10.5 g; Trans Fat: 0 g
Protein: 65.3 g; Net Carbs: 19.9 g
Total Carbs: 21.3 g; Dietary Fiber: 1.4 g; Sugars: 2.7 g
Cholesterol: 178 mg; Sodium: 1288 mg; Potassium: 873 mg;
Vitamin A: 17%; Vitamin C: 14%; Calcium: 37%; Iron: 189%

Ingredients:

- ☐ 1 1/2-1 3/4 pounds ground beef (grass-fed preferred)
- ☐ 1 clove garlic, peeled and then minced
- ☐ 1 teaspoon salt
- ☐ 1/2 cup Parmesan, freshly grated
- ☐ 1/3 cup fresh flat-leaf parsley, finely chopped, loosely packed
- ☐ 1/4 teaspoon black pepper, freshly ground
- ☐ 2 tablespoons tomato paste
- ☐ 4 slices Provolone or mozzarella cheese, cut in halves
- ☐ 8 mini buns, sliced into halves

Optional toppings:
- ☐ Ketchup
- ☐ Lettuce
- ☐ Mayonnaise
- ☐ Tomato slices

Directions:

1. Grease a pan and preheat on medium heat. Alternatively, you can preheat a charcoal or a gas grill.
2. Put the ground beef, parsley, garlic, tomato paste, parmesan cheese, salt, and pepper into a mixing bowl. With clean hands, combine the ingredients until well mixed, making sure not to compress the ingredients.
3. Divide the mix into 8 portions and shape into equal thickness and size patties.
4. Put the burgers on the pan or on the grill; cook for about 3 to 4 minutes per side or until cooked through.
5. Top each warm burger with 1/2 slice cheese; serve on buns with your toppings of choice.

Freezing: You can shape the burger patties ahead of time. Put the uncooked patties into a gallon freezer bag, arranging them in a single layer with parchment paper between each patties. Put the buns into another gallon freezer bag. Wrap each cheese slice tightly with plastic wrap and put into the bag with the bans. Freeze until ready to cook.

When ready to serve, transfer in the fridge and let thaw overnight. Alternatively, you can submerge the patties in cool water until thawed; replace the water every 30 minutes. Cook the patties according to directions.

Slow Cooked Balsamic Beef

Prep Time: 15 minutes; **Cook Time:** 8 hours	
Serving Size: 289 g; **Serves:** 6; **Calories:** 448	
Total Fat: 14.4 g **Saturated Fat:** 5.4 g; **Trans Fat:** 0 g	
Protein: 69.9 g; **Net Carbs:** 4.6 g	
Total Carbs: 4.6 g; **Dietary Fiber:** 0 g; **Sugars:** 3.6 g	
Cholesterol: 203 mg; **Sodium:** 456 mg; **Potassium:** 974 mg;	
Vitamin A: 1%; **Vitamin C:** 1%; **Calcium:** 1%; **Iron:** 238%	

Ingredients:
- 1 tablespoon soy sauce
- 3-4 pound roast beef, boneless (round roast or chuck)
- 1/4 cup balsamic vinegar
- 2 teaspoons steak seasoning, all natural
- 1/2 teaspoon red pepper flakes (increase if you want more heat)
- 4 cloves garlic, minced
- 1 tablespoon Worcestershire sauce
- 1 cup beef broth
- 1 tablespoon honey

Directions:
1. Put the roast beef in a slow cooker.
2. In a small-sized bowl, mix the remaining ingredients together until combined; pour over the roast beef.
3. Cook on LOW for about 8 hours or until the meat shreds easily apart.
4. With 2 forks, shred the beef meat apart in the slow cooker.
5. Serve warm on top of mashed potatoes or in buns with a little sauce over the top.

Freezing: Let the shredded cooked beef cool completely. Make sure that you don't let the meat sit for more than 2 hours on the counter. When completely cooled, transfer into a freezer bags or freezer containers and freeze.

When ready to serve, you can transfer into the fridge, let that for about 24-48 hours, and then gently warm in the microwave or on a stove top.

Alternatively, put the still frozen meat and sauce directly into a pot on a stove over medium low heat. Pour 1 cup beef broth or water over the top, cover the pot, and periodically stir until warmed through.

Another way is to put the frozen meat and sauce into a microwavable bowl; using the DEFROST setting, thaw in the microwave, occasionally stirring. Once thawed, heat on COOK setting with 30 to 60 second increments until warmed through.

Chicken, Black Bean, and Cheese Enchiladas

Prep Time: 30 minutes; **Cook Time:** 15 minutes	

Serving Size: 300 g; **Serves:** 6; **Calories:** 722
Total Fat: 23.9 g **Saturated Fat:** 10.5 g; **Trans Fat:** 0 g
Protein: 52.5 g; **Net Carbs:** 59.7 g
Total Carbs: 77.9 g; **Dietary Fiber:** 18.2 g; **Sugars:** 10.5 g
Cholesterol: 108 mg; **Sodium:** 677 mg; **Potassium:** 1833 mg;
Vitamin A: 120%; **Vitamin C:** 114%; **Calcium:** 37%; **Iron:** 38%

Ingredients:

- 1 1/3 cups Monterey Jack and or Cheddar cheese, shredded
- 1 can (15-ounce) black beans, rinsed and then drained
- 1 can (4-ounce) diced green chilies
- 1 pound boneless, skinless chicken breasts, cut into 1-inch pieces
- 1/2-1 cup red enchilada sauce
- 1/3 cup salsa, prepared mild, medium, or hot
- 1/4 cup onion, chopped
- 2 cloves garlic, minced
- 2 teaspoons olive oil
- 4-6 pieces (8-inch) whole-wheat tortillas
- Homemade taco seasoning

Directions:

1. Preheat the oven to 400F. Grease a 9x9-inch casserole dish with cooking spray.
2. Inside a large-sized skillet, heat the oil on medium heat.
3. Add the garlic and the onion, sauté for 2 minutes.
4. Add the chicken; sauté for about 5 minutes or till cooked through and golden brown. Add the taco seasoning.
5. Stir in the black beans, salsa, and green chilies; simmer for about 5 minutes or till the sauce is reduced and thick.
6. Put 1/2 of the enchilada sauce into the bottom of the prepared dish.
7. Arrange 6 tortillas on a clean, flat surface. Divide the chicken-bean mix between each tortilla and top each with about 1 to 2 tablespoons cheese. Roll each tortilla, and with the seam side down, put side by side in the baking dish. Drizzle the remaining enchilada sauce over the rolled tortillas. Sprinkle with the remaining cheese.
8. Bake in the oven for about 15 minutes or till the cheese topping is golden.

Notes: You can assemble the enchiladas ahead of time and freeze. When ready to serve, just thaw in the fridge overnight and bake.

Asian Lettuce Wraps

Prep Time: 15 minutes; **Cook Time:** 25 minutes		
Serving Size: 343 g; Serves: 4; Calories: 451		
Total Fat: 12.9 g Saturated Fat: 2.4 g; Trans Fat: 0 g		
Protein: 37.1 g; Net Carbs: 40.9 g		
Total Carbs: 44.4 g; Dietary Fiber: 3.5 g; Sugars: 12.9 g		
Cholesterol: 88 mg; Sodium: 1078 mg; Potassium: 707 mg;		
Vitamin A: 96%; Vitamin C: 49%; Calcium: 8%; Iron: 19%		

Ingredients:
- 16 Boston Bibb, butter leaf, or Romaine lettuce leaves
- 1 pound ground chicken, lean (or turkey or beef)
- 1 can (8 ounce) water chestnuts, drained and finely chopped
- 1 cup cabbage, shredded
- 1 cup carrots, shredded
- 1 large yellow onion, finely chopped (I usually cut this back to ½ onion)
- 1 tablespoon cooking oil
- 1/2 bunch green onions, chopped
- 1/2 cup hoisin sauce
- 2 cloves fresh garlic, minced
- 2 tablespoons rice wine vinegar
- 2 tablespoons soy sauce, or to taste
- 2 teaspoons freshly grated ginger
- Asian Chile pepper sauce or any hot sauce, to taste
- 4 teaspoons Asian (dark) sesame oil
- 2 cups brown rice, cooked, optional

Directions:
1. Rinse the whole lettuce leaves clean and then pat dry carefully so you don't tear them; set a aside.
2. Inside a large-skillet or in a pot, brown the chicken with 1 tablespoon oil, frequently stirring. When browned, drain excess grease and set aside to cool.
3. In the same pan, sauté the yellow onion over medium heat, stirring frequently, until tender. Add the garlic, hoisin sauce, soy sauce, rice wine, ginger, and the chili pepper; stir to combine and simmer for 1 to 2 minutes.
4. Stir in the green onions, water chestnuts, cabbage, carrots, browned chicken, and sesame oil; continue cooking for about 3 to 4 minutes or till carrots, cabbage, and onion just start to soften. If the mix seems to dry, just add more hoisin and/or soy sauce to taste; add carefully or it can become too salty.
5. To serve, spoon the chicken mix into a lettuce leaf, wrap it like a burrito, and enjoy.

Freezing: Cook the chicken mix, let cool completely, put in a freezer bag or container, and freeze.
When ready to serve, thaw in the fridge overnight or in a microwave and then warm in a microwave or on a stove. Rinse and pat dry fresh lettuce leaves, fill with the meat mix, and enjoy.

Optional: You can add cooked rice on the lettuce first and then top with the mix.

Slow Cooker: Cook the chicken and onions as directed. Put into a slow cooker. Add the rest of the ingredients into the cooker, except for the rice, and if using, the rice. Cook on LOW for 5 to 6 hours or on HIGH for 2 to 3 hours. When cooked, set to warm unti ready to serve or freeze to serve later.

Chicken, Salsa, Corn, and Mozzarella Cheese Fajitas

Prep Time: 30 minutes; **Cook Time:** 15 minutes	

Serving Size: 190 g; **Serves:** 8; **Calories:** 236
Total Fat: 8.9 g **Saturated Fat:** 2.2 g; **Trans Fat:** 0 g
Protein: 17.3 g; **Net Carbs:** 20.1 g
Total Carbs: 23.7 g; **Dietary Fiber:** 3.6 g; **Sugars:** 3.7 g
Cholesterol: 41 mg; **Sodium:** 187 mg; **Potassium:** 383 mg;
Vitamin A: 20%; **Vitamin C:** 69%; **Calcium:** 4%; **Iron:** 12%

Ingredients:

- 1 1/2 cups mozzarella cheese, shredded (or cheddar cheese or Monterey jack)
- 1 can corn (or 5-6 ears of roasted corn)
- 2-3 chicken breasts (4 ounces each), cooked and diced
- 2 tablespoons olive oil
- 2 garlic cloves, minced
- 1/2 onion, chopped
- 1/2 cup salsa
- 1 tablespoon taco seasoning
- 1 red bell pepper, small-medium, diced
- 1 green bell pepper, small-medium, diced
- 8 tortillas, medium-sized

Directions:

1. Preheat the oven to 400F.
2. Grease a 9x9-inch casserole dish and a 9x12-inch dish with cooking spray.
3. Inside a large-sized skillet, heat the oil over medium heat. Add the garlic and the onion; sauté for about 1 to 2 minutes. Add the bell peppers; continue cooking for about 5 to 7 minutes or till starting to soften.
4. Add the chicken, corn, and the salsa. Sprinkle taco seasoning all over; toss until well combined. Remove from the heat.
5. Lay a tortilla out in a clean surface; sprinkle with some shredded cheese. Add a generous 1/2 cup chicken filling; roll the tortilla and with the same side down, put into the prepared dishes. Repeat the process with the remaining tortilla, cheese, and filling.
6. Sprinkle the top with a generous amount of shredded cheese; bake at 400F for about 15 minutes or till the cheese is melted.

Freezing: You can assemble the fajitas ahead of time. Do not bake. Freeze them in an airtight container.

When ready to serve, transfer to the fridge, et thaw for 24 hours, and bakes as directed.

Chicken Burritos

Prep Time: 30 minutes; **Cook Time:** 25 minutes	
Serving Size: 210 g; **Serves:** 8; **Calories:** 449	
Total Fat: 17.1 g **Saturated Fat:** 7.6 g; **Trans Fat:** 0 g	
Protein: 31.5 g; **Net Carbs:** 37.5 g	
Total Carbs: 42.7 g; **Dietary Fiber:** 5.3 g; **Sugars:** 1.6 g	
Cholesterol: 80 mg; **Sodium:** 383 mg; **Potassium:** 614 mg;	
Vitamin A: 8%; **Vitamin C:** 3%; **Calcium:** 24%; **Iron:** 17%	

Ingredients:

- 3/4 cup frozen corn
- 3/4 cup cooked black beans (or half of 15 ounce can of black beans, drained)
- 3/4 cup brown rice, cooked
- 2/3 cups water
- 2 pieces (about 1 pound total) chicken breasts, diced and then patted very dry
- 1-2 tablespoons olive oil
- 1/2-1 cup mild salsa (adjust to taste)
- 1 packet store-bought mild taco seasoning (or use this homemade taco seasoning)
- 1 1/2 cups shredded cheddar cheese
- 8 pieces (8-inch) whole wheat tortillas

Optional toppings:
- Guacamole or creamy avocado dip
- Sour cream or plain Greek yogurt
- Pico de Gallo

Directions:

1. Inside a large-sized skillet, heat 1-2 tablespoons olive oil on medium to medium-high heat. Add the chicken, sauté for about 3 to 4 minutes or till cooked through.
2. Add the water, salsa, brown rice, corn, black beans, and taco seasoning; reduce the heat to low and simmer for 5 minutes, occasionally stirring.
3. To assemble the burritos, put a generous 1/3 cup meat mix and 3 tablespoon shredded cheese into each tortilla. Pull in each end and then roll up tightly.
4. If serving immediately, wrap each tortilla with foil, heat in a 350F oven for about 15-20 minutes. Alternatively, you can wrap each tortilla with moist paper towel; warm in 30 second increments in the microwave until heated through. Serve with the optional toppings, if desired.

Freezing: If preparing ahead of time, individually wrap each burrito with foil, put into gallon sized freezer bags, and freeze.

When ready to serve, transfer into the fridge, thaw overnight, and then warm in a 350F oven for about20-25 minutes. Alternatively, you can warm in the microwave as directed; just open the burrito halfway through reheating to let the inside ingredients warm.

Chicken and Bacon Sandwiches

Prep Time: 15 minutes, plus 15 minutes marinating; **Cook Time:** 8 minutes

Serving Size: 184 g; **Serves:** 6; **Calories:** 535	
Total Fat: 34 g **Saturated Fat:** 10.8 g; **Trans Fat:** 0 g	
Protein: 37.5 g; **Net Carbs:** 18.6 g	
Total Carbs: 20.9 g; **Dietary Fiber:** 3.2 g; **Sugars:** 3.6 g	
Cholesterol: 112 mg; **Sodium:** 1686 mg; **Potassium:** 414 mg;	
Vitamin A: 12%; **Vitamin C:** 1%; **Calcium:** 26%; **Iron:** 14%	

Ingredients:

- 3 large boneless, skinless chicken breasts
- 3 tablespoons cider vinegar
- 6 slices bacon, cooked and then broken in halves
- 6 slices cheddar cheese
- 6 tablespoons olive oil
- 1 tablespoon salt
- 1 tablespoon garlic powder
- 1 1/2 teaspoon powdered ginger
- 1 1/2 teaspoon paprika
- 1 1/2 teaspoon ground black pepper
- 6 hamburger whole-wheat buns

Optional toppings:

- Lettuce
- Tomato slices
- Onion slices
- Mayonnaise
- Dijon mustard

Directions:

1. Into a gallon-sized freezer bag, combine the oil with the vinegar, salt, pepper, garlic powder, paprika, and ginger. Gently shake the bag to mix and set aside.
2. Carefully cut the chicken breast lengthwise, cutting through the center to make 2 thin chicken breast halves. Put the chicken breast halves into the freezer with marinade, seal, and shake to coat the meat. Put the bag I the fridge and let marinate for at least 15 minutes up to several hours.
3. Preheat a grill or a grill pan to medium-high heat.
4. Lightly grease the grill or grill pan with cooking spray. Put the chicken on the pan or grill; discard the marinade. Grill for about 3-4 minutes or till there are prominent grill marks on the bottom. Carefully flip the chicken. Reduce the heat to medium, cover the pan/grill; grill for another 3-4 minutes or till cooked through. The chicken is done when the internal temperature is 165F and the meat juices run clear.
5. Sandwich 1 chicken, 1 cheese, 1 bacon cut into 3 pieces, and your choice of optional toppings in the buns.

Freezing: Put the chicken into the marinade, seal, and freeze immediately. Individually wrap each cheese and bacon with plastic wrap or foil; put into another gallon-sized freezer bag. Put the buns in the freezer bag with the cheese and bacon; freeze together in the freezer.

When ready to make the sandwiches, transfer all the sandwich ingredients into the fridge, and let thaw overnight. Alternatively, you can submerge the sealed marinated chicken in cool water for about 2-3 hours, replacing the water every 30 minutes until thawed. Cook as directed.

Mini Herbed Chicken Burgers

Prep Time: 30 minutes; **Cook Time:** 10 minutes per batch		
Serving Size: 133 g; **Serves:** 8; **Calories:** 232		
Total Fat: 7.4 g **Saturated Fat:** 1.6 g; **Trans Fat:** 0 g		
Protein: 33.9 g; **Net Carbs:** 5 g		
Total Carbs: 5.5 g; **Dietary Fiber:** 0.5 g; **Sugars:** 0.5 g		
Cholesterol: 87 mg; **Sodium:** 415 mg; **Potassium:** 256 mg;		
Vitamin A: 7%; **Vitamin C:** 12%; **Calcium:** 4%; **Iron:** 9%		

Ingredients:
- [ ] 2 pounds chicken, ground (or turkey)
- [ ] 1/2 teaspoon dried oregano
- [ ] 1/2 teaspoon black pepper
- [ ] 1/2 cup whole-wheat panko breadcrumbs
- [ ] 1/2 cup fresh flat-leaf parsley, finely chopped
- [ ] 1 teaspoon kosher salt
- [ ] 1 1/2 teaspoons garlic, finely chopped
- [ ] 2 tablespoons fresh lemon juice
- [ ] 2 tablespoons olive oil

Directions:
1. Inside a large-sized bowl, combine the ground chicken with the parsley, garlic, oregano, and the lemon juice using a fork; season with the salt and the pepper. Divide the mix into 16 portions and form into patties.
2. Put the breadcrumbs into a shallow dish, coat each patty with the breadcrumbs; turn to coat and gently press to adhere the crumbs. Set aside.
3. Inside a large-sized skillet, heat 1 tablespoon oil over medium heat. Add just enough patties that will fit in the skillet; cook for about 5 minutes each side or until cooked through and browned. When you notice them browning before they are cooked through, reduce the heat to medium-low, cover the pan, and cook for a couple minutes more. Repeat the process with the remaining oil and patties. Serve plain or on mini whole-wheat buns or hotdog buns cut into halves to make miniature buns for the small patties.

Freezing: Make the patties ahead of time up to coating with the breadcrumbs. Put the patties in a single layer on a baking sheet lined with wax paper or parchment paper. Flash freeze in the freezer for about 1 hour. When frozen, transfer into a re-sealable freezer bag and freeze for about 3 months.

When ready to cook, transfer needed patties in the fridge and let thaw overnight before cooking.

Southwest Chicken and Bacon Wrap

Prep Time: 30 minutes; Cook Time: 12-14 minutes	

Serving Size: 168 g; Serves: 8; Calories: 230	
Total Fat: 10.2 g Saturated Fat: 3.8 g; Trans Fat: 0 g	
Protein: 22.7 g; Net Carbs: 9.7 g	
Total Carbs: 11.5 g; Dietary Fiber: 1.8 g; Sugars: 1.8 g	
Cholesterol: 66 mg; Sodium: 442 mg; Potassium: 337 mg;	
Vitamin A: 9%; Vitamin C: 7%; Calcium: 8%; Iron: 11%	

Ingredients:
- 8 pieces bacon, baked or fried, then crumbled
- 8 whole-wheat tortillas
- 4 boneless, skinless chicken breasts
- 1/2 cup mozzarella cheese (could sub Pepper Jack or Mexican cheese blend)
- 1/2 cup cheddar cheese (could sub Mexican cheese blend)
- Lettuce, shredded
- Southwest chicken marinade (recipe below)
- Southwest ranch sauce (recipe below)

For the sauce:
- 1/2 cup ranch dressing
- 1/2 cup salsa

For the Southwest chicken marinade:
- 4 teaspoons chili powder
- 2/3 cup oil
- 2 teaspoons garlic powder
- 2 teaspoon Italian seasoning
- 2 tablespoon fresh cilantro or parsley, chopped
- 1/3 cup vinegar
- 1 teaspoon salt
- 1 teaspoon ground cumin
- 1/2 teaspoon ground black pepper

Directions:
1. Combine all the marinade ingredients inside a large-sized Ziploc bag and shake to mix. Add the chicken; transfer into the fridge and marinate for at least 1 hour or longer.
2. Grill the chicken on medium-high heat for about 6 to 7 minutes each side or until cooked through and no longer pink. Let rest for a couple of minutes and then slice into thin, long strips.
3. Divide the chicken between each tortilla. Add with the bacon pieces, shredded lettuce, cheese, and tomatoes. Roll the tortillas like a burrito.
4. Ina bowl or in a glass jar, combine the southwest ranch sauce ingredients until mixed.
5. Dip each burrito in the sauce or add the sauce inside the wraps.

Freezing: After rolling the tortillas into burritos, wrap with plastic wrap and then with foil; freeze. When ready to serve, remove the foil and plastic wrap. Wrap each with moist paper towel and microwave for about 2-3 minutes on HIGH until heated through.

Crab Cakes

Prep Time: 20 minutes, plus 30 minutes cooling; **Cook Time:** 8 minutes per batch	
Serving Size: 167 g; **Serves:** 4; **Calories:** 353	
Total Fat: 23.1 g **Saturated Fat:** 4.8 g; **Trans Fat:** 0 g	
Protein: 14.4 g; **Net Carbs:** 18.8 g	
Total Carbs: 19.8 g; **Dietary Fiber:** 1 g; **Sugars:** 3.6 g	
Cholesterol: 102 mg; **Sodium:** 987 mg; **Potassium:** 79 mg;	
Vitamin A: 8%; **Vitamin C:** 12%; **Calcium:** 34%; **Iron:** 12%	

Ingredients:

- [ ] 1 egg, beaten
- [ ] 2 cans (6-ounces each) crab meat, drained well
- [ ] 1/2 teaspoon Old Bay seasoning
- [ ] 1/2 teaspoon garlic powder
- [ ] 1/2 cup real mayonnaise
- [ ] 1/2 cup panko breadcrumbs, plus more for coating cakes before cooking
- [ ] 1 teaspoon Worcestershire sauce
- [ ] 1 teaspoon dried parsley (crush in hand)
- [ ] 1 teaspoon Dijon mustard
- [ ] 1 tablespoon unsalted butter
- [ ] 2 tablespoons celery, finely diced
- [ ] 2 tablespoons olive oil, divided
- [ ] 2 tablespoons onion, finely diced
- [ ] 2 tablespoons red bell pepper, finely diced
- [ ] Salt and pepper, to taste

Optional garnishes:
- [ ] Seafood sauce or lemon wedges

Directions:

1. In a medium-sized pan, sauté the celery, onion, and pepper in 1 tablespoon olive oil on medium heat for about 2 to 3 minutes or till soft; lightly season with salt and pepper. Remove from the pan; set aside and let cool.
2. In a medium-sized bowl, mix the mayo with the Worcestershire sauce, mustard, seasoning, egg, parsley, and garlic powder. Stir in the slightly cooled sautéed veggies. Gently fold in the crab meat and the breadcrumbs. Cover the bowl; refrigerate and let cool for 30 minutes.
3. Divide the mix into 4 or 8 portions, form into 4 regular-sized or 8 mini-sized patties. Lightly coat both sides of each patty with breadcrumbs.
4. In a medium pan, melt the butter with 1 tablespoon olive oil on medium heat. Add patties, just enough to fit the pan; cook for about 3 to 4 minutes each side. Turn the patties when the bottom is nicely browned. Continue cooking until the next side is browned.
5. Serve with seafood sauce or lemon wedges.

Freezing: Store the patties in an airtight container with parchment paper between each patty; freeze.

When ready to serve, transfer in the fridge and let thaw overnight or you can thaw in the microwave on DEFROST setting. Cook as directed.

Sweet Potato and Salmon Cakes

Prep Time: 40 minutes; **Cook Time:** 6 minutes per batch	
Serving Size: 206 g; **Serves:** 6; **Calories:** 327	
Total Fat: 14.8 g **Saturated Fat:** 2.4 g; **Trans Fat:** 0 g	
Protein: 22.6 g; **Net Carbs:** 24.1 g	
Total Carbs: 26.7 g; **Dietary Fiber:** 2.6 g; **Sugars:** 4 g	
Cholesterol: 65 mg; **Sodium:** 754 mg; **Potassium:** 596 mg;	
Vitamin A: 9%; **Vitamin C:** 23%; **Calcium:** 10%; **Iron:** 21%	

Ingredients:

- 3 pieces (6-ounce each) salmon fillet
- 1 egg, lightly beaten
- 1 large sweet potato, peeled and cut into small chunks
- 1 1/2 cups whole-wheat crackers, crushed into crumbs
- 1 bay leaf
- 1 cup chicken broth
- 1 tablespoon seafood seasoning (I used Old Bay)
- 1 tablespoon thyme leaves, finely chopped
- 1 teaspoon hot sauce
- 2 scallions, finely chopped
- 3 tablespoons extra-virgin olive oil
- 3-4 tablespoons fresh parsley, finely chopped
- Freshly ground black pepper
- Salt

Directions:

1. Put the potatoes into a small-sized pot. Cover with water and bring to a boil on high heat. When boiling, salt the water and cook for about 10 to 12 minutes or till tender. Drain the potatoes and then return into the pot and then mash.
2. Put the salmon fillets into a skillet. Add the broth, bay leaf, and just enough water come level with the salmon top, but do not cover; bring to a boil on medium heat. When boiling, reduce the heat to a simmer; poach for about 8-10 minutes or till opaque.
3. Remove the skin from the salmon; transfer the salmon meat into a bowl and discard the skin.
4. Using a fork, flake the salmon; season with salt and pepper to taste. Add the mashed sweet potatoes, seafood seasoning, 1/2 of the cracker crumbs, thyme, egg, scallions, hot sauce, and parsley; mix to combine. The fish cakes need to be just firm enough. If the mix is too wet, add a bit more crumbs.
5. Form the salmon mix into 4 pieces 4-inch patties or 8 pieces 2-inch patties. Coat the patties with the remaining breadcrumbs.
6. In a skillet, heat 2 tablespoons extra-virgin olive on medium heat.
7. Put the patties into the pan; cook for about 2-3 minutes per side or until light golden.
8. Serve with tartar sauce for dipping or serve on buns with cheese topping like burger.

Freezing: Make the patties ahead of time. Put them in a freezer bag with a parchment paper between each patty.

When ready to cook, transfer into the fridge and let thaw for at least 24 hours. Cook according to directions.

Fish Sticks

Prep Time: 20 minutes; **Cook Time:** 10 minutes	
Serving Size: 157 g; **Serves:** 4; **Calories:** 251	
Total Fat: 10.5 g **Saturated Fat:** 2.9 g; **Trans Fat:** 0 g	
Protein: 28.4 g; **Net Carbs:** 10.3 g	
Total Carbs: 11.8 g; **Dietary Fiber:** 1.5 g; **Sugars:** 1.3 g	
Cholesterol: 103 mg; **Sodium:** 538 mg; **Potassium:** 82 mg;	
Vitamin A: 3%; **Vitamin C:** 1%; **Calcium:** 15%; **Iron:** 12%	

Ingredients:

- ☐ 4 pieces (4 ounces) tilapia filets
- ☐ 3/4 teaspoon garlic powder
- ☐ 1/4 teaspoon pepper, to taste
- ☐ 1/4 cups pecans, pulsed in food processor until finely chopped
- ☐ 1/2 teaspoon salt
- ☐ 1/2 teaspoon dried parsley
- ☐ 1/2 cups whole-wheat breadcrumbs
- ☐ 1/2 cups Parmesan cheese, freshly grated
- ☐ 1 egg

Directions:

1. Preheat the oven to 475F. Liberally grease a cookie sheet with cooking spray.
2. In a shallow dish, combine the breadcrumbs with the parmesan cheese, pecans, salt, garlic powder, pepper, and dried parsley.
3. In another shallow bowl, whisk the eggs.
4. Cut the fish into nugget pieces or into strips; pat dry with paper towel. Dip each fish in the egg and then in the breading mix; make sure each piece is coated well.
5. Line the coated fish in the prepared cookie sheet; bake for about 10 minutes or till cooked through, easily flakes when tested with a fork, crispy outside, and browned.

Freezing: If not serving right away, prepare the fish until putting them in the prepared cookie sheet. Flash freeze for about 1 hour. Put the flash frozen fish into a freezer bag, squeeze all the air out from the bag, seal, and freeze for 3 months.

When ready to serve, put on a greased cookie sheet and bake as directed at 475F for about 15 minutes.

Cancer Fighting Soup

Prep Time: 30 minutes; **Cook Time:** 30 minutes	
Serving Size: 255 g; **Serves:** 16; **Calories:** 325	
Total Fat: 4.7 g **Saturated Fat:** 1.2 g; **Trans Fat:** 0 g	
Protein: 40.4 g; **Net Carbs:** 20.5 g	
Total Carbs: 29.7 g; **Dietary Fiber:** 9.2 g; **Sugars:** 5.8 g	
Cholesterol: 81 mg; **Sodium:** 185 mg; **Potassium:** 858 mg;	
Vitamin A: 67%; **Vitamin C:** 35%; **Calcium:** 10%; **Iron:** 23%	

Ingredients:
- 1 can (15 ounces) black beans, drained and rinsed
- 1 can (28-ounce) crushed tomatoes
- 1 cup broccoli, chopped finely
- 1 cup cauliflower, chopped finely
- 1 cup mushrooms, diced
- 1 onion, diced
- 1 teaspoon Italian seasoning (or other dried herbs like basil, oregano, and parsley)
- 1 zucchini, diced
- 1/2 cup lentils
- 1/4-1/2 teaspoon red pepper flakes
- 12 cups (or 3 cartons 32-ounces each) chicken or vegetable broth
- 1-2 cups frozen green peas
- 1-2 tablespoons olive oil
- 2 bay leaves
- 2 cups carrots, diced
- 2 tablespoons tomato paste
- 2-3 celery stalks, sliced
- 2-3 cups spinach, chopped
- 3 garlic cloves
- Salt and pepper, to taste

Directions:
1. Inside a large-sized stockpot, heat 1 to 2 tablespoons olive oil over medium-high heat.
2. Add the onion, celery, carrots, and garlic; sauté for about 3 to 4 minutes or till tender. Season with the salt, pepper, Italian seasoning, and red pepper flakes to taste.
3. Add the broth, tomato paste, crushed tomatoes, lentils, and black beans; bring to a boil. When boiling, reduce the heat to a simmer; lightly season again with salt and pepper and cook, simmering, for about 10 to 15 minutes.
4. Except for the frozen peas, add all the remaining veggies; simmer for about 5 to 10 minutes more. Stir in the frozen peas; turn the heat off. Remove the bay leaf and adjust seasoning, if needed.
5. Serve with crusty bread or whole-grain crackers and/or freshly shredded parmesan cheese.

Freezing: When cooked, let the soup cool; make sure you do not leave for more than 2 hours on the counter. Divide the soup into portions in freezer bags or containers and freeze.

When ready to serve, transfer in the fridge and let thaw for about 24 to 48 hours. Gently reheat over low heat in a crockpot or stovetop pot. Alternatively, you can put frozen soup block in a crockpot or stovetop pot over low to medium-low heat. Add about 1 to 2 cups of broth or water over the top; gently warm, occasionally stirring.

Slow Cooked Chili Turkey with Black Beans and Sweet Potato

Prep Time: 15 minutes; Cook Time: 3-4 hours on high, 6-8 hours on low
Serving Size: 308 g; Serves: 4-6; Calories: 424
Total Fat: 11.3 g Saturated Fat: 1.9 g; Trans Fat: 0 g
Protein: 30.2 g; Net Carbs: 42.6 g
Total Carbs: 54.7 g; Dietary Fiber: 12.1 g; Sugars: 4.1 g
Cholesterol: 58 mg; Sodium: 566 mg; Potassium: 1666 mg;
Vitamin A: 18%; Vitamin C: 33%; Calcium: 11%; Iron: 28%

Ingredients:

- 1 can (15 ounce) cooked black beans, drained and rinsed
- 1 can (15 ounces) petite diced tomatoes, liquid and all
- 3 cups sweet potatoes, peeled and then diced
- 1 pound ground turkey, lean
- 1 large onion, finely diced
- 2 tablespoons olive oil, divided
- 2 garlic cloves, minced
- 2 cups vegetable or chicken broth
- 11/4 teaspoon black pepper
- 1/4 teaspoon paprika
- 1/4 teaspoon dried oregano
- 1/2 tablespoon ground cumin
- 1 teaspoon salt
- 1 teaspoon jalapeño pepper, minced
- 1 tablespoon tomato paste
- 1 tablespoon chili powder

Optional toppings:
- Avocado, diced
- Cheddar cheese, shredded
- Greek yogurt, plain or sour cream
- Green onion, thinly sliced, etc.
- Onions, diced
- Salsa

Directions:

1. Inside a large-sized pan, heat 1 tablespoon olive oil. Add the sweet potato dices, sauté for about 5 minutes or till just softened; lightly season with salt and pepper while sautéing. After 15 minutes, add the sweet potato mix into the slow cooker.
2. Increase the heat of the stove to medium-high. In the same pan, add 1 tablespoon olive oil. Add the onion, garlic, jalapeno pepper, and ground turkey; sauté for about 4 to 5 minutes, breaking the meat, until the turkey is cooked through and the onion is soft. Lightly season with salt and pepper while sautéing. Drain off any excess grease.
3. Add the turkey mix and the remaining ingredients into the slow cooker; stir well to combine. Slow cook for about 6 to 8 hours on LOW and for about 3 to 4 hours on HIGH.
4. Adjust the salt and pepper, if desired. If desired, add hot sauce for more heat. Serve topped with your choice of chili toppings.

Freezing: Cook as directed and let cool completely. Put in airtight, freezable bag or container and freeze.

When ready to serve; transfer in the fridge and let thaw overnight. Gently warm on the stove top, or in a slow cooker on LOW setting, or in a microwave until warmed through.

Lunch Wraps

Prep Time: 25 minutes; **Cook Time:** 15-20 minutes

Serving Size: 154 g; **Serves:** 6; **Calories:** 380

Total Fat: 8.4 g **Saturated Fat:** 4.4 g; **Trans Fat:** 0 g

Protein: 16.4 g; **Net Carbs:** 53.2 g

Total Carbs: 61.6 g; **Dietary Fiber:** 8.4 g; **Sugars:** 2.5 g

Cholesterol: 20 mg; **Sodium:** 261 mg; **Potassium:** 752 mg;

Vitamin A: 5%; **Vitamin C:** 3%; **Calcium:** 21%; **Iron:** 19%

Ingredients:

- 1 cup black beans, cooked or canned, drained and then rinsed (or kidney beans)
- 1 cup brown rice, cooked
- 1 cup cheddar cheese, shredded
- 1 cup corn, frozen or canned (drained)
- 1/2 cup salsa (your favorite)
- 6 pieces 8-inch whole-wheat or multigrain tortillas

Directions:

1. Preheat the oven to 350F.
2. Lay out the tortillas in a clean, flat surface. Evenly distribute the rice, corn, beans, salsa, and the cheese between each tortilla; roll neatly and wrap each with foil.
3. Bake in the oven for about 15 to 20 minutes or till hot.

Freezing: If not serving immediately, after the tortillas are wrapped in foil, put them into a freezer bag and freeze for up to 3 months.

When ready to serve, just bake, adding about 10 to 15 minutes to the original baking time, a total of about 25-35 minutes. Alternatively, you can remove the foil, wrap each with moist paper towel, and microwave in 30 to 60 second increments or until heated through.

20-Minute Chili Pumpkin

Prep Time: 30 minutes; **Cook Time:** 20 minutes

Serving Size: 320 g; **Serves:** 12; **Calories:** 397	
Total Fat: 5.9 g **Saturated Fat:** 0.8 g; **Trans Fat:** 0 g	
Protein: 21.3 g; **Net Carbs:** 48.4 g	
Total Carbs: 68.2 g; **Dietary Fiber:** 19.8 g; **Sugars:** 10.9 g	
Cholesterol: 0 mg; **Sodium:** 241 mg; **Potassium:** 1473 mg;	
Vitamin A: 192%; **Vitamin C:** 30%; **Calcium:** 14%; **Iron:** 37%	

Ingredients:

- 1 can (28 ounces) diced tomatoes (do not drain)
- 1 can (15 ounces) pumpkin puree
- 1 can (15 ounces) pinto beans, drained and then rinsed
- 1 can (15 ounces) garbanzo beans, drained and then rinsed
- 1 can (15 ounces) black beans, drained and then rinsed
- 1/2 cup dried lentils, rinsed (or your choice of beans)
- 4 cups (1 carton) vegetable stock or broth (more if the chili is too thick)
- 3 large carrots, diced
- 2 tablespoons tomato paste
- 2 tablespoons olive oil
- 2 tablespoons chili powder
- 2 large onions, diced
- 1-2 teaspoons sea salt, to taste
- 1/2-1 teaspoon black pepper, to taste
- 1/2 teaspoon paprika
- 1/2 teaspoon onion powder
- 1/2 teaspoon garlic powder
- 1/2 teaspoon dried oregano
- 1/2 teaspoon crushed red pepper flakes
- 1 tablespoon ground cumin
- 1 bay leaf
- 4 garlic cloves, minced

Directions:

1. Inside a large-sized pot or in a Dutch oven, sauté the onions, garlic, and carrots in olive oil for about 4-5 minutes or till tender; lightly season with salt and pepper while sautéing.
2. In the same pot, add the rest ingredients; lightly season with salt and pepper. Bring the mix to a boil; stirring almost constantly. When boiling, reduce the heat to a low simmer; cook, simmer, regularly stirring, for about 20 minutes, to avoid burning the bottom.
3. Taste, and if needed, adjust the salt and pepper. Remove the bay leaf and serve with your preferred chili toppings.

Freezer: Cook as directed and let cool completely. Put in freezable, airtight container or bag and freeze.

When ready to serve, transfer in the fridge and let thaw overnight. Gently warm on the stovetop. Alternatively, you can put frozen soup inside a large-sized stockpot, add 1-2 cups of broth or water over the top and gently warm on low to medium-low heat, occasionally stirring to prevent the bottom from burning.

Dinner

Turkish Beef Kebabs

Prep Time: 30 minutes; **Cook Time:** 10-15 minutes	

Prep Time: 30 minutes; **Cook Time:** 10-15 minutes
Serving Size: 119 g; **Serves:** 8; **Calories:** 206
Total Fat: 4.4 g **Saturated Fat:** 1.8 g; **Trans Fat:** 0 g
Protein: 22.4 g; **Net Carbs:** 16.8 g
Total Carbs: 17.8 g; **Dietary Fiber:** 1 g; **Sugars:** 1.8 g
Cholesterol: 52 mg; **Sodium:** 487 mg; **Potassium:** 319 mg;
Vitamin A: 1%; **Vitamin C:** 1%; **Calcium:** 5%; **Iron:** 64%

Ingredients:
- 1 pound ground beef (93-percent lean)
- 1 small onion, very finely chopped
- 1 teaspoon salt
- 1/2 teaspoon ground cumin
- 1/2 teaspoon smoked or sweet ground paprika
- 1/4 teaspoon freshly ground pepper
- 1/4 teaspoon ground cinnamon
- 3/4 cup Greek yogurt, plain
- 3/4 teaspoon garlic powder
- 8 pitas, pocketless, warmed
- White onion, chopped tomato, and parsley, for garnish

Directions:
1. In a mixing bowl, combine the beef with the paprika, cumin, garlic powder, cinnamon, pepper, salt, and onion; stir with a fork until very well blended. Divide the mix into 8 portions. Put a portion into the pal of 1 hand, press with the other hand into a 3x2-inch patty. Lay a skewer lengthwise down the center of the patty; press the meat gently around it, forming a 6-inch long 1-inch thick hot dog. Repeat the process with the remaining meat mix. For maximum flavor, put the kebabs into a plate, cover, and refrigerate for at least 1 hour up to 12 hours.
2. If serving immediately, preheat the boiler or set a toaster oven on broil. Arrange the kebabs on a broiler pan; broil for about 8-10 minutes, turning them after 5 minutes. If cooking in a toaster oven, cook the kebabs for about 15 minutes, turning them after 8 minutes.
3. To serve, slide the meat off from the skewers. Put 1 kebab in the center of each warmed pita.
4. Stir the yogurt and season with the salt and pepper. Drizzle about 2 tablespoons of the yogurt mix over each kebab and then spoon some white onion, chopped tomato, and parsley.

Freezing: If making ahead of time, chill on the plate, covered, for about 1 hour. Individually wrap with plastic wrap and then wrap each with foil; label and freeze. Alternatively, you can open-freeze the kebabs, vacuum seal in pairs, and then return them into the freezer.

When ready to serve, transfer the kebabs in the fridge and let thaw for about 4-8 hours. Broil and serve as directed.

Notes: When the kebabs are defrosted, taste of the cumin will disappear and will taste mostly of garlic. Refresh the cumin flavor aby adding 1/4 teaspoon cumin into the yogurt mix.

Baked Ziti

Prep Time: 30 minutes; **Cook Time:** 20-30 minutes	

Prep Time: 30 minutes; **Cook Time:** 20-30 minutes

Serving Size: 278 g; **Serves:** 16; **Calories:** 443

Total Fat: 17.6 g **Saturated Fat:** 7.8 g; **Trans Fat:** 0 g

Protein: 24.4 g; **Net Carbs:** 45.7 g

Total Carbs: 47.5 g; **Dietary Fiber:** 1.8 g; **Sugars:** 1.2 g

Cholesterol: 91 mg; **Sodium:** 4136 mg; **Potassium:** 663 mg;

Vitamin A: 8%; **Vitamin C:** 9%; **Calcium:** 21%; **Iron:** 16%

Ingredients:

For the sauce:

- 8 ounces cremini mushrooms, sliced
- 24 ounces spaghetti sauce, traditional, jarred
- 2 cloves garlic, minced or pressed
- 1/2 onion, diced
- 1 tablespoon Italian seasoning
- 1 pound ziti noodles, cooked al dente according to pack directions
- 1 pound Italian ground sausage
- 1 can (14 ounces) diced tomatoes

For the cheese mixture:

- 2 eggs
- 16 ounces mozzarella cheese, shredded
- 15 ounces ricotta cheese
- 1/4 teaspoon black pepper
- 1/2 teaspoon salt
- 1/2 cup parmesan cheese, shredded
- 1 tablespoon dried parsley

Directions:

For the sauce:

1. Inside a large-sized skillet or in a Dutch oven, brown and crumble the sausage over medium-high heat. Add the garlic and onions; cook until tender. Stir in the mushrooms; cook until softened.
2. Add the sauce, tomatoes, and the Italian seasoning; bring to a gentle boil. Reduce the heat and simmer, occasionally stirring, for 10 minutes. If your pan is large enough, add the pasta and then stir to coat. If needed, transfer the pasta inside a large bowl. Add the sauce and stir to coat.

For the cheese mixture:

1. In a small dish, combine the ricotta with the remaining cheese mixture ingredients.

To assemble the caked ziti:

1. Lightly grease a 13x9-inch casserole dish with nonstick spray. Layer 1/2 of the pasta mix on the bottom of the casserole dish, spreading in an even layer, and then top with the cheese mix, spreading in an even layer. Sprinkle 1/2 of the shredded mozzarella on top. Spread the remaining pasta mix and the remaining mozzarella cheese.

If serving right away: Cover the dish with foil and bake in a preheated 350F oven for 25 minutes. Remove the foil and bake for another 15-20 minutes or till the center is bubbly.

If serving later: Let cool to room temperature and then cover with an airtight lid. If the dish has no lid, cover with plastic wrap and then cover with a double layer of tin foil. Freeze.

To bake: Take the dish out from the freezer and remove the lid or the plastic wrap. Cover with foil and bake in a preheated 350F oven for 1 hour. Remove the foil and bake for another 10-15 minutes or till the center is bubbly.

Macaroni, Broccoli, and Cheese Bake

Prep Time: 30 minutes; Cook Time: 17-24 minutes			
Serving Size: 221 g; Serves: 8; Calories: 342			
Total Fat: 14.5 g Saturated Fat: 8.5 g; Trans Fat: 0 g			
Protein: 17.4 g; Net Carbs: 34 g			
Total Carbs: 35.5 g; Dietary Fiber: 1.5 g; Sugars: 4.2 g			
Cholesterol: 72 mg; Sodium: 321 mg; Potassium: 350 mg;			
Vitamin A: 16%; Vitamin C: 65%; Calcium: 35%; Iron: 13%			

Ingredients:

- 12 ounces broccoli florets, frozen or fresh
- 12 ounces pasta, whole-wheat (elbows, shells, rotini, etc.)
- 8 ounces (2 cups) reduced-fat sharp cheddar cheese
- 2 tablespoons Parmesan cheese grated
- 1/4 cup onion, freshly minced
- 2 tablespoons of butter
- 1/4 cup panko bread crumbs
- 2 cups fat-free milk
- 1/4 cup flour
- 1 cup chicken broth, low-sodium (you can use vegetable broth)
- Nonstick cooking spray
- Salt and black pepper

Directions:

1. Preheat the oven to 375F. With the cooking spray, grease a 9x9-inch baking dish.
2. Bring a large-sized pot with salted water to a boil. Add the pasta and the broccoli; cook following the direction on the pasta package till al dente.
3. Melt the butter inside a large-sized skillet over medium heat. Add the onion; cook for 1 minutes. Whisk in the flour; cook for 1 minute. Whisk the milk in and the chicken broth; increase the heat to medium-high heat and bring to boil. When boiling, reduce the heat to medium; cook the sauce for 5 minutes or till thick and smooth; season with the salt and the pepper. Once thick, remove from the heat. Add the cheddar cheese; stir until blended well.
4. Add the pasta and the broccoli; mix well. Pour into the prepared the baking dish; top with the grated parmesan, then the breadcrumbs. Lightly coat the top with the cooking spray; bake for about 15 to 20 minutes. After baking, broil for about 2 to 4 minutes or till the breadcrumbs are golden.

Freezing: Just assemble. Cover the unbaked dish with foil and freeze. Reheat from frozen, covered with foil, in preheated 350F oven for about 30 to40 minutes

117

Stuffed Taco Shells

Prep Time: 30 minutes; **Cook Time:** 45-60 minutes	

Serving Size: 59 g; **Serves:** 40-45; **Calories:** 161
Total Fat: 8.2 g **Saturated Fat:** 3.7 g; **Trans Fat:** 0 g
Protein: 11.2 g; **Net Carbs:** 9 g
Total Carbs: 10.4 g; **Dietary Fiber:** 1.4 g; **Sugars:** 2.1 g
Cholesterol: 35 mg; **Sodium:** 260 mg; **Potassium:** 206 mg;
Vitamin A: 16%; **Vitamin C:** 2%; **Calcium:** 11%; **Iron:** 27%

Ingredients:

- ☐ 1 can (4 ounces) diced green chilies
- ☐ 1 cup corn and black bean salsa (or any of your favorite variety salsa)
- ☐ 1 package (16 ounces) large taco shells
- ☐ 2 pounds ground beef (or ground turkey)
- ☐ 4 cup Mexican blend cheese, shredded
- ☐ 6 tablespoons taco seasoning (homemade or 2 packages)
- ☐ Salsa, for bottom of baking dish

Toppings (optional):

- ☐ Avocado
- ☐ Lettuce
- ☐ Sour cream
- ☐ Tomato

Directions:

1. Cook the large shell pasta following directions on the package. When cooked, drain, separate, and then put on a parchment paper on the counter; set aside.
2. While the pasta is cooking, brown the ground beef/turkey Inside a large-sized skillet. When browned, drain excess grease and return to the skillet. Add the corn and black been salsa, green chilies, and taco seasoning. Fold in the shredded cheese; set aside.
3. With a large-sized spoon, stuff each shell pasta with the meat mix until filled.
4. If baking right away, pour 1 cup salsa on the bottom of the baking dish; choose a dish that can hold the number of shells you are going to cool, about 2-3 shells per serving. Put the stuffed shells on top of the salsa layer. Cover the dish with foil; bake at preheated 350F oven for 45 minutes. Remove the foil; bake for about 5 to 15 minutes more or until the salsa is bubbly and the filling is fully heated. If desired, serve with additional toppings.

Freezing: If not baking immediately, put the stuffed pasta in Ziploc bag and freeze until ready to use. When ready to serve, assemble and cook as directed.

Slow Cooked Chicken Fajitas

Prep Time: 20 minutes; **Cook Time:** 5-6 hours	
Serving Size: 351 g; **Serves:** 5; **Calories:** 366	
Total Fat: 7.2 g **Saturated Fat:** 0 g; **Trans Fat:** 0 g	
Protein: 60.4 g; **Net Carbs:** 10.3 g	
Total Carbs: 14.5 g; **Dietary Fiber:** 4.2 g; **Sugars:** 7.3 g	
Cholesterol: 156 mg; **Sodium:** 808 mg; **Potassium:** 796 mg;	
Vitamin A: 58%; **Vitamin C:** 170%; **Calcium:** 6%; **Iron:** 18%	

Ingredients:

- 4 cups onions, sliced (a mixt of red or white and sweet)
- 4 cups bell peppers, sliced (stems and seeds discarded)
- 2 pounds boneless, skinless chicken breast (and/or thigh), sliced into 1/2-inch wide strips
- 3/4 teaspoon cumin
- 1/4 teaspoon paprika
- 1/2 teaspoon red pepper flakes, or to taste
- 1/2 teaspoon onion powder
- 1/2 teaspoon garlic powder
- 1/2 tablespoon coarse sea salt
- 1 tablespoon chili powder
- Chopped cilantro and fresh lime wedges, optional

Directions:

1. Into the bowl of the slow cooker, toss the peppers with the chicken and the onions.
2. In a small-sized bowl, stir the remaining ingredients together until combined. Sprinkle the spice mix evenly over the chicken mix; toss to evenly distribute the spice mix.
3. Cover the slow cooker; cook for about 5 to 6 hours on LOW until the juices run clear.
4. Serve immediately over grain-free tortillas, cauliflower rice, or rice. If desired, squeeze with fresh lime juice and with garnish with some chopped cilantro.

Notes: If making ahead of time, store into an airtight container at room temperature for up to 3-4 weeks. If serving later than 1 month, store in the fridge.

Slow Cooked Veggie Lasagna

Prep Time: 40 minutes; **Cook Time:** 3 hours on high, 5-6 hours on low

Serving Size: 312 g; **Serves:** 8; **Calories:** 309
Total Fat: 10.1 g **Saturated Fat:** 4.9 g; **Trans Fat:** 0 g
Protein: 17.4 g; **Net Carbs:** 34.2 g
Total Carbs: 38.9 g; **Dietary Fiber:** 4.7 g; **Sugars:** 13 g
Cholesterol: 36 mg; **Sodium:** 935 mg; **Potassium:** 841 mg;
Vitamin A: 36%; **Vitamin C:** 68%; **Calcium:** 24%; **Iron:** 12%

Ingredients:

- 1 bell pepper (I used half a red and half a yellow)
- 1 cup PLUS 1 1/2 cups shredded mozzarella cheese
- 1 medium yellow squash
- 1 medium zucchini
- 4 ounces mushrooms
- 23 ounces jarred pasta sauce
- 2 cloves garlic, minced
- 15 ounces container Ricotta
- 15 ounces canned tomato sauce (our just use additional pasta sauce)
- 14 1/2 ounces canned diced tomatoes, drained
- 1/8 teaspoon pepper
- 1/2 teaspoon salt
- 1/2 pound (about 9-10) lasagna noodles
- 1/2 medium yellow sweet onion, diced
- 1/2 cup Parmesan cheese
- 1 teaspoon Italian seasoning
- Pinch red pepper flakes

Directions:

1. Chop the pepper, mushrooms, squash, and zucchini into small bite-sized pieces; put inside a large-sized bowl. Add the garlic, onion, and the drained diced tomatoes.
2. In another bowl, mix the ricotta with the parmesan, 1 cup mozzarella, and the seasonings until well combined.
3. Add the cheese mix into the bowl with veggies. Add the tomato sauce and the spaghetti sauce; toss until well combined.
4. Equally divide between 2 large freezer bags, label, and freeze until ready to use.
5. When ready to serve, transfer into the fridge and let thaw overnight to 24 hours.
6. Put 1 cup of sauce on the bottom of a large-sized oval crock.
7. Break about 2 to 3 noodles to fit the oval rock and form the first noodle layer.
8. Add 1 cup of sauce over the first layer noodles. Repeat the process with the last layer of sauce on top; sprinkle the top with additional 1 1/2 cups cheese.
9. Cover the crock and cook for 3 hours on HIGH and for 5 to 6 hours on LOW. Uncover and let sit for 30 minutes with the heat off. Slice and serve.

Notes: If making ahead of time, store into an airtight container at room temperature for up to 3-4 weeks. If serving later than 1 month, store in the fridge.

Pork and Herbed White Beans

Prep Time: 30 minutes, plus 1 hour standing; **Cook Time:** 1 1/2 hours	
Serving Size: 504 g; **Serves:** 6; **Calories:** 284	
Total Fat: 6.7 g **Saturated Fat:** 1.6 g; **Trans Fat:** 0 g	
Protein: 29 g; **Net Carbs:** 20.3 g	
Total Carbs: 27.6 g; **Dietary Fiber:** 7.3 g; **Sugars:** 2.9 g	
Cholesterol: 55 mg; **Sodium:** 410 mg; **Potassium:** 1048 mg;	
Vitamin A: 33%; **Vitamin C:** 9%; **Calcium:** 16%; **Iron:** 40%	

Ingredients:

- 1 piece (1-pound) boneless picnic roast pork, cut into 1/2-inch pieces
- 1 cup dried white beans
- 1/2 cup carrot, coarsely chopped
- 1 fresh sage sprig
- 1 1/2 tablespoons olive oil, divided
- 1/2 cup water
- 1/2 teaspoon black pepper
- 1/2 teaspoon salt, divided
- 2 cups fat-free, lower-sodium chicken broth
- 2 cups onion, coarsely chopped
- 2 fresh thyme sprigs
- 6 cups boiling water
- 6 garlic cloves, coarsely chopped

Directions:

1. Put the beans in the Dutch oven; cover with 6 cups of boiling water. Let stand for 1 hour and drain.
2. Preheat the oven to 325F.
3. Heat a Dutch oven on medium-high heat. Put 1 tablespoon olive oil into the pan; swirl to coat.
4. Evenly sprinkle the pork with 1/4 teaspoon and 1/4 teaspoon pepper. Put the pork into the Dutch oven; sauté for about6 minutes, turning to brown all sides. Stir in the beans, remaining salt, water, thyme, and sage.
5. Heat a skillet on medium-high heat. Add the remaining 1 1/2 teaspoon oil; swirl to coat.
6. Add the onion and the carrot; sauté for 4 minutes, occasionally stirring. Add the garlic; sauté for 1 minute, constantly stirring. Stir the onion mix into the bean mix; bake at 325F for 1 1/2 hours or until the beans are tender.
7. Drain through a sieve over a bowl. Reserve the solids and the cooking liquid. Skim the fat from the top of the cooking liquid and discard. Stir the cooking liquid back into the pork mix.

Notes: Prepare this dish on a weekend and you have instant pork and beans throughout the week; just reheat.

Smokey Turkey Mole with Almond

Prep Time: 30 minutes; **Cook Time:** 21 minutes	

Serving Size: 258 g; **Serves:** 6; **Calories:** 330
Total Fat: 10.6 g **Saturated Fat:** 1.9 g; **Trans Fat:** 0 g
Protein: 28.2 g; **Net Carbs:** 22.6 g
Total Carbs: 34.7 g; **Dietary Fiber:** 12.1 g; **Sugars:** 18.3 g
Cholesterol: 53 mg; **Sodium:** 401 mg; **Potassium:** 1107 mg;
Vitamin A: 185%; **Vitamin C:** 30%; **Calcium:** 6%; **Iron:** 55%

Ingredients:

- 1 1/2 cups crushed tomatoes, fire-roasted (I used Muir Glen)
- 3 cups turkey breast, cooked, chopped
- 1 can (14 1/2-ounce) vegetable broth
- 1 can (7-ounce) chipotle chilies in adobo sauce
- 2 pieces corn tortillas (6-inch), torn to small-sized pieces
- 2 dried Anaheim chilies, stemmed, seeded, and chopped
- 1/8 teaspoon ground cloves
- 1/4 teaspoon salt
- 1/2 teaspoon vegetable oil
- 1/2 teaspoon ground cumin
- 1/2 cup almonds, roasted
- 1 tablespoon vinegar (white wine)
- 1 tablespoon sugar
- 1 garlic clove, crushed
- 1 cup onion, chopped
- Cilantro sprigs, for garnish, optional

Directions:

1. Put the almonds into a food processor, process for 2 1/2 minutes or till smooth, scraping the sides of the processor bowl one time. Set aside.
2. Inside a large-sized nonstick skillet, heat the oil on medium-high heat. Put the Anaheim chilies; sauté for 1 minute or till soft. Add the garlic and the onion; sauté for 4 minutes or till the onion is slightly browned.
3. Remove 1 chipotle chili from the can, cut into halves. Add 1 chili half into the onion mix. Reserve the remaining chilies and the adobo sauce for a different use.
4. Add the tomatoes, sugar, cumin, salt, cloves, corn tortillas, and the broth. Reduce the heat to a simmer and cook, simmering, for 15 minutes, occasionally stirring.
5. Spoon the mix into the food processor, process till smooth. Return the mix into the pan. Stir in the almond butter, then vinegar; cook for 1 minutes. Stir in the turkey. If desired, garnish with the cilantro.

Notes: If making ahead of time; let cool and freeze. Just reheat when ready to serve.

Green Chile Chili

Prep Time: 20 minutes; Cook Time: 1 hour	
Serving Size: 264 g; Serves: 12; Calories: 537	
Total Fat: 20.8 g Saturated Fat: 6.7 g; Trans Fat: 0 g	
Protein: 39.1 g; Net Carbs: 34 g	
Total Carbs: 50 g; Dietary Fiber: 16 g; Sugars: 16.1 g	
Cholesterol: 91mg; Sodium: 212 mg; Potassium: 1573 mg;	
Vitamin A: 189%; Vitamin C: 34%; Calcium: 8%; Iron: 43%	

Ingredients:

- 12 ounces ground sirloin
- 1/4 cup (1 ounce) sharp cheddar cheese, shredded
- 1/2 cup salsa verde
- 1 teaspoon hot paprika
- 1 tablespoon chili powder
- 1 tablespoon canola oil
- 1 green onion, sliced
- 1 can (4-ounce) diced green chilies, undrained
- 1 can (15-ounce) tomatoes, no-salt-added, undrained and crushed
- 1 can (15-ounce) kidney beans, organic, rinsed and drained
- 1 bottle (12-ounce) dark beer
- 1 1/2 cups chopped onion
- 5 garlic cloves, minced

Directions:

1. Heat a large-sized Dutch oven on medium-high heat. Add the oil to the pan; swirl to coat. Add the beef; sauté for 5 minutes or till no longer to pink, stirring to crumble. Add the onion, paprika, and the chili powder; sauté for 4 minutes; occasionally stirring. Add the garlic, sauté for 1 minute, occasionally stirring.
2. Stir in the beer; bring to a boil and cook for 15 minutes or till the liquid is almost evaporated. Add the salsa green chilies, tomatoes, and the kidney beans; bring to a boil. Reduce the heat and simmer for 30 minutes, occasionally stirring. Ladle into bowls and top each serve with 1 tablespoon cheese. Sprinkle with green onion. Serve with corn muffins or corn bread.

Notes: If making ahead of time, just freeze and then reheat when ready to serve.

Beef, Okra, and Tomato Stew

Prep Time: 15 minutes; **Cook Time:** 25 minutes	

Serving Size: 438 g; **Serves:** 6; **Calories:** 509
Total Fat: 15.1 g Saturated Fat: 3.9 g; Trans Fat: 0 g
Protein: 41.5; **Net Carbs:** 44.7 g
Total Carbs: 49.9 g; **Dietary Fiber:** 5.2 g; **Sugars:** 5.6 g
Cholesterol: 101 mg; **Sodium:** 219 mg; **Potassium:** 1139 mg;
Vitamin A: 41%; **Vitamin C:** 72%; **Calcium:** 10%; **Iron:** 137%

Ingredients:

- ☐ 1 1/2 cups rice
- ☐ 1 1/2 pounds beef sirloin, cut into 3/4-inch cubes
- ☐ 1 bag (16 ounce) cut frozen okra
- ☐ 1 can (28 ounce) fire-roasted tomatoes, diced
- ☐ 1 cup beef broth
- ☐ 1 onion, chopped
- ☐ 1/2 cup parsley, chopped
- ☐ 3 tablespoons extra-virgin olive oil
- ☐ Salt and pepper
- ☐ 3 cups water

Directions:

1. In a medium-sized saucepan, combine the rice with the water; bring to a simmer. Cover and then cook for about 20 minutes on medium-low heat until the water is absorbed. Remove from the heat; let stand for 5 minutes, covered, and then fluff using a fork.
2. While the rice is cooking, heat 2 tablespoons olive oil Inside a large-sized pot on medium-high heat.
3. Season the beef with the salt and the pepper. Cooking in batches, add the beef into the pot, cook for about 2 minutes or till browned; transfer to a bowl. When all the beef is cooked, lower the heat to medium. Add the onions and the remaining 1 tablespoon olive oil; cook for 3-4 minutes or till the onion is translucent.
4. Stir in the tomatoes, the okra, and the beef broth; bring to a boil; occasionally stirring. Lower the heat to simmer and cook, simmering for 15 minutes or till thick. Return the beef and any juice in the bowl into the pot. Stir in the parsley. Serve with the rice.

Notes: Makethis ahead of time. Let cool completely and freeze in freezable, airtight containers or bags for up to 1 month.

Spaghetti and Shrimp Coconut Broth

Prep Time: 10 minutes; **Cook Time:** 25 minutes	

Serving Size: 311 g; **Serves:** 12; **Calories:** 498

Total Fat: 19.3 g **Saturated Fat:** 14.5 g; **Trans Fat:** 0 g

Protein: 43.2 g; **Net Carbs:** 36 g

Total Carbs: 37.5 g; **Dietary Fiber:** 1.5 g; **Sugars:** 2.3 g

Cholesterol: 360 mg; **Sodium:** 640 mg; **Potassium:** 574 mg;

Vitamin A: 11%; **Vitamin C:** 5%; **Calcium:** 16%; **Iron:** 20%

Ingredients:
- 1 1/2 pounds spaghetti
- 2 cans (13 1/2 ounces each) coconut milk
- 2 bags (2 pounds each) frozen, raw shrimp (31- 40 per pound), thawed and tails removed
- 1 tablespoon garlic, finely chopped
- 1 tablespoon Asian fish sauce
- 1 can (14 1/2 ounce) chicken broth
- 1 bunch cilantro, coarsely chopped
- 2 teaspoons ginger, finely chopped
- 2 teaspoons hot chili sauce

Directions:
1. Inside a large-sized, deep skillet, combine the coconut milk with the chicken broth; bring to a simmer on medium heat. Stir in the dish sauce, ginger, garlic, lime juice, and chili sauce; cook for 2 minutes.
2. Stir in the shrimp; cook for about 4 minutes or till just opaque. Stir in the cilantro and then remove the skillet from the heat.
3. Cook the spaghetti Inside a large-sized pot of boiling salted water until al dente; drain and let cool.

Freezing: Divide the shrimp mix between 3 re-sealable 1 gallon-sized freezer bags and seal. Divide the spaghetti between 3 more freezable bag; seal and label. Freeze.

When ready to serve, thaw needed bag of shrimp mix and pasta in the fridge overnight. Toss the pasta and the shrimp in the skillet; simmer for about 1-2 minutes until warmed through.

Beef Kebabs, Almonds ,and Roasted Green Beans

Prep Time: 15 minutes; **Cook Time:** 15 minutes	
Serving Size: 285 g; **Serves:** 4; **Calories:** 327	
Total Fat: 14.1 g **Saturated Fat:** 3.6 g; **Trans Fat:** 0 g	
Protein: 38.1 g; **Net Carbs:** 7.3 g	
Total Carbs: 13.3 g; **Dietary Fiber:** 6 g; **Sugars:** 2.6 g	
Cholesterol: 101 mg; **Sodium:** 86 mg; **Potassium:** 837 mg;	
Vitamin A: 32%; **Vitamin C:** 61%; **Calcium:** 8%; **Iron:** 130%	

Ingredients:

- ☐ 1 pound ground beef
- ☐ 1 1/4 pounds green beans
- ☐ 1 1/2 tablespoons extra-virgin olive oil
- ☐ 1 tablespoon garlic, finely chopped
- ☐ 1 teaspoon smoked paprika
- ☐ 1/2 lemon, cut into 4 wedges
- ☐ 1/4 cup flat-leaf parsley, chopped
- ☐ 2 tablespoons almonds, sliced
- ☐ Salt and pepper

Directions:

1. Preheat the oven to 450F.
2. Inside a large-sized bowl, crumble the beef and then mix in the garlic, parsley, paprika, 1/2 teaspoon pepper, and 1 teaspoon salt. Form the mix into 1 1/4-inch thick balls. Thread 4 balls into 1 skewer.
3. On a rimmed baking sheet, toss the green beans with the olive oil, 1/4 teaspoon salt, and 1/4 teaspoon pepper; spread the beans in a single layer in the baking sheet; roast for 10 minutes. Stir in the almonds; roast for about 5 minutes more or until the green beans are lightly browned and the almonds are toasted.
4. Preheat a grill pan to medium-high. Grill the beef skewers for about 8-10 minutes, turning, until just cooked through. Serve with the green bean mix and with lemon wedges. You can also serve the meat balls in a pita with sliced cucumbers and plain Greek yogurt.

Notes: You can double the meatballs and make ahead of time. Freeze in airtight container for up to3 months. Add into stews and soups.

Lemon Chicken with Sweet Pea Tortellini

Prep Time: 35 minutes; **Cook Time:** 40 minutes	
Serving Size: 284 g; **Serves:** 4; **Calories:** 731	
Total Fat: 11.5 g **Saturated Fat:** 3 g; **Trans Fat:** 0 g	
Protein: 39.9 g; **Net Carbs:** 109 g	
Total Carbs: 112.7 g; **Dietary Fiber:** 3.7 g; **Sugars:** 0 g	
Cholesterol: 83 mg; **Sodium:** 1173 mg; **Potassium:** 337 mg;	
Vitamin A: 3%; **Vitamin C:** 3%; **Calcium:** 15%; **Iron:** 43%	

Ingredients:

- 4 chicken leg quarters
- 24 wonton wrappers
- 1/4 cup ricotta cheese
- 1/2 ounce peas, thawed
- 1 tablespoon vegetable oil
- 1 tablespoon fresh tarragon, chopped
- 1 lemon, 1/2 thinly sliced crosswise, 1/2 squeezed into juice
- Salt and pepper

Directions:

1. Preheat the oven to425F.
2. In a single layer, arrange the lemon slices down the center of a roasting pan.
3. Rub the chicken with oil and then season with salt and pepper. With the skin side up, put the chicken on the lemon slices; bake for 35 minutes. Transfer to the broiler; broil for 3 minutes or till the skin is crisp. Drizzle the chicken with the lemon juice.
4. While he chicken is cooking, put the peas, ricotta, 1/4 teaspoon salt, and 1/2 teaspoon tarragon; process until mixed.
5. On a clean, work surface, working with 2 wonton wrappers at a time, spoon 2 teaspoon of the pea mix into the center of each wrapper. Moisten the edges with water, fold the wrapper diagonally into half, forming a triangle; push out any air pockets and press the edges firmly to seal. With the long side of the triangle facing towards you, fold the top point back towards you and then fold the left and the right points to meet it; firmly press all the 3 points together, securing them with more water.
6. Inside a large-sized pot of boiling salted water, cook the tortellini for about 5 minutes or till they float to the top. With a slotted spoon, transfer them into 4 plates.
7. Divide the chicken and the roasted slices of lemon between the plates and then top with the juices in pan. Sprinkle with the remaining 2 1/2 teaspoons tarragon.

Notes: You can prepare the tortellini ahead of time. Put them in a baking sheet and flash freeze until solid. Transfer to a freezer bag and freeze until ready to use. When ready to serve, just cook frozen tortellini in frozen boiling salted water for 6 minutes.

Skillet Sausage and Shrimp

Prep Time: 20 minutes; **Cook Time:** 30 minutes

Serving Size: 405 g; **Serves:** 12; **Calories:** 508	
Total Fat: 11.1 g **Saturated Fat:** 3.3 g; **Trans Fat:** 0 g	
Protein: 42.7 g; **Net Carbs:** 53.8 g	
Total Carbs: 55.6 g; **Dietary Fiber:** 1.8 g; **Sugars:** 2.4 g	
Cholesterol: 327 mg; **Sodium:** 802 mg; **Potassium:** 574 mg;	
Vitamin A: 25%; **Vitamin C:** 39%; **Calcium:** 17%; **Iron:** 20%	

Ingredients:

- 2 bags (2 pounds) shrimp, raw, frozen (31-40 per pound)
- 1 can (14 1/2 ounces) diced tomatoes
- 4 links chicken-apple sausage, precooked, cut into 1-inch pieces
- 4 cups long-grain white rice
- 2 teaspoons garlic, finely chopped
- 2 tablespoons butter
- 1/4 cup extra-virgin olive oil
- 1 large onion, chopped
- 1 large green bell pepper, chopped
- 6 cups chicken broth
- Salt and pepper

Directions:

1. Inside a large-sized, deep skillet, heat the butter and the olive oil on medium-high heat. Add the rice and the onion; cook, occasionally stirring, for about 5 minutes or till the onion is soft. Add the garlic, bell pepper, and the sausage; cook, stirring, for about 3 minutes or till the veggies are soft. Remove from the heat, stir in the tomatoes along with their juices; season with salt and pepper to taste. Let completely.
2. Divide the rice mix into 3 portions, put into 3 re-sealable 1 gallon-sized freezer bags, pour 2 cups chicken broth into each freezer bag, label, and freeze.
3. Divide the shrimp into 3 portions, put into 3 re-sealable 1 gallon-sized freezer bags, label, and freeze.
4. When ready to serve, take out a portion of the rice mix and the shrimp from the freezer. Put the shrimp inside a large bowl of cold water and let thaw.
5. Put the frozen rice mix into a skillet; heat the skillet, thawing the mix and then bring to a boil. When boiling, lower the heat, cover the skillet, and simmer for about 17 minutes or till the rice is tender.
6. Drain the thawed shrimp. Add to the rice mix; cook on medium heat, frequently stirring, for about 5 minutes or till the shrimp is opaque. Serve.

Cheddar Cheesy Beef Potpie

Prep Time: 40 minutes; Cook Time: 35 minutes
Serving Size: 483 g; Serves: 5; Calories: 750
Total Fat: 38.8 g Saturated Fat: 22 g; Trans Fat: 0 g
Protein: 59.9 g; Net Carbs: 35.7 g
Total Carbs: 39 g; Dietary Fiber: 3.3 g; Sugars: 6.4 g
Cholesterol: 208 mg; Sodium: 643 mg; Potassium: 1291 mg;
Vitamin A: 44%; Vitamin C: 38%; Calcium: 47%; Iron: 158%

Ingredients:
- ☐ 1 1/2 pounds ground beef
- ☐ 1 1/2 cups flour
- ☐ 1 can (28 ounces) diced tomatoes, drained
- ☐ 1 cup beef broth
- ☐ 1 small onion, chopped
- ☐ 1/2 cup milk
- ☐ 2 cups sharp cheddar cheese, shredded (8 ounces)
- ☐ 2 teaspoons baking powder
- ☐ 6 tablespoons butter, chilled
- ☐ Salt and pepper

Directions:
1. Preheat the oven to 375F. Grease an 8x12-inch baking dish; set aside.
2. Heat 2 tablespoons of butter Inside a large-sized skillet over medium-high heat. Add onion; cook for about 3-5 minutes, stirring, until soft.
3. Add the beef; cook, crumbling with the back of a spoon, for about 5 minutes or till no longer pink.
4. Stir in the beef broth and the tomatoes; season with salt and pepper to taste. Lower the heat; cook, occasionally stirring, for about 20 minutes or till most of the liquid has evaporated. Pour the mix into the greased baking dish, spreading evenly.
5. Inside a large-sized bowl, combine the flour with the baking powder and 1/2 teaspoon salt. With a pastry blender or your fingertips, blend the remaining 4 tablespoons butter and cheese into the flour mix until the mix resembles coarse crumbs. Pour the milk in; quickly stir using a fork to from a dry, shaggy dough. Gather the dough together and knead lightly inside the bowl. Transfer into a floured surface; pat or roll the dough inside a large 1/2-inch thick round. With a 3-inch cookie cutter, cut out 8 biscuits from the dough. Gather the leftover dough and again shape into 1/2-inch think round; cut out more biscuits. Repeat the process until all the dough is used.
6. Put the biscuits on top of the beef mixture, placing them as close together as possible; bake for about 35 minutes or till the biscuits are lightly browned.

Freezing: You can assemble this potpie ahead of time. Tightly cover the dish with plastic wrap and freeze for up to 4 months. When ready to serve, remove the plastic wrap, cover the dish with foil, and bake at 375F for 1 hour. Remove the foil and bake for 15 minutes more or until biscuit is lightly brown and the filling is heated through.

When baked, this meal also freezes real well. Just reheat when ready to serve.

Cheeseburger Meatloaf with Mashed Potatoes

Prep Time: 20 minutes; **Cook Time:** 35 minutes	

Serving Size: 307 g; **Serves:** 8; **Calories:** 499

Total Fat: 24.3 g **Saturated Fat:** 11.6 g; **Trans Fat:** 0 g

Protein: 38.3 g; **Net Carbs:** 28 g

Total Carbs: 31.6 g; **Dietary Fiber:** 3.6 g; **Sugars:** 7.3 g

Cholesterol: 168 mg; **Sodium:** 667 mg; **Potassium:** 973 mg;

Vitamin A: 14%; **Vitamin C:** 44%; **Calcium:** 25%; **Iron:** 98%

Ingredients:
- ☐ 1 1/2 pounds ground beef
- ☐ 1/2 cup bread-and-butter pickle chips, chopped
- ☐ 2 large eggs
- ☐ 2 pounds new red potatoes
- ☐ 8 ounces cheddar cheese, cut into 1/3-inch cubes
- ☐ 3/4 cup heavy cream
- ☐ 2/3 cup ketchup
- ☐ 2/3 cup breadcrumbs
- ☐ 1 red onion, finely chopped
- ☐ 2 tablespoons extra-virgin olive oil, plus more for greasing

Directions:
1. Preheat the oven to 400F. Lightly grease a rimmed baking sheet; set aside.
2. Heat 2 tablespoons olive oil in a medium-sized skillet over medium heat. Add the onion, cook, stirring for about 3 minutes or till soft.
3. Inside a large-sized bowl, combine the ketchup with the eggs, breadcrumbs, and pickles. Mix the onion into the ketchup mix.
4. Crumble the beef and the cheese; mix together with the ketchup mix. Transfer the beef mix into the greased baking sheet. Shape into a 4x12-inch loaf; bake for about 35 minutes or till an instant-read thermometer registers 160F when inserted into the center of the loaf.
5. While the meatloaf is cooking, cut the potatoes into halves. Put them inside a large-sized pot. Pour water to cover the potatoes by 1 inch. Salt the water and bring to a boil. When boiling, reduce the heat to a simmer; cook for about 10 to 15 minutes or till tender. Drain and then return the potatoes into the pot. Mash with the cream.
6. When the meatloaf is cooked, let rest for 5 minutes, slice, and serve with the mashed potatoes.

Freezing: You can bake this meatloaf ahead of time. Freeze for up to 1 month. When ready to serve, just reheat in a 350F oven.

130

Meaty Moussaka

Prep Time: 30 minutes; **Cook Time:** 45 minutes	
Serving Size: 409 g; **Serves:** 4; **Calories:** 673	
Total Fat: 39.3 g **Saturated Fat:** 21.1 g; **Trans Fat:** 0 g	
Protein: 63.9 g; **Net Carbs:** 12.1 g	
Total Carbs: 14.2 g; **Dietary Fiber:** 2.1 g; **Sugars:** 6.9 g	
Cholesterol: 322 mg; **Sodium:** 674 mg; **Potassium:** 1106 mg;	
Vitamin A: 25%; **Vitamin C:** 9%; **Calcium:** 22%; **Iron:** 188%	

Ingredients:
- 1 1/2 pounds ground beef
- 1 can (8 ounces) tomato sauce
- 1 cup whole milk
- 1 small onion, chopped
- 1 teaspoon ground nutmeg
- 1/2 cup ricotta cheese
- 2 large eggs
- 2 tablespoons flour
- 2 teaspoons ground cinnamon
- 4 ounces cream cheese
- 4 tablespoons butter
- Salt and pepper

Directions:
1. Preheat the oven to 350F.
2. Heat 2 tablespoons of butter Inside a large-sized skillet over medium-high heat. Add the onion; cook for about 3-5 minutes or till soft.
3. Add the beef; cook for 5 minutes or till no longer pink.
4. Stir in the nutmeg and the cinnamon; season with salt and pepper to taste.
5. Add the tomato sauce; cook for about 3-5 minutes or till most of the liquid has evaporated. Pour the mix into an 8x8-inch baking dish; set aside.
6. In a medium-sized bowl, lightly beat the eggs; set aside.
7. In a small-sized saucepan, melt the remaining 2 tablespoons of butter on medium-high heat. Whisk in the flour; cook for about 30 seconds, whisking often, until the mix is smooth. Slowly whisk in the milk until the mix is thick. Lower the heat to medium; stir in the cream cheese, the ricotta cheese, and season with salt and pepper to taste.
8. Whisk 1/4 of the cheese sauce into the egg until smooth. Whisk the egg mix into the cheese sauce in the saucepan. Pour the sauce over the meat in the baking dish; spread evenly. Bake for about 40-45 minutes or till the top is light brown and frim to the touch; let cool for 10 minutes and then cut into squares. Serve.

Freezing: You can assemble the moussaka ahead of time. Tightly wrap the dish with plastic wrap and freeze for up to 1 month. When ready to serve, remove the plastic wrap, cover with foil, and bake at 350F for 1 ½ hours. Remove the foil and bake for another 15 minutes or till the top is golden and the filling is heated through.

Notes: If you have leftover ricotta cheese, drizzle it with honey and then sprinkle with chopped nuts and serve as a dessert.

Beef Ravioli Bake a.k.a Fake-Out Lasagna

Prep Time: 30 minutes; **Cook Time:** 1 hour, plus 10 minutes sitting

Serving Size: 212 g; **Serves:** 16; **Calories:** 527		
Total Fat: 9.6 g **Saturated Fat:** 4.1 g; **Trans Fat:** 0 g		
Protein: 19.6 g; **Net Carbs:** 24 g		
Total Carbs: 25.7 g; **Dietary Fiber:** 1.7 g; **Sugars:** 4.6 g		
Cholesterol: 72 mg; **Sodium:** 737 mg; **Potassium:** 575 mg;		
Vitamin A: 11%; **Vitamin C:** 14%; **Calcium:** 8%; **Iron:** 43%		

Ingredients:
- 1 can (15 ounces) crushed Italian tomatoes
- 1 pounds ground beef (preferably grass-fed, organic)
- 1/2 medium-sized onion, diced
- 1/2 pounds pork sausage (preferably local, organic)
- 2 cups Italian mix cheese, shredded (Romano, Parmesan, Asiago, etc)
- 2 cups mozzarella cheese, shredded
- 2 jars (28 ounce each) spaghetti sauce
- 2 packages (10 ounces each) fresh cheese ravioli, cooked al dente
- 2-3 garlic cloves, minced
- Grated Parmesan cheese, for serving, optional

Directions:
1. Preheat the oven to 375F. grease a 9x13-inch baking pan with cooking spray.
2. Inside a large-sized skillet, sauté the onions over medium heat until soft. Add the garlic; sauté for 1 minute, making sure it does not burn. Add the beef and the sausage; increase the heat to medium-high. Cook until the beef is no longer pink and the sausage is browned. Drain the grease. Stir in the sauce and the crushed tomatoes; remove the skillet from the heat.
3. Spread a thin layer of the meat sauce onto the bottom of the baking dish. Arrange a layer of cooked ravioli over the sauce, sprinkle with the mozzarella cheese and the Italian cheese.
4. Repeat the layers with the sauce as the final top layer. Cover the baking dish with the foil; bake for 45 minutes or till heated through. Remove the foil and bake for another 15 minutes or till the edges are bubbly. Let rest for 10 minutes, slice, sprinkle with parmesan cheese, and serve.

Freezing: You can assemble the dish ahead of time. Tightly wrap with foil and freeze.

When ready to serve, transfer into the fridge and let thaw for about 48 hours. Alternatively, you can thaw in the microwave on DEFROST setting. Bake as directed.

If baking from frozen, adjust baking time by 1-1 ½ hours, making total baking time to 2-2 1/2 hours.

Baked Italian Meatballs

Prep Time: 10 minutes; **Cook Time:** 20 minutes	
Serving Size: 154 g; **Serves:** 6; **Calories:** 304	
Total Fat: 9.1 g **Saturated Fat:** 3.2 g; **Trans Fat:** 0 g	
Protein: 38.4 g; **Net Carbs:** 13.6 g	
Total Carbs: 14.8 g; **Dietary Fiber:** 1.2 g; **Sugars:** 2.2 g	
Cholesterol: 133 mg; **Sodium:** 615 mg; **Potassium:** 579 mg;	
Vitamin A: 7%; **Vitamin C:** 8%; **Calcium:** 5%; **Iron:** 126%	

Ingredients:

- 1 1/2 pounds ground beef (or ground turkey)
- 1 cup whole-wheat breadcrumbs (or panko)
- 1 large egg, beaten
- 1 teaspoon salt
- 1/2 teaspoon garlic powder
- 1/2 teaspoon ground pepper
- 1/2 teaspoon Italian seasoning
- 1/4 cup fresh parsley, finely chopped, loosely packed
- 2 tablespoons milk
- 2 tablespoons tomato paste

Directions:

1. Preheat the oven to 350F. Line a sheet pan with foil or with parchment paper.
2. With clean hands, gently combine all the ingredients in a medium-sized bowl.
3. With a spoon or a medium-sized dough scooper, scoop and roll the mix into 1 1/2-inch meatballs. Line the meatballs on the prepared sheet pan, leaving a space between each; bake for about 20 minutes or till the inside is no longer pink or the internal temperature is 160F.

Freezing: Make the meatballs ahead of time. After placing them into the prepared sheet pan, flash freeze for about 1 hour or more until frozen. When frozen, put the meatballs into a gallon-sized freezer bag and freeze.

When ready to serve, transfer the meatballs into the fridge and let thaw overnight or submerge the freezer bag in cool water until thawed, replacing the water every 30 minutes. Cook as directed.

133

Slow Cooked Pot Roast

Prep Time: 20 minutes; **Cook Time:** 7 hours	
Serving Size: 354 g; **Serves:** 8-10; **Calories:** 330	
Total Fat: 7.6 g **Saturated Fat:** 0 g; **Trans Fat:** 0 g	
Protein: 38.5 g; **Net Carbs:** 21.9 g	
Total Carbs: 26.4 g; **Dietary Fiber:** 4.5 g; **Sugars:** 5.3 g	
Cholesterol: 1 mg; **Sodium:** 339 mg; **Potassium:** 694 mg;	
Vitamin A: 93%; **Vitamin C:** 45%; **Calcium:** 4%; **Iron:** 7%	

Ingredients:

- 4-6 medium russet potatoes, chopped into 1-inch pieces (or about 5-7 cups)
- 4 celery stalks, chopped
- 3-5 large carrots, chopped into 1-inch pieces (or about 2 cups)
- 3 garlic cloves, minced
- 2-3 pounds rump roast (trim off visible fat)
- 2 tablespoons whole-wheat flour
- 2 onions, diced
- 1/4 teaspoon garlic powder
- 1/4 teaspoon black pepper
- 1/4 cup red wine
- 1/2 teaspoon salt
- 1 tablespoon Italian seasoning
- 1 cup low sodium chicken stock
- 1 can (8 ounces) no-salt tomato sauce
- 1 bay leaf
- All-natural steak seasoning
- Olive oil
- Salt and pepper

Directions:

1. In a skillet, heat a couple tablespoons of olive oil on medium-high heat.
2. Season all the sides of the roast with the seasoning steaks. Put in the skillet and brown all sides, about 2 minutes each side. Put the browned roast into the slow cooker.
3. Add a bit more oil into the skillet, if necessary. Add the celery, onion, and garlic; sauté for about 3 to 5 minutes or till tender. Season with salt and pepper while sautéing and with a wooden spoon, scrape the browned bits from the bottom of the pan.
4. Meanwhile, in a medium-mixing bowl, whisk the tomato sauce with the chicken stock, red wine, Italian seasoning, bay leaf, black pepper, garlic powder, salt, and whole-wheat flour; pour the mix into the slow cooker.
5. Add the celery mix into the slow cooker; stir to mix and coat the meat and the veggies with the sauce.
6. Slow cook for about 4 to 5 hours on LOW, or, if desired, longer. Add the potatoes and the carrots into the sauce; cook for 2 hours more or until the veggies are tender.
7. Remove the roast, let rest for about 10 minutes on a wooden cutting board. Turn off the slow cooker, remove the lid, and allow to rest. With 2 forks, shred the roast and then gently stir in the veggie and the sauce in the cooker. Adjust the seasoning, if desired.

134

Freezing: Let the pot roast cool completely; make sure not to leave in the fridge or the freezer for more than 2 hours. Put in freezable containers or bags; remove as much air as possible, seal, and freeze.

When ready to serve, transfer into the fridge and let thaw for about 24-48 hours or in the microwave on DEFROST setting. When thawed, warm over low to medium-low heat on the stove, occasionally stirring gently.

Casserole Chicken Parmesan

Prep Time: 20 minutes; Cook Time: 20-25 minutes	

Serving Size: 213 g; Serves: 4; Calories: 309
Total Fat: 9.8 g Saturated Fat: 2.4 g; Trans Fat: 0 g
Protein: 30.8 g; Net Carbs: 20.6 g
Total Carbs: 23.8 g; Dietary Fiber: 3.2 g; Sugars: 9.6 g
Cholesterol: 73 mg; Sodium: 670 mg; Potassium: 531 mg;
Vitamin A: 10%; Vitamin C: 3%; Calcium: 11%; Iron: 13%

Ingredients:

- ☐ 4 cups chicken, fully cooked, shredded or cubed
- ☐ 1-2 tablespoons olive oil
- ☐ 1/2 cup Parmesan cheese, shredded or grated
- ☐ 1 jar (28 ounces) marinara sauce
- ☐ 1 cup whole-wheat breadcrumbs (or panko)
- ☐ 1 1/2 cups mozzarella cheese, shredded
- ☐ Fresh herbs, chopped (oregano, basil, parsley, etc.), to taste
- ☐ Salt and pepper, to taste

Directions:

1. Preheat the oven to 350F. Grease an 8x8-inch dish with cooking spray.
2. Layer the chicken onto the bottom of the dish. Pour the marinara sauce over; mix until the chicken is coated. Top with the cheeses until the chicken is covered.
3. In a small-sized bowl, mix thee breadcrumbs with the fresh herbs olive oil, dash salt, and dash pepper; sprinkle the seasoned crumbs over the top.
4. Bake for about 20 to 25 minutes or till the top is golden and the sides are bubbling.

Freezing: Assemble the casserole ahead of time. Cover and freeze. When ready to serve, transfer into the fridge and let thaw overnight. Remove the cover and bake as directed. If the center is still slightly frozen, bake for longer or defrost in the microwave before baking. If the top gets too browned, cover with foil.

Chicken Piccata

Prep Time: 40 minutes; **Cook Time:** 5-10 minutes	
Serving Size: 319 g; **Serves:** 4-6; **Calories:** 680	
Total Fat: 30.8 g **Saturated Fat:** 14.9 g; **Trans Fat:** 0 g	
Protein: 43.5 g; **Net Carbs:** 41.4 g	
Total Carbs: 43.8 g; **Dietary Fiber:** 2.4 g; **Sugars:** 4.1 g	
Cholesterol: 240 mg; **Sodium:** 563 mg; **Potassium:** 520 mg;	
Vitamin A: 14%; **Vitamin C:** 31%; **Calcium:** 12%; **Iron:** 26%	

Ingredients:

- 4 pieces (4 ounces each) boneless, skinless chicken breasts
- 2/3 cup lemon juice, freshly squeezed (2 lemons), lemon halves reserved
- 2 extra-large eggs
- 1/2 cup whole-wheat flour
- 1 tablespoon water
- 1 cup dry white wine (choose one that you'd drink)
- 1 1/2 cups whole-wheat breadcrumbs (or panko)
- 6 tablespoons unsalted butter, room temperature, divided
- Fresh parsley, chopped, for serving
- Olive oil
- Kosher salt and freshly ground black pepper
- Sliced lemon, for serving

Directions:

1. Preheat the oven to 400F. Line a sheet pan with parchment paper.
2. Put each chicken breast between 2 sheets plastic wrap or parchment paper; pound into ¼-inch thickness and then season both sides with salt and pepper.
3. In a shallow plate; mix the flour with ½ teaspoon pepper and 1 teaspoon salt.
4. In another plate, beat the eggs with 1 tablespoon water.
5. Pour the breadcrumbs into a third plate.
6. Dip each chicken breast into the flour; shake off excess. Dip in the egg and then in the breadcrumb mix.
7. Heat 2 tablespoons olive oil inside a large-sized sauté pan over medium to medium-low heat. Working 2 breasts at a time, put into chicken into the pan; cook for 2 minutes per side or until browned. Put the browned chickens on the sheet pan.
8. Wipe the pan clean. Put 2 tablespoons olive oil, heat, and then cook the remaining chicken breasts as directed above; put on the sheet pan. Bake for about 5-10 minutes or till the insides of the chickens are no longer pink.
9. Meanwhile, wipe the sauté pan clean using dry paper towel. Melt the butter in pan over medium heat. Add the lime juice, the wine, reserved lemon halves, 1/2 teaspoon pepper, and 1 teaspoon salt; bring to boil over high heat for about 2 to 3 minutes or till reduced by half. Turn the heat off, add the remaining 4 tablespoons butter; swirl to combine. Discard the lemon halves.
10. Serve 1 chicken breast into each plate; spoon the sauce over the chickens. Serve with lemon slice and a sprinkle of fresh parsley.

Freeze: You can cook the sauce ahead of time, let cool completely, and freeze; when ready to serve, just warm on low heat. You can also freeze the uncooked, breaded chicken. When ready to eat, transfer into the fridge and let thaw overnight. Sauté and bake as directed.

Parmesan Chicken Tenders

Prep Time: 5 minutes; Cook Time: 15 minutes
Serving Size: 173 g; Serves: 4; Calories: 393
Total Fat: 19.4 g Saturated Fat: 4.8 g; Trans Fat: 0 g
Protein: 46.2 g; Net Carbs: 6.4 g
Total Carbs: 6.4 g; Dietary Fiber: 0 g; Sugars: 0 g
Cholesterol: 138 mg; Sodium: 417 mg; Potassium: 380 mg;
Vitamin A: 2%; Vitamin C: 0%; Calcium: 7%; Iron: 12%

Ingredients:
- 1 1/3 pounds chicken tenders
- 1 1/2 teaspoons Old Bay seasoning
- 1/2 teaspoon garlic powder
- 1/4 cup Parmesan cheese, finely grated
- 1/4 cup whole-wheat flour
- 2 tablespoons olive oil
- Salt and pepper

Directions:
1. Preheat the oven to 425F.
2. Cover a metal sheet pan with foil. Put the pan into the preheated oven to heat.
3. Put the flour, Old Bay seasoning, parmesan, and garlic powder inside a large-sized Ziploc plastic bag; shake until well combined and set aside.
4. In a small-sized bowl, lightly season the chicken tenders with the salt and the pepper and then toss with the olive oil coated.
5. Several chicken tenders at a time, add into the bag with the flour mix; seal and shake until each piece are coated.
6. Carefully remove the hot sheet pan from the oven; generously grease with the cooking spray. Arrange the seasoned chicken tenders in pan, arranging with a space between each piece; bake at 425F for about 15 minutes or till the chicken tenders are done, turning once halfway baking. The chicken is done when the insides are no longer pink or the internal temperature 165F. Serve immediately.

Freezing: Bread the chicken tenders as directed. Put in a baking sheet and flash freeze for about 1 to 2 hours. When frozen, put into a gallon-sized freezable bag, and freeze until ready to cook.

When ready to serve, bake from frozen as directed in a preheated, foil-covered sheet pan at 425F for about 20 to 25 minutes; turning once. The chicken is done when the insides are no longer pink or the internal temperature 165F. Serve immediately.

Chicken Parmesan

Prep Time: 20 minutes; Cook Time: 20-25 minutes
Serving Size: 243 g; Serves: 4; Calories: 408
Total Fat: 15.2 g Saturated Fat: 5.2 g; Trans Fat: 0 g
Protein: 42.7 g; Net Carbs: 20.5 g
Total Carbs: 23.1 g; Dietary Fiber: 2.6 g; Sugars: 6.9 g
Cholesterol: 153 mg; Sodium: 835 mg; Potassium: 537 mg;
Vitamin A: 10%; Vitamin C: 3%; Calcium: 15%; Iron: 17%

Ingredients:
- ☐ 4 chicken breasts, pounded out to about ½ inch thickness
- ☐ 2/3 cup Italian seasoned breadcrumbs
- ☐ 1/3 cup Parmesan cheese
- ☐ 1 egg, lightly beaten
- ☐ 1 cup mozzarella cheese
- ☐ 1 cup marinara sauce
- ☐ Salt and pepper
- ☐ Splash milk

Directions:
1. Preheat oven to 350F.
2. Grease a 9x13 baking pan or dish with cooking spray or rub with vegetable; set aside.
3. Put the chicken breasts between sheets of plastic wrap. With the flat side of the meat mallet or with the bottom of a glass or heavy pan, pound into 1/2-inch thick
4. Sprinkle both sides of the chicken breasts with a pinch of salt and pepper.
5. In a shallow dish, whisk the egg with a splash of milk.
6. In another shallow dish, combine the parmesan cheese with the breadcrumbs.
7. One piece at time, dip the chicken breasts in the egg mixture, turning to coat; let excess drip off. Drip into the parmesan mix, turning to coat; shake excess.
8. Put the breaded chicken into a greased 13x9-inch casserole dish; bake at 350F for about 20-25 minutes or till the center is no longer pink and the juices run clear. To check for doneness, cut a small slit in the center of 1 chicken breast using a knife; pull open to see if the meat is white and no longer pink.
9. Top each chicken breast with 1 spoonful or more of pasta sauce; spread the sauce around the top of each chicken piece, sprinkle about 1 to 2 tablespoons of mozzarella cheese over the top as well.
10. Return the chicken into the oven; bake for 5 minute more or until the cheese is melted. Serve warm with pasta.

Freezing: Bread the chicken as directed. Put into a freezable bag or in casserole dish tightly covered with plastic wrap. Put the marinara sauce in another freezable bag and the cheese into another bag; freeze together with the breaded chicken.

When ready to serve, transfer the breaded chicken and the marinara into the fridge and let thaw overnight. Alternatively, you can thaw the chicken in the microwave on DEFROST setting. Run the frozen marinara bag under warm water to defrost. Do not defrost cheese. Bake the chicken as directed.

Herb Roasted Pork Tenderloin

Prep Time: 5 minutes; **Cook Time:** 20 minutes	
Serving Size: 149 g; **Serves:** 4; **Calories:** 240	
Total Fat: 8.7 g **Saturated Fat:** 2.2 g; **Trans Fat:** 0 g	
Protein: 37.4 g; **Net Carbs:** 1.4 g	
Total Carbs: 1.4 g; **Dietary Fiber:** 0 g; **Sugars:** 0 g	
Cholesterol: 103 mg; **Sodium:** 373 mg; **Potassium:** 626 mg;	
Vitamin A: 1%; **Vitamin C:** 1%; **Calcium:** 2%; **Iron:** 13%	

Ingredients:

- 1 1/4 pounds pork tenderloin
- 1 tablespoon olive oil
- 1 teaspoon dried oregano
- 1 teaspoon garlic powder
- 1 teaspoon ground coriander
- 1 teaspoon ground cumin
- 1/2 teaspoon ground thyme
- 1/2 teaspoon onion powder
- 1/2 teaspoon salt
- 1/4 teaspoon pepper

Directions:

1. Preheat the oven to 450F.
2. In a small-sized bowl, combine the garlic powder with the cumin, oregano, thyme, coriander, salt, onion powder, and pepper; set aside.
3. Put the pork tenderloin roasting pan lined parchment paper or foil. Rub the pork tenderloin all over with seasoning mix, gently pressing so the seasoning adheres.
4. Bake for about 20 to 25 minutes or till the internal temperature is 145F and the inside is slightly pink; make sure not overcook. Let rest for about 5 to 10 so the juices redistribute. Slice at an angle and serve.

Freezing: Season the pork as directed. Put the uncooked, seasoned pork into a gallon-sized freezable bag, seal, and then freeze. When ready to cook, transfer into the fridge and let thaw overnight. Just before cooking, set for about 30 minutes at room temperature on the counter. Cook as directed.

Slow cooker instructions: Season the pork as directed. Put the pork into slow cooker; cook for about 5-6 hours on LOW or until the internal temperature is 145F. let rest as directed above, slice, and serve.

Mexican Pulled Pork

Prep Time: 15 minutes; **Cook Time:** 4 hours, 50 minutes, plus 15 minutes resting

Serving Size: 257 g; **Serves:** 8; **Calories:** 707

Total Fat: 52.1 g **Saturated Fat:** 18.3 g; **Trans Fat:** 0 g

Protein: 53.1 g; **Net Carbs:** 0 g

Total Carbs: 4.2 g; **Dietary Fiber:** 1.2 g; **Sugars:** 1 g

Cholesterol: 204 mg; **Sodium:** 1902 mg; **Potassium:** 797 mg;

Vitamin A: 2%; **Vitamin C:** 5%; **Calcium:** 7%; **Iron:** 19%

Ingredients:

- 4-7 pounds pork shoulder
- 4 cloves garlic
- 2 tablespoons white cooking wine
- 2 tablespoons salt
- 2 tablespoons olive oil
- 1/4 cup brown sugar (mix 1/4 tablespoon molasses + 1/4 cup sweetener)
- 1/2 teaspoon chili powder
- 1 teaspoon ground cumin
- 1 teaspoon dried oregano
- 1 medium onion
- Pepper, to taste

Directions:

1. Rinse the pork shoulder and then pat dry.
2. Put the cumin, dried oregano, salt, chili powder, black pepper, olive oil, garlic, brown sugar substitute, white wine, and the onion quarter into blender or food processor; blend or process until well combined. Pour the cumin mix over the pork shoulder; rub the mix on every surface of the meat.
3. Put the pork into a Dutch oven or into a roasting pan. Pour 2 cups water. Tightly cover; roast the pork at 300F for about 4 1/2 hours, turning once halfway through cooking.
4. When the pork is tender and pulls away easily, increase the heat 425F, remove the lid; roast with the skin side up for another 15-20 minutes to get the skin crispy. When done, let rest for about 15 minutes. With 2 forks, shred the pork and pour the juices over the shredded meat.
5. Serve with warm tortillas, sour cream, lime wedges, guacamole, pico de gallo, salsa, or your choice of Mexican fixings.

Freezing: Prepare the pork up to its marinade; put in a freezable bag, seal, and freeze until ready to cook. When ready to cook, transfer into the fridge and let thaw overnight. Cook as directed.

Broiled Parmesan Tilapia

Prep Time: 20 minutes; **Cook Time:** 6 minutes	
Serving Size: 146 g; **Serves:** 8; **Calories:** 171	
Total Fat: 8.1 g **Saturated Fat:** 4.9 g; **Trans Fat:** 0 g	
Protein: 23.6 g; **Net Carbs:** 1.3 g	
Total Carbs: 2 g; **Dietary Fiber:** 0.7 g; **Sugars:** 0.6 g	
Cholesterol: 74 mg; **Sodium:** 131 mg; **Potassium:** 66 mg;	
Vitamin A: 6%; **Vitamin C:** 13%; **Calcium:** 10%; **Iron:** 9%	

Ingredients:

- 2 pounds tilapia fillets
- 1/8 teaspoon celery salt
- 1/4 teaspoon ground black pepper
- 1/4 teaspoon garlic powder
- 1/4 cup fresh herbs, minced
- 1/4 cup butter, softened
- 1/2 cup Parmesan cheese, freshly grated
- 3 tablespoons Greek yogurt (or mayo)
- Juice of 1 lemon
- Salt and pepper
- Zest of 1 lemon

Directions:

1. Preheat the broiler.
2. Grease a rimmed sheet pan with olive oil.
3. In a bowl, mix the parmesan cheese, with the Greek yogurt, butter, lemon juice, lemon zest, 1/4 teaspoon black pepper, basil, celery salt, and onion powder; set aside.
4. Rinse the tilapia and then pat dry. Lay the fillets into the prepared pan, season both sides with a little salt and pepper.
5. Broil a couple of inches from the source for 2 minutes, flip, and broil for 2 minutes more.
6. Remove from the oven; generously spread parmesan cheese topping over the top.
7. Return to the oven; broil for another 2 minutes or till the top is golden. The fish is done when they flake easily when tested; do not overcook.

Freezing: Make the parmesan topping ahead of time and freeze in a separate bag with the fish. When ready to cook, just thaw the topping and the fish overnight in the fridge or run under warm water in the freezer bag until thawed. Bake as directed.

Parmesan and Cracker Crusted Tilapia

Prep Time: 30 minutes; **Cook Time:** 5 minutes per batch	

Serving Size: 248 g; **Serves:** 4; **Calories:** 280
Total Fat: 10.2 g **Saturated Fat:** 4.7 g; **Trans Fat:** 0 g
Protein: 40.8 g; **Net Carbs:** 0 g
Total Carbs: 7.7 g; **Dietary Fiber:** 1 g; **Sugars:** 0.6 g
Cholesterol: 192 mg; **Sodium:** 1201 mg; **Potassium:** 108 mg;
Vitamin A: 17%; **Vitamin C:** 16%; **Calcium:** 23%; **Iron:** 25%

Ingredients:

- ☐ 1 1/2 pounds tilapia fillets (or sole), rinsed and patted dry
- ☐ 1 cup oyster crackers
- ☐ 1 tablespoon Old Bay seasoning
- ☐ 1 teaspoon garlic powder
- ☐ 1/3 cup multigrain crackers
- ☐ 1/3cup flat-leaf parsley
- ☐ 2 large eggs, beaten
- ☐ 2 tablespoons fresh thyme leaves (or 2 teaspoons of dried thyme leaves)
- ☐ 3 tablespoons fresh chives, chopped
- ☐ 3/4 cup Parmesan cheese
- ☐ Lemon wedges, for serving
- ☐ Olive oil, for frying
- ☐ Salt and pepper, to taste
- ☐ Splash of heavy cream or half-and-half
- ☐ Whole-wheat flour, for coating

Directions:

1. Preheat the oven to 200F.
2. With a food processor, grind the multigrain crackers with the oyster crackers, parmesan cheese, thyme, chives, garlic powder, and Old Bay seasoning; transfer into a shallow bowl.
3. Put the flour into a different shallow bowl.
4. In another bowl, beat the eggs with the cream.
5. Fill a large-sized skillet with 1/4-inch deep of oil; heat over medium flame/heat.
6. Season the fish fillets with the salt and pepper.
7. Coat the fish with the flour; shake of excess. Coat with the egg mix and then with the cracker crumb mix. Cooking 2 fillets at a time, fry the fish in the skillet for about 5 minutes, turning once through frying, until deep golden.
8. Transfer each batch into the oven to keep warm. Serve with lemon wedges.

Freezing: Bread the fish as directed, put in freezable bags, and freeze. When ready to serve, transfer into the fridge and let thaw overnight. Cook according to directions.

Firecracker Asian Salmon (Grilled or Roasted)

Prep Time: 20 minutes, plus 1 hour marinating; **Cook Time:** 10 minutes grilling or 20 minutes roasting

Serving Size: 149 g; **Serves:** 8; **Calories:** 289		
Total Fat: 21.2 g **Saturated Fat:** 3.4 g; **Trans Fat:** 0 g		
Protein: 22.7 g; **Net Carbs:** 2.8 g		
Total Carbs: 2.8 g; **Dietary Fiber:** 0 g; **Sugars:** 1.4 g		
Cholesterol: 50 mg; **Sodium:** 650 mg; **Potassium:** 485 mg;		
Vitamin A: 6%; **Vitamin C:** 2%; **Calcium:** 5%; **Iron:**6%		

Ingredients:

- 8 pieces (4 ounce) fillets salmon
- 4 tablespoons soy sauce
- 4 tablespoons green onions, chopped
- 4 tablespoons balsamic vinegar (or sub rice vinegar or red wine vinegar)
- 3 teaspoons brown sugar
- 2 teaspoons crushed red pepper flakes
- 2 cloves garlic, minced
- 1/2 teaspoon salt
- 1/2 cup peanut oil
- 1 teaspoon sesame oil
- 1 1/2 teaspoons ground ginger

Directions:

1. In a gallon Ziploc bag, put all the ingredients except for the salmon fillets; zip and shake until well combined.
2. Add the salmon fillets into the marinade, seal, and marinate in the fridge for 1 hour. You can freeze the fillets at this point.

For grilling:
1. Prepare the outdoor grill with coals 5 inches from the grate; lightly grease the grate. Grill the fish 5 inches from the coals for 10 minutes per 1 inch of thickness, measured at the thickest part, or until the fish easily flakes when tested with a fork. Turn the fish fillets halfway through grilling.

For roasting:
1. Preheat the oven to 400F; roast for 20 minutes.

Freezing: Prepare the marinade as directed. Add the salmon, seal the bag, and freeze for up to 3 months. When ready to serve, thaw under running cold water or in a sink of cold water. When thawed, do not marinate the fish very long before cooking. Grill or roast as directed.

145

Mediterranean Shrimp

Prep Time: 35 minutes; **Cook Time:** 5 minutes	
Serving Size: 141 g; **Serves:** 4; **Calories:** 247	
Total Fat: 14.7 g **Saturated Fat:** 2.5 g; **Trans Fat:** 0 g	
Protein: 26 g; **Net Carbs:** 2.3 g	
Total Carbs: 2.3 g; **Dietary Fiber:** 0 g; **Sugars:** 0 g	
Cholesterol: 239 mg; **Sodium:** 862 mg; **Potassium:** 215 mg;	
Vitamin A: 8%; **Vitamin C:** 9%; **Calcium:** 11%; **Iron:** 3%	

Ingredients:
- ☐ 1 pound shrimp, large-sized, raw, deveined, shell on or shelled (16-20 per pound)

For the marinade:
- ☐ 1 teaspoon salt
- ☐ 1/2 teaspoon dried basil
- ☐ 1/2 teaspoon dried oregano
- ☐ 1/2 teaspoon garlic, minced (2-3 garlic cloves, minced)
- ☐ 1/4 cup olive oil
- ☐ 1/4 teaspoon freshly ground black pepper
- ☐ 1/8 teaspoon red pepper flakes
- ☐ 3 tablespoons lemon juice, fresh (juice of about 1½ lemons)
- ☐ Feta cheese, crumbled, for garnish
- ☐ Fresh parsley, chopped, for garnish
- ☐ Lemon wedges, for garnish

Directions:
1. In a medium-sized bowl, combine all the ingredients until well mixed.
2. Pat the shrimp dry using paper towels. Add into the marinade, toss, let marinate in the fridge for 30 minutes, occasionally stirring.
3. Preheat the oven broiler. Line a baking sheet with foil.
4. Put the shrimps into the baking sheet. Alternatively, you can thread about 4-5 shrimp into skewers. Discard the marinade.
5. Broil for 2 minutes, flip, and broil for 2 minutes more. The shrimps are cooked when they are pink; do not overcook. Garnish with minced parsley, squeeze of lemon juice, and crumbled feta. Serve while the dish is still warm or at room temperature.

Notes: You can save the remaining marinade. Put into a small-sized pot and boil for about 4 to 5 minutes; pour over the shrimp and rice or pasta. Top with parsley, lemon, and feta.

Freezing: Makethe marinade ahead of time. Freeze in a separate bag with the shrimps. If desired, you can rinse, pat dry, and thread the shrimps in skewers. When ready to cook, submerge sealed freezer bags in cold water for about 15 minutes or till the shrimps are mostly thawed. Marinate, cook, and serve as directed.

Rosemary Shrimp Scampi

Prep Time: 15 minutes, plus 30 minutes marinating; **Cook Time:** 4 minutes		

Serving Size: 205 g; **Serves:** 4; **Calories:** 485

Total Fat: 34.7 g **Saturated Fat:** 6.9 g; **Trans Fat:** 0 g

Protein: 27.8 g; **Net Carbs:** 0 g

Total Carbs: 22.6 g; **Dietary Fiber:** 12.6 g; **Sugars:** 0.6 g

Cholesterol: 239 mg; **Sodium:** 1459 mg; **Potassium:** 524 mg;

Vitamin A: 27%; **Vitamin C:** 51%; **Calcium:** 48%; **Iron:** 50%

Ingredients:

- 1 pound (about 40 large-sized) shrimp, peeled and then deveined (about 1 pound)
- Cooking spray
- Lemon wedges, optional

For the marinade:

- 1/2 teaspoon freshly ground black pepper
- 1/2 teaspoon red pepper flakes
- 2 pieces (6-inch) rosemary sprig, stems discarded and finely chopped
- 2 teaspoon salt
- 6 garlic cloves, minced
- 6 tablespoons fresh lemon juice
- 8 tablespoons olive oil

Directions:

1. Combine the marinade ingredients into Ziploc bag. Add the shrimp, seal, and shake to coat. Put in the fridge and marinate for 30 minutes, occasionally turning the bag.
2. Broil or grill the shrimps for 2 minutes each side or until pink. If desired, serve with lemon wedges.

Freezing: Make the marinade as directed, add the shrimp, seal the bags, and freeze. When ready to cook, run the sealed bag under warm water until the shrimps are thawed. Grill or broil as directed.

Sweet and Savory Salmon

Prep Time: 15 minutes; **Cook Time:** 20 minutes		
Serving Size: 270 g; **Serves:** 4; **Calories:** 411		
Total Fat: 17.5 g **Saturated Fat:** 2.5 g; **Trans Fat:** 0 g		
Protein: 44.8 g; **Net Carbs:** 20.2 g		
Total Carbs: 20.2 g; **Dietary Fiber:** 0 g; **Sugars:** 17.7 g		
Cholesterol: 100 mg; **Sodium:** 549 mg; **Potassium:** 933 mg;		
Vitamin A: 5%; **Vitamin C:** 2%; **Calcium:** 9%; **Iron:** 11%		

Ingredients:
- 2 pounds salmon
- 1/4 teaspoon salt
- 1/4 teaspoon red pepper flakes
- 1/4 teaspoon black pepper
- 1/4 cup honey
- 1 tablespoon thinly sliced green onion, plus more for garnish
- 1 tablespoon sesame oil
- 1 tablespoon rice vinegar
- 1 tablespoon freshly grated ginger
- 2 tablespoons reduced-sodium soy sauce
- 3 cloves garlic, minced

Directions:
1. Inside a large-sized Ziploc bag, combine the honey with the sesame oil, soy sauce, rice vinegar, garlic, ginger, red pepper, green onion, salt, and pepper; seal and shake until combined.
2. Add the salmon fillets, seal, and turn to coat. Put in the fridge and marinate for about 15 to 30 minutes, turning 1-2 times during marinating.
3. Preheat the oven to 375F. Line a baking sheet with heavy-duty foil.
4. Remove the salmon from the marinade; lay into the prepared baking sheet; fold up all the 4 sides of the foil. Pour the marinade over the salmon. Pinch the foil sides, covering the salmon completely and sealing closed, making sure to leave a little space at the top.
5. Put the baking sheet in the oven; bake for about 15 to 20 minutes or till almost cooked through. Remove from the oven and open the packet. Turn the broiler on; broil for about 2 to 3 minutes or till slightly charred or until caramelized.
6. Garnish with some green onions. Serve the salmon and thee cooked sauce from the foil over brown rice.

Notes: Cooking time of the fish will vary depending on the thickness of the fillets. The salmon is cooked with it easily flakes when tested with a fork, no longer translucent, and cloudy, pink in color.

Freezing: Prepare the marinade. If the salmon is not frozen, put in another freezer bag. Squeeze as much air as you can out from the bags, seal, and freeze. When ready to cook, thaw the bags in the fridge or submerge the sealed bags in cold water until thawed; replace the water every 30 minutes. Prepare and cook according to directions.

Italian Sausage and Tortellini Soup

Prep Time: 30 minutes; Cook Time: 15-20 minutes, plus 3-5 minutes for tortellini		

Serving Size: 534 g; Serves: 10; Calories: 419

Total Fat: 18.4 g Saturated Fat: 5.8 g; Trans Fat: 0 g

Protein: 24.4 g; Net Carbs: 32.3 g

Total Carbs: 41.2 g; Dietary Fiber: 8.9 g; Sugars: 9.1g

Cholesterol: 56 mg; Sodium: 1650 mg; Potassium: 1065 mg;

Vitamin A: 50%; Vitamin C: 41%; Calcium: 14%; Iron: 26%

Ingredients:

- 1 can (28 ounces) tomato sauce
- 1 cans (14 ounces) diced tomatoes (liquid and all)
- 1 cup carrots, sliced (about 2-3 medium carrots)
- 1 cup frozen corn
- 1 jalapeno pepper, diced (or add to the soup whole and you can pull it out later)
- 1 onion, diced
- 1 package (16 ounces) frozen cheese multi-colored tortellini (I used Trader Joe's tortellini)
- 1 teaspoon Italian Seasoning
- 1/2 teaspoon dried basil
- 1/2 teaspoon ground black pepper (or more to taste)
- 1-2 stalks celery, sliced
- 16 ounce Italian sausage, crumbled and browned
- 2 bay leaves
- 2 cans (non-marinated 14 ounces) quartered artichoke hearts (liquid and all)
- 2 cans French Onion Soup (or 1 sautéed diced onion and 4 cups broth)
- 3 garlic cloves, minced
- 4 cups vegetable broth or chicken broth
- Olive oil

Directions:

1. Inside a large-sized stockpot, brown the Italian sausage over medium-high heat, until cooked through. Add the seasonings; set aside. Wipe the pot clean.
2. Put about 1 to 2 tablespoons olive oil into the pot; swirl to coat the bottom and heat over medium high heat. Add the celery, carrots, garlic, and onion; sauté for about 3 to 4 minutes or till soft; lightly season with salt and pepper to taste while sautéing.
3. Return the cooked sausage into the pot. Add the artichoke hearts, tomato sauce, tomatoes, broth, French onion soup, corn, and the bay leaves; stir to combine and bring to a boil. Reduce the heat to a simmer; cook for about 15 to 20 minutes.
4. Add the tortellini; cook according to the directions on the package, just a couple minutes before serving. Remove the bay leaves. Serve topped with parmesan cheese.

Freezing: Cook the soup; do not add the tortellini. Let cool and freeze. When ready to serve, just thaw in the fridge, bring to a simmer in a pot on a stove. Add tortellini and cook according to package instructions.

149

Szechuan Steak Stir-Fry

Prep Time: 20 minutes; **Cook Time:** 15 minutes

Serving Size: 218 g; **Serves:** 4; **Calories:** 356	
Total Fat: 15.1 g **Saturated Fat:** 3.4 g; **Trans Fat:** 0 g	
Protein: 44.1 g; **Net Carbs:** 7.3 g	
Total Carbs: 9.3 g; **Dietary Fiber:** 2 g; **Sugars:** 3.3 g	
Cholesterol: 102 mg; **Sodium:** 1075 mg; **Potassium:** 565 mg;	
Vitamin A: 33%; **Vitamin C:** 19%; **Calcium:** 2%; **Iron:** 27%	

Ingredients:

- 1 pound steak (any kind), sliced thin, 1-2" long pieces
- 1 tablespoon sesame oil
- 1 teaspoon sugar
- 1/3 cup fresh cilantro, chopped
- 1/4 cup soy sauce, all natural
- 1/4 cup water
- 1/4 teaspoon red pepper flakes
- 1-2 tablespoon vegetable or peanut oil
- 2 garlic cloves, minced
- 2 tablespoons dry-roasted peanuts, chopped
- 2 tablespoons stir-fry sauce, all natural
- 2 teaspoons cornstarch
- 2-3 cups (about 1 small package) frozen stir-fry vegetables

Directions:

1. Inside a large-sized Ziploc bag, combine the garlic cloves with the soy sauce, red pepper flakes, stir-fry sauce, and the sesame oil; seal and shake until well combined. Add the steak in the bag, put in the fridge, ad marinate for at least 1 hour.
2. In a bowl, combine the cornstarch with the water and sugar; set aside.
3. Heat a large-sized skillet or a wok on medium-high heat. add the veggies; stir-fry for about 2 to 3 minutes or till tender crisp, making sure not to overcook. Transfer into a plate.
4. Add the beef and the marinade into the skillet or wok; stir-fry until the meat is cooked through, about 1 to 2 minutes.
5. Return the veggies into the pan; toss with the sauce and the meat; bring the sauce to a simmer. Add the cornstarch mix, continue stir-frying for 1 minute or so or until the sauce is thick. Top with the peanuts and the cilantro. Serve over cauliflower rice.

Freezing: Prepare the uncooked ingredients. Put them into separate freezer safe bags/containers as follows: the marinade and the steak Inside a large freezable bag, the cornstarch mix in a small Ziploc bag, and the chopped peanuts in another small Ziploc bag. Put all the bags into a 1 gallon-sized freezable bag. Do not prepare and freeze the cilantro ahead of time.

When ready to cook, thaw the steak, cornstarch, and chopped peanuts overnight in the fridge or under running cold water for a couple of minutes. DO NOT THAW the frozen vegetables. Cook as directed.

150

Snacks

Peanut Butter, Oats, and Flaxseed Granola Bars

Prep Time: 10 minutes; Cook Time: 30 minutes
Serving Size: 43 g; Serves: 12; Calories: 181
Total Fat: 8.8 g Saturated Fat: 2.8 g; Trans Fat: 0 g
Protein: 5.2 g; Net Carbs: 19.1 g
Total Carbs: 21.7 g; Dietary Fiber: 2.6 g; Sugars: 10 g
Cholesterol: 2 mg; Sodium: 96 mg; Potassium: 173 mg;
Vitamin A: 0%; Vitamin C: 0%; Calcium: 3%; Iron: 12%

Ingredients:
- 1 cup oat flour, or ground rolled oats, use gluten-free, if needed
- 1 cup rolled oats, use gluten-free, if needed
- 1/2 cup peanut butter, natural, smooth
- 1/3 cup sugar-free maple syrup
- 1/4 teaspoon sea salt
- 1-2 tablespoons water, as needed
- 2 tablespoons flaxseed, ground

Optional:
- 1/2 cup chocolate chips (I use dairy-free Enjoy Life chocolate chips)

Directions:
1. Preheat the oven to 350F. Line an 8x8-inch baking dish with parchment paper or grease/spray with coconut oil.
2. Inside a large-sized bowl, combine the oat flour with the rolled oats, ground flaxseeds, and the sea salt. Add the peanut butter and the maple syrup; mix to combine. The batter needs to be slightly sticky, but not wet. If needed, add water to achieve the right consistency. If using, mix in the chocolate chips.
3. With wet hands, spread the batter into the prepared pan, packing the batter tight and evening the top; bake for about 18 to 20 minutes or till the edges are slightly browned.
4. Let sit for 20 minutes, remove from the pan, and then cut into 12 bars.

Notes: Store into airtight containers and keep in the countertop for up to 4 days or freeze for up to a couple of months.

Baked Protein Peanut Butter Chocolate Oatmeal Cups

Prep Time: 10 minutes; Cook Time: 25 minutes
Serving Size: 94 g; Serves: 12; Calories: 212
Total Fat: 9.2 g Saturated Fat: 5.2 g; Trans Fat: 0 g
Protein: 6.8 g; Net Carbs: 24.7 g
Total Carbs: 28.6 g; Dietary Fiber: 3.9 g; Sugars: 9 g
Cholesterol: 5 mg; Sodium: 48 mg; Potassium: 444 mg;
Vitamin A: 0%; Vitamin C: 5%; Calcium: 8%; Iron: 12%

Ingredients:
- 3 bananas, ripe, medium to large, mashed (the more ripe the better)
- 3 cups oats, old fashioned (gluten-free if necessary)
- 2 tablespoons cocoa powder
- 2 tablespoons chia seeds plus 6 tablespoons water (or 2 eggs)
- 1/4 cup peanut butter, creamy
- 1/4 cup maple syrup, pure, (or 15 drops of liquid stevia), optional for sweetness
- 1/2 teaspoon vanilla extract
- 1 tablespoon baking powder
- 1 scoop protein powder, chocolate, plant-based (I use Vega Chocolate Protein + Greens)
- 1 cup cashew milk, silk, unsweetened (almond or coconut are great, too)
- Pinch salt

Directions:
1. Preheat the oven to 350F. Grease a muffin tin with the cooking spray.
2. In a small-sized bowl, stir the chia seeds with the water to create chia eggs. Alternatively, you can use 2 eggs; set aside.
3. Put the bananas inside a large-sized bowl; mash with fork. Add the peanut butter, cashew milk, vanilla, and if using, stevia or maple syrup; stir until well combined. Stir in the chia eggs or the 2 eggs. Add the oats, protein powder, baking powder, cocoa powder, and salt; stir until combined.
4. Evenly spoon the mixture between the muffin cups; you can fill the cups to the top. There may be some excess batter.
5. Bake for 25 minutes, remove from the oven, put the muffin tin on a wire rack and let cool completely.

Notes: When completely cool, store in airtight containers and keep in the fridge.

Chocolate Streusel Coffee Cake

Prep Time: 30 minutes; **Cook Time:** 70-80 minutes		

Serving Size: 110 g; **Serves:** 16; **Calories:** 440
Total Fat: 39.3 g Saturated Fat: 15.1 g; Trans Fat: 0 g
Protein: 9.5 g; **Net Carbs:** 16.1 g
Total Carbs: 24.3 g; Dietary Fiber: 8.2 g; Sugars: 8.3 g
Cholesterol: 90 mg; Sodium: 359 mg; Potassium: 342 mg;
Vitamin A: 12%; Vitamin C: 1%; Calcium: 14%; Iron: 8%

Ingredients:

For the chocolate streusel:

- 1 cup chocolate chips, semisweet
- 1 cup walnuts, chopped
- 2 teaspoons ground cinnamon
- 1/2 cup light brown sugar, packed (mix 1/2 tablespoons molasses + 1/2 cup low carb sweetener)
- Pinch kosher salt

For the cake and assembly:

- 4 large eggs
- 4 cups almond flour, plus more for pan
- 2 teaspoons vanilla extract
- 2 teaspoons baking soda
- 2 teaspoons baking powder
- 2 cups sour cream
- 2 cups granulated sugar (equal amount Swerve sweetener)
- 1/2 teaspoon kosher salt
- 1 cup unsalted butter, (2 sticks) at room temperature, plus more for pan

Special equipment:

- 12-cup Bundt pan

Directions:

1. Inside a large-sized bowl, combine the walnuts with the brown sugar substitute, chocolate chips, and salt.
2. Preheat the oven to 350F. Butter and flour a Bundt pan, tapping out any excess flour.
3. In a medium-sized bowl, whisk 4 cups flour with the baking soda, baking powder, and salt.
4. Inside a large-sized bowl, with an electric mixer on MEDIUM-HIGH speed, beat in the granulated sugar and 1 cup of butter for about 5 minutes or till fluffy and light. One at a time, add the eggs, beating until blended and scraping the sides of the bowl with every addition. Reduce the speed to LOW. Add the dry ingredients in 2 additions, alternating with the sour cream with every addition. Add the vanilla; beat to combine.
5. Transfer 1/2 of the batter into the prepared pan; smooth the surface. Sprinkle 1/2 of the streusel mix evenly over the layer. Scrape in the remaining 1/2 batter; smooth the surface and then sprinkle the remaining streusel mix.
6. Bake for about 70 to 80 minutes or till golden brown and a tester come out clean when inserted in the center.

7. Transfer the pan on a wire rack; let cool in pan for 30 minutes. Invert onto a wire rack and let cool completely.

Notes: Make this cake ahead of time; just store tightly covered for up to 3 days at room temperature.

Nutty Fruit Cookies

Prep Time: 30 minutes; **Cook Time:** 8-9 minutes

Serving Size: 24 g; **Serves:** 20; **Calories:** 78

Total Fat: 2.5 g **Saturated Fat:** 0 g; **Trans Fat:** 0 g

Protein: 2.3 g; **Net Carbs:** 11.1 g

Total Carbs: 12.1 g; **Dietary Fiber:** 1 g; **Sugars:** 4.3 g

Cholesterol: 9 mg; **Sodium:** 75 mg; **Potassium:** 67 mg;

Vitamin A: 0%; **Vitamin C:** 0%; **Calcium:** 1%; **Iron:** 4%

Ingredients:

- [ ] 1 cup whole-wheat flour
- [ ] 1 large egg
- [ ] 1 teaspoon vanilla
- [ ] 1/2 cup nuts, chopped, such as almonds, walnuts, or pecans
- [ ] 1/2 teaspoon baking soda
- [ ] 1/4 cup dried fruit, such as cranberries or raisins
- [ ] 1/4 cup unsweetened applesauce
- [ ] 1/4 teaspoon salt
- [ ] 2 tablespoons peanut butter, smooth
- [ ] 3 tablespoons honey
- [ ] 3/4 cup oats, old-fashioned

Directions:

1. Preheat the oven to 375F.
2. In a mixing bowl, beat the egg lightly with the honey, applesauce, vanilla, and peanut butter until combined.
3. In another bowl, combine the flour with the baking soda, oats, and salt.
4. Add the dry ingredients into the egg mix; stir to combine.
5. Stir in the dried fruit and the nuts.
6. Grease a cookie sheet with butter.
7. With a spoon, drop batter into the cookie sheet; slightly flatten and then bake for about 8 to 9 minutes.

Notes: Double or triple the batch. Let cool completely, put in freezer bags, and freeze.

No-Cook Coconut-ty Chocolate Date Bars

Prep Time: 20 minutes; **Cook Time:** 0 minutes

Serving Size: 48 g; **Serves:** 12; **Calories:** 144		
Total Fat: 4.5 g **Saturated Fat:** 3.3 g; **Trans Fat:** 0 g		
Protein: 2.4 g; **Net Carbs:** 24.6 g		
Total Carbs: 29.8 g; **Dietary Fiber:** 5.2 g; **Sugars:** 29.3 g		
Cholesterol: 0 mg; **Sodium:** 200 mg; **Potassium:** 325 mg;		
Vitamin A: 0%; **Vitamin C:** 1%; **Calcium:** 2%; **Iron:** 14%		

Ingredients

- ☐ 2 cups dates, pitted
- ☐ 1/4 cup cacao nibs
- ☐ 1 teaspoon kosher salt
- ☐ 1 cup shredded coconut, unsweetened, divided
- ☐ 2 tablespoons agave syrup
- ☐ 3/4 cup raw cacao powder or unsweetened cocoa powder
- ☐ Nonstick vegetable oil spray

Directions:

1. Grease an 8x8-inch baking pan with vegetable oil spray and then line with parchment paper, leaving overhang on every side.
2. Put the dates, 3/4 cup shredded coconut, cocoa powder, agave syrup, cocoa nibs, 2 tablespoons water, and salt into a food processor; process till smooth, stopping and scraping the sides a couple of time as needed.
3. Press the mix firmly into the prepared baking pan.
4. Scatter the remaining 1/4 cup shredded coconut over the top, pressing to adhere. Cut into bars.

Notes: Make ahead of time and store in airtight containers for up to 2 weeks at room temperature.

Hazelnut, Almonds, Oats, Sunflower Seeds, and Coconut Granola

Prep Time: 20 minutes; **Cook Time:** 20-25 minutes	

Serving Size: 51 g; **Serves:** 8; **Calories:** 259	
Total Fat: 19.3 g **Saturated Fat:** 3.7 g; **Trans Fat:** 0 g	
Protein: 4.8 g; **Net Carbs:** 16.4 g	
Total Carbs: 19.8 g; **Dietary Fiber:** 3.4 g; **Sugars:** 9.8 g	
Cholesterol: 0 mg; **Sodium:** 150 mg; **Potassium:** 186 mg;	
Vitamin A: 0%; **Vitamin C:** 2%; **Calcium:** 4%; **Iron:** 11%	

Ingredients:
- 1 cup hazelnuts, blanched, very coarsely chopped
- 1 cup oats, old-fashioned
- 1/2 cup almonds, sliced
- 1/2 cup shredded coconut, unsweetened
- 1/2 cup sunflower seeds, raw, shelled
- 1/2 teaspoon kosher salt
- 1/4 cup honey
- 1/4 cup vegetable oil
- Dried fruit, for serving
- Whole Greek yogurt, plain, for serving

Directions:
1. Preheat the oven to 350F.
2. Inside a large-sized bowl, toss the oats with the almonds, hazelnuts, coconut, sunflower seeds, oil, honey, and salt. Spread the mix into a rimmed baking sheet lined with parchment paper; bake, occasionally tossing, for about 20 to 25 minutes or till golden and crisp. Let cool and serve with yogurt and dried fruit.

Notes: Make ahead of time and stored in airtight container for up to 1 week at room temperature.

Nutty Sunflower Cherry-Quinoa Bars

Prep Time: 30 minutes; **Cook Time:** 20-25 minutes

Serving Size: 33 g; **Serves:** 12; **Calories:** 114	
Total Fat: 6.2 g **Saturated Fat:** 0.6 g; **Trans Fat:** 0 g	
Protein: 3.7 g; **Net Carbs:** 10.6 g	
Total Carbs: 12.3 g; **Dietary Fiber:** 1.7 g; **Sugars:** 2.5 g	
Cholesterol: 0 mg; **Sodium:** 153 mg; **Potassium:** 138 mg;	
Vitamin A: 1%; **Vitamin C:** 1%; **Calcium:** 3%; **Iron:** 6%	

Ingredients:
- ☐ 1 cup chopped almonds
- ☐ 1 cup tart cherries, dried
- ☐ 1/2 cup quinoa, raw, rinsed
- ☐ 1/4 cup pumpkin seeds, raw
- ☐ 1/4 cup sunflower seeds, raw
- ☐ 2 tablespoons brown rice syrup
- ☐ 3/4 teaspoon kosher salt
- ☐ Nonstick vegetable oil spray

Directions:
1. Preheat the oven to 350F. Grease an 8x8 baking pan with vegetable cooking spray and then line with parchment paper, leaving overhang on every side.
2. In a rimmed baking sheet, toast the almonds, pumpkin seeds, quinoa, and the sunflower seeds in the oven, occasionally stirring, for about 10 to 12 minutes or till golden brown; let cool.
3. Reduce the oven temperature to 200F.
4. Put the cherries, 2 tablespoons water, and brown rice syrup in a food processor; process till smooth and then transfer into a medium-sized bowl. Stir in the toasted almond mix. Firmly press into the prepared baking dish; bake for about 20 to 25 minutes or till no longer sticky. Let cool and then cut into bars.

Notes: Make ahead of time and store in airtight containers for up to 2 weeks at room temperature.

Low-fat Pumpkin Oatmeal Chocolate Chip Muffins

Prep Time: 0 minutes; **Cook Time:** 23-28 minutes

Serving Size: 81 g; **Serves:** 12; **Calories:** 153	
Total Fat: 8.8 g **Saturated Fat:** 2.1 g; **Trans Fat:** 0 g	
Protein: 4.9 g; **Net Carbs:** 13.5 g	
Total Carbs: 18.2 g; **Dietary Fiber:** 4.7 g; **Sugars:** 6.2 g	
Cholesterol: 2 mg; **Sodium:** 126 mg; **Potassium:** 288 mg;	
Vitamin A: 64%; **Vitamin C:** 2%; **Calcium:** 10%; **Iron:** 8%	

Ingredients:

- 1 1/2 cups almond flour
- 1 1/2 teaspoons baking powder
- 1 cup canned pumpkin
- 1 cup oatmeal
- 1/2 banana, ripe, mashed
- 1/2 cup chocolate chips, plus 2 tablespoons
- 1/2 teaspoon baking soda
- 1/3 cup applesauce, unsweetened, all natural
- 1/3 cup dark brown sugar (1 teaspoon molasses + 1/3 cup low carb sweetener)
- 1/4 teaspoon salt
- 2 egg whites, slightly beaten
- 2 teaspoons pumpkin pie spice
- 2/3 cup almond milk, unsweetened
- Extra oatmeal, for sprinkling on muffins

Directions:

1. Preheat the oven to 350F. Line a 12 cups muffin tin with paper cups or grease with nonstick spray. If greasing, make sure to spray the insides of the cups.
2. Inside a large-sized bowl, mix the flour with the pumpkin pie spice, oatmeal, baking soda, baking powder, and salt.
3. In another bowl, combine the mashed banana with the pumpkin, almond milk, brown sugar substitute, applesauce, and egg whites.
4. Add the flour mix into the pumpkin mix; stir to combine. Fold the chocolate chips gently into the mix.
5. Fill each muffin cup to 3/4 full and then sprinkle each with a bit of oatmeal on top. Put the muffin tin in the oven; bake for about 23 to 28 minutes or till a toothpick come out clean when inserted in the center of the muffins. Serve warm.

Notes: Make these ahead of time. When ready to serve, just reheat for 20 seconds in the microwave; spread with your choice of topping.

Nutty Honeycomb Ice Cream

Prep Time: 30 minutes; **Cook Time:** 10-15 minutes, plus 6-8 hours freezing
Serving Size: 154 g; **Serves:** 10; **Calories:** 542
Total Fat: 45.7 g **Saturated Fat:** 25 g; **Trans Fat:** 0 g
Protein: 6.1 g; **Net Carbs:** 30.3 g
Total Carbs: 32.5 g; **Dietary Fiber:** 2.2 g; **Sugars:** 23.6 g
Cholesterol: 145 mg; **Sodium:** 213 mg; **Potassium:** 259 mg;
Vitamin A: 30%; **Vitamin C:** 3%; **Calcium:** 18%; **Iron:** 2%

Ingredients:
- 1 can (14-ounce) sweetened condensed milk, low-fat or regular
- 1 quart heavy cream
- 1 teaspoon baking soda
- 2 teaspoons vanilla extract
- 3 tablespoons dark corn syrup
- 3/4 cup pecans
- Heaping 1/2 cup superfine sugar (equal amount Swerve sweetener or more)
- Vegetable oil, for greasing

Directions:
1. Preheat the oven to 375D. Coarsely break the pecans in your hands and then spread them out into a baking sheet. Put in the oven and toast for about 5 minutes. Remove ad let cool.
2. Grease a sheet of wax paper with oil and put into a baking sheet.
3. In a saucepan, combine the sugar substitute and the syrup, gently heat, swirling the pan until the sugar is melted. Increase the heat and boil the mix for about 4 minutes or till the color is rich caramel, carefully watching to avoid burning. Remove the pan from the heat. Add the nuts into the caramel. Very carefully sprinkle the baking soda into the pan. The mix will suddenly increase in volume and look frothy. Stir and then immediately pour into the oiled wax paper before the mix sets. Let set and cool. When cooled, transfer into aplastic bag and then with a rolling pin, bash to break into smallish chunks.
4. With a hand mixer, inside a large-sized bowl, whip the cream with the vanilla extract until slightly thick. The mix should be floppy, but should not reach the peaks stage. With the mixer running, pour in the sweetened condensed milk; continue beating until just stiff.
5. Fold in the pieces of the nutty honeycombs with any crumbs.
6. Transfer into a 3-quart container and then freeze for about 6-8 hours.
7. When ready to serve, remove from the freezer 20 minutes before serving and let thaw in a cool place.

Almond Fudge Brownies

Prep Time: 30 minutes; **Cook Time:** 25 minutes, plus 4 hours cooling

Serving Size: 47 g; **Serves:** 16; **Calories:** 206		
Total Fat: 13 g **Saturated Fat:** 3.6 g; **Trans Fat:** 0 g		
Protein: 4.5 g; **Net Carbs:** 18.5 g		
Total Carbs: 20.1 g; **Dietary Fiber:** 1.6 g; **Sugars:** 17.5 g		
Cholesterol: 41 mg; **Sodium:** 66 mg; **Potassium:** 155 mg;		
Vitamin A: 2%; **Vitamin C:** 0%; **Calcium:** 6%; **Iron:** 5%		

Ingredients:

- 5 ounces bittersweet chocolate (70- to 72-percent cacao), chopped
- 3 large eggs, at room temperature
- 2 tablespoons unsalted butter
- 2 tablespoons canola oil
- 1/4 teaspoon salt
- 1/2 cup walnuts, chopped, optional
- 1 teaspoon vanilla extract
- 1 teaspoon baking powder
- 1 cup sugar
- 1 1/4 cups almond flour, plus 1 tablespoon

Directions:

1. Preheat the oven to350F. Grease an 8x8-inch baking pan with nonstick spray or with butter and then lightly flour.
2. In a small-sized bowl, combine the butter with the chocolate and the oil; microwave at 50 percent power for 1 minute until melted or melt over hot water. Let cool to room temperature.
3. Sift the flour, the baking powder, and the salt onto a wax paper.
4. In a mixing bowl, with a handheld mixer on MEDIUM speed, lightly beat the eggs. Add the vanilla and the sugar in; beat for about 3 minutes or till thick. Blend the chocolate mix. Sprinkle the dry ingredients over the mix. With a rubber spatula, blend until the batter is just mixed and then spread the batter into the greased pan; if using, sprinkle the walnuts over the top.
5. Bake for about 25 minutes or till the top is shiny and hard and a knife comes out almost clean when inserted in the center. Let the brownies cool in pan for 4 hours. Unmold, wrap with foil, and store overnight, or ideally, for 24 hours. Cut into 16 brownies.
6. If serving, cut as many brownies as needed and keep the rest wrapped in foil for up to 5 days at room temperature.

Freezing: Cut the cooled brownies into 4 quarters. Wrap each quarter with freezer plastic wrap and then with heavy-duty foil and freeze. When ready to serve, unwrap a quarter, let stand for 15 minutes at room temperature, cut into 4 pieces, and serve cold.

161

Blueberry Scones

Prep Time: 20 minutes; **Cook Time:** 25 minutes	
Serving Size: 106 g; **Serves:** 8; **Calories:** 413	
Total Fat: 29 g **Saturated Fat:** 11.4 g; **Trans Fat:** 0 g	
Protein: 6.3 g; **Net Carbs:** 33 g	
Total Carbs: 36.5 g; **Dietary Fiber:** 3.5 g; **Sugars:** 30.2 g	
Cholesterol: 0 mg; **Sodium:** 0 mg; **Potassium:** 0 mg;	
Vitamin A: 0%; **Vitamin C:** 0%; **Calcium:** 0%; **Iron:** 0%	

Ingredients:

- 1 heaping cup blueberries (190 grams), fresh or frozen, do not thaw
- 1 large egg
- 1 teaspoon vanilla extract
- 1/2 cup granulated sugar (100 grams), (or use equal amount Swerve sweetener)
- 1/2 cup heavy cream (120ml)
- 1/2 cup unsalted butter, frozen (115 grams)
- 1/2 teaspoon ground cinnamon
- 1/2 teaspoon salt
- 2 baking powder plus 1/2 teaspoons baking powder
- 2 cups almond flour (250 grams), do not to over-measure
- Coarse sugar for sprinkling on top before baking

For the glaze:

- 1 cup confectioners' sugar (120g), or use equal amount Swerve sweetener
- 1/4 teaspoon vanilla extract
- 3 tablespoons heavy cream (45 ml), or half-and-half or milk

Directions:

1. Preheat the oven to 400F or 204 C. Place the baking rack to the middle-low position. Line a large-sized baking sheet with silicone baking mat or parchment paper; set aside.
2. Inside a large-sized bowl, whisk the flour with the baking powder, sugar substitute, salt, and cinnamon.
3. Grate the frozen butter and add into the flour mix. With 2 knives, a pastry cutter, or your fingers, combine until the mixture resembles coarse meal; set aside.
4. In a small-sized bowl, whisk the cream with the egg and the vanilla. Drizzle over the flour mix; toss the mix using a rubber spatula until everything is moistened. Gently and slowly fold the blueberries in the mix, making sure not to overmix the dough; the dough will be slightly wet.
5. With floured hands, work the dough as best as you can into a ball; transfer into the prepared baking pan. Press into a neat 8-inch disk and then cut into 8 equal wedges with a very sharp knife. Sprinkle the top with coarse sugar. Separate the scones, making a little space between each wedge. Bake for about 20 to 25 minutes or till cooked through or lightly golden.
6. Remove from the oven; let cool for a couple of minutes.
7. Meanwhile, whisk all the glaze ingredients until well combined. Just before serving, lightly drizzle the scones with the glaze.

Notes: Scones are best when serve immediately. However, Makethem ahead of time and keep at room temperature for up to2 days. They can also be frozen for

162

up to 3 months. When ready to serve, thaw in the fridge overnight, and warm to your liking.

No Bake Chewy Peanut Butter Flax Seed, Rice Crispies, and Chocolate Chips Granola Bars

Prep Time: 15 minutes; Cook Time: 5 minutes	
Serving Size: 39 g; Serves: 35; Calories: 166	
Total Fat: 7.6 g Saturated Fat: 3.2 g; Trans Fat: 0 g	
Protein: 3.5 g; Net Carbs: 21.1 g	
Total Carbs: 23.2 g; Dietary Fiber: 2.1 g; Sugars: 14.3 g	
Cholesterol: 1 mg; Sodium: 71 mg; Potassium: 107 mg;	
Vitamin A: 0%; Vitamin C: 0%; Calcium: 1%; Iron: 12%	

Ingredients:
- 4 cups crisp rice cereal (use organic)
- 2/3 cups ground flax seed
- 2 teaspoons vanilla extract
- 2 2/3cups old fashioned oats
- 1/4 teaspoon fine sea salt
- 1/3 cup coconut oil
- 1/2-1 cup mini chocolate chips
- 1/2 cup raw sugar or brown sugar (equal amount Swerve sweetener)
- 1 cup peanut butter, crunchy, 100% all-natural
- 1 1/2 cups honey

Directions:
1. Inside a large-sized bowl, combine the oats with the rice cereal and the flax seed; stir using a large spoon until well combined and set aside.
2. Measure the honey, sugar, sea salt, and the coconut oil into a saucepan. Turn the heat of the stove on to medium; bring to a boil, constantly stirring the mixture, and then boil for 1 minute or so or until the sugar is dissolved. Remove the pan from the heat, add the peanut butter and vanilla extract; stir until smooth.
3. Pour the honey mix over the oat mix; stir until well mixed and let sit for about 5 to 8 minutes.
4. Meanwhile, take a large-sized 17 1/2x12 1/2-inch cookie sheet or a jellyroll pan and parchment paper. Put the cookie sheet on top of a large piece parchment paper; trace around the outside. Cut the cookie sheet outline and put it inside the cookie sheet; the sheet should fit perfectly. The parchment will help keep the granola bar in 1 piece before you cut I up.
5. Pout the granola mix into the prepared cookie sheet. Press the top with a second cookie sheet to flatten the top. Immediately spread the chocolate chips on to and then press to adhere. Let the layer cool on the counter or in the fridge. When completely cool, slide the layer out of the pan and then cut into your preferred size. I cut 7 bars down and then 5 across to make 35 bars.

Freezing: Individually wrap each bar with plastic wrap, put into a freezable Ziploc bag, and freeze. Take out a bar in the morning and they will be thawed by morning snack time and by lunch hour.

French Toast Baked Sticks

Prep Time: 30 minutes; Cook Time: 16-18 minutes		

Serving Size: 26 g; Serves: 12; Calories: 39	
Total Fat: 2.4 g Saturated Fat: 1.1 g; Trans Fat: 0 g	
Protein: 1.9 g; Net Carbs: 2.2 g	
Total Carbs: 2.2 g; Dietary Fiber: 0 g; Sugars: 0.7 g	
Cholesterol: 44 mg; Sodium: 47 mg; Potassium: 25 mg;	
Vitamin A: 2%; Vitamin C: 0%; Calcium: 2%; Iron: 2%	

Ingredients:

- 4 slices Texas Toast (or any thick-cut, hearty bread)
- 3 eggs
- 1/2 teaspoon cinnamon
- 1/2 cup milk
- 1 teaspoon vanilla
- 1 tablespoon butter, melted, slightly cooled

Directions:

1. Preheat the oven to 350F. Generously grease a baking sheet with nonstick spray; set aside.
2. Cut the slices of bread into thirds; set aside.
3. Inside a large-sized shallow dish, whisk the eggs with the melted butter, milk, cinnamon, and vanilla.
4. Dunk the bread sticks into the batter; let the excess drip off and then put them into the greased baking sheet, arranging in a single layer. Bake for about 16 to 18 minutes, spraying the top with the nonstick spray halfway through cooking and then flip.

Freeing: Let the baked toasts cool. Put them into a baking sheet and flash freeze until hard. Transfer into a freezer container or bag. When ready to serve, just microwave for about 30 seconds to 1 minute or until heated.

No-Bake Peanut Butter, Chocolate, Date, Oat Bars

Prep Time: 30 minutes, plus 4 hours firming; Cook Time: 0 minutes
Serving Size: 58 g; Serves: 16; Calories: 277
Total Fat: 16.6 g Saturated Fat: 7.3 g; Trans Fat: 0 g
Protein: 6.2 g; Net Carbs: 25.3 g
Total Carbs: 29 g; Dietary Fiber: 3.7 g; Sugars: 14.2 g
Cholesterol: 0 mg; Sodium: 75 mg; Potassium: 202 mg;
Vitamin A: 0%; Vitamin C: 0%; Calcium: 1%; Iron: 13%

Ingredients:
- ☐ 1 cup peanut butter, creamy
- ☐ 1 cup semisweet chocolate chips
- ☐ 1 teaspoon vanilla extract, pure
- ☐ 1/4 cup coconut oil
- ☐ 10 dates, medjool, pitted
- ☐ 3 cups oats, old-fashioned
- ☐ 3 tablespoons raw honey, or maple syrup

Directions:
1. Line a 9x9-inch baking pan with wax paper, leaving a 1-inch or so hangover on the edges.
2. Put 3/4 of the peanut butter, honey, coconut oil, vanilla, and dates into a food processor; pulse until smooth. Add the oats in; pulse until well combined. The mixture will be crumbly, but it will hold its shape when formed into a ball.
3. Press 3/4 of the oat mix into the bottom of the prepared pan.
4. In a small-sized saucepan, melt the chocolate chips with the remaining peanut butter over low heat, stirring until smooth. Pour the chocolate mix over the layer in pan and using a rubber spatula or a spoon, spread the chocolate mix.
5. Crumble the remaining 1/4 of the oat mix over the chocolate; pressing it gently to adhere.
6. Cover and then refrigerate for at least 4 hours or until firm. When firm, remove from the pan by lifting the wax paper by the edges and then cut into bars. Store in airtight containers and keep in the fridge.

Notes: These healthy no refined sugar and no butter bars are freezable. Just let thaw for 10 minutes when ready to serve.

Banana Foster Bread

Prep Time: 40 minutes; **Cook Time:** 1 hour		

Serving Size: 52 g; **Serves:** 16; **Calories:** 150

Total Fat: 11.6 g **Saturated Fat:** 3.5 g; **Trans Fat:** 0 g

Protein: 4.1 g; **Net Carbs:** 6.4 g

Total Carbs: 10.8 g; **Dietary Fiber:** 4.4 g; **Sugars:** 2.7 g

Cholesterol: 35 mg; **Sodium:** 178 mg; **Potassium:** 174 mg;

Vitamin A: 4%; **Vitamin C:** 2%; **Calcium:** 5%; **Iron:** 6%

Ingredients:

- 1 1/2 cups banana, ripe, mashed
- 6.75 ounces almond flour (about 1 1/2 cups)
- 6 tablespoons butter, melted and divided
- 3/4 teaspoon baking soda
- 2 large eggs
- 1/8 teaspoon ground allspice
- 1/4 cup ground flaxseed
- 1/4 cup cognac or dark rum, divided
- 1/3 cup yogurt, plain, fat-free
- 1/3 cup powdered sugar (equal amount Swerve Sweetener)
- 1/2 teaspoon salt
- 1/2 teaspoon ground cinnamon
- 1 1/2 cup packed brown sugar, divided (mix 1 tablespoon molasses + 1 cup low carb sweetener)
- Cooking spray

Directions:

1. Preheat the oven to 350F.
2. In a nonstick skillet, combine the banana with 5 tablespoons of butter, 1 cup brown sugar substitute, and 3 tablespoons cognac; cook on medium heat or until the mix starts to bubble. Remove from the heat and let cool. Put the banana mix inside a large-sized bowl. Add the yogurt, the remaining 1/2 cup brown sugar substitute, and the eggs; beat at MEDIUM speed with a mixer.
3. Measure the flour and put into a small-sized bowl. Add the flaxseed, baking soda, salt, cinnamon, and allspice; mix until combined. Add the flour mix into the banana mix; beat until the mixtures are just blended.
4. Pour the batter into a 5x9 inch loaf pan greased with cooking spray; bake at 350F for 1 hour or until a toothpick come out clean when inserted in the center. Remove from the pan, put the pan in the wire rack and let cool for 10 minutes. Remove the bread from the pan and put on the wire rack.
5. Combine the remaining 1 tablespoon of melted butter with the remaining 1 tablespoon of cognac, and the powdered sugar substitute; stir until the mix is well blended. Drizzle over the still warm bread.

Freezing: Like most banana breads, this adult version freezes well. Just drizzle the glaze after you have thawed the loaf.

167

Heart Smart Chocolate-Cherry and Oats Cookies

Prep Time: 30 minutes; **Cook Time:** 12 minutes

Serving Size: 23 g; **Serves:** 30; **Calories:** 73		
Total Fat: 3.6 g **Saturated Fat:** 2.1 g; **Trans Fat:** 0 g		
Protein: 1.3 g; **Net Carbs:** 8.7 g		
Total Carbs: 9.9 g; **Dietary Fiber:** 1.2 g; **Sugars:** 1.5 g		
Cholesterol: 13 mg; **Sodium:** 102 mg; **Potassium:** 39 mg;		
Vitamin A: 2%; **Vitamin C:** 0%; **Calcium:** 1%; **Iron:** 2%		

Ingredients:
- ☐ 1 1/2 cups rolled oats, old-fashioned
- ☐ 1 cup dried cherries
- ☐ 1 large egg, lightly beaten
- ☐ 1 teaspoon baking soda
- ☐ 1 teaspoon vanilla extract
- ☐ 1.5 ounces all-purpose flour (about 1/3 cup)
- ☐ 1.5 ounces whole-wheat flour (about 1/3 cup)
- ☐ 1/2 teaspoon salt
- ☐ 3 ounces bittersweet chocolate, coarsely chopped
- ☐ 3/4 cup packed light brown sugar (mix 3/4 tablespoon molasses + 3/4 cup low carb sweetener)
- ☐ 6 tablespoons unsalted butter
- ☐ Cooking spray

Directions:
1. Preheat the oven to 350F.
2. Measure the flours and put inside a large-sized bowl. Add the rolled oats, baking soda, and the salt; stir with a whisk until combined.
3. In a small-sized saucepan, melt the butter on low heat; remove from the heat and then add the brown sugar substitute, stirring until the mix smooth.
4. Add the butter mix into flour mix; with a mixer, beat at MEDIUM speed until blended. Add the egg, cherries, and vanilla, beat until combined. Fold the chopped chocolate in the mix.
5. By 1 tablespoonfuls, scoop the dough and drop into the cooking spray coated baking sheets, placing them 2 inches apart; bake at 350F for 12 minutes. Let cool in the baking sheet for about 3 minutes or till almost firm. Transfer onto wire racks and let cool completely.

Notes: Make ahead of time or double the batch. Just freeze for a healthy treat any time.

Pepperoni Pizza Puffs

Prep Time: 15 minutes; Cook Time: 25 minutes	
Serving Size: 193 g; Serves: 4; Calories: 428	
Total Fat: 33.7 g Saturated Fat: 12.1g; Trans Fat: 0 g	
Protein: 20.9 g; Net Carbs: 8.7 g	
Total Carbs: 12.1 g; Dietary Fiber: 3.4 g; Sugars: 5.6 g	
Cholesterol: 105 mg; Sodium: 796 mg; Potassium: 479 mg;	
Vitamin A: 29%; Vitamin C: 69%; Calcium: 37%; Iron: 13%	

Ingredients:
- 1 egg, lightly beaten
- 1 red bell pepper, sliced
- 1/2 cup pizza sauce, store-bought
- 2 tablespoons fresh basil, finely chopped
- 3/4 cup almond flour
- 3/4 cup whole milk
- 3/4 teaspoon baking powder
- 4 ounces cheese, shredded (about 1 cup)
- 4 ounces pepperoni, cut into small cubes (about 1 cup)

Directions:
1. Preheat the oven 375F. Grease a 24-cup mini muffin pan.
2. Inside a large-sized bowl, whisk the flour with the baking powder. Whisk in the milk and then the egg. Stir in the pepperoni and the mozzarella cheese; let the mix stand for 10 minutes.
3. Stir the batter and then divide between the muffin pans; bake for about 20-25 minutes or till golden and puffed.
4. Meanwhile, microwave the pizza sauce until warmed through. Stir in 1 tablespoon of basil into the sauce. When baked, sprinkle the top of the puffs with the remaining basil. Serve the puffs and the slices of red pepper flakes with the pizza sauce for dipping.

Freezing: Put the cooled, baked in a baking sheet, arranging in a single layer; flash freeze until frozen. Transfer into a freezer bag and freeze. When ready to serve, put the frozen puffs into a baking sheet; bake in a preheated 350F oven for about 8-10 minutes.

Veggie Beef Meatballs

Prep Time: 40 minutes; **Cook Time:** 18-20 minutes	

Serving Size: 56 g; **Serves:** 15; **Calories:** 105
Total Fat: 3.1 g **Saturated Fat:** 1.3 g; **Trans Fat:** 0 g
Protein: 11.6 g; **Net Carbs:** 6.4 g
Total Carbs: 7 g; **Dietary Fiber:** 0.6 g; **Sugars:** 1.5 g
Cholesterol: 40 mg; **Sodium:** 333 mg; **Potassium:** 180 mg;
Vitamin A: 17%; **Vitamin C:** 5%; **Calcium:** 4%; **Iron:** 35%

Ingredients:

- ☐ 1 pound ground beef
- ☐ 1 egg
- ☐ 1 cup whole-wheat bread crumbs
- ☐ 1 carrot, medium, finely shredded or food processor minced
- ☐ 1 1/4 teaspoons salt
- ☐ 1/2 cup Parmesan cheese, fresh, finely grated
- ☐ 1/2 onion, small, finely chopped or food processor minced
- ☐ 1/2teaspoon pepper
- ☐ 1/3 cup fresh parsley, finely chopped or food processor minced, loosely packed,
- ☐ 2 cloves garlic, minced (by hand or in food processor)
- ☐ 3 tablespoons ketchup

Directions:

1. Preheat the oven to 400F. Line a 9x13-inch casserole dish or a rimmed sheet pan with foil or parchment paper.
2. Inside a large-sized bowl, combine the carrot with the onion, parsley, garlic, egg, parmesan, ketchup, breadcrumbs, salt, and pepper. Mix the ground beef in; with your hands combine well until mixed. With about 2 tablespoon measure, form the mixture into meatballs, about 1 1/2-inch diameter. Put them in the prepared dish/pan, placing them with a little space between each meatball.
3. Bake for about 18 to 20 minutes or till cooked through and the center is no longer pink. The meatballs are cooked when the internal temperature is 160F.

Freezing:

Before baking: Roll into meatballs, put into freezer containers or bags, arranging in a single layer. If stacking in a container, layer with a parchment between each stack. When ready to cook, thaw for 2 hours in the fridge and bake as directed. If cooking directly from frozen, bake for 30 minutes more than original baking time, to a total of 50 minutes. If the outside are getting to browned, cover with foil.

After baking: Let cool, put into freezer containers or bags, arranging in a single layer. If stacking in a container, layer with a parchment between each stack. When ready to cook, thaw for 24 hours in the fridge. Warm on the stove over low to medium-low heat with some marinara sauce. Alternatively, you can warm the frozen meatballs in the microwave in 30-second intervals until warmed through; be careful not to overcook them.

Whole-Wheat Calzones

Prep Time: 1 hour; **Cook Time:** 10-13 minutes	
Serving Size: 114 g; **Serves:** 16; **Calories:** 246	
Total Fat: 13.1 g **Saturated Fat:** 5 g; **Trans Fat:** 0 g	
Protein: 13.4 g; **Net Carbs:** 17.4 g	
Total Carbs: 18.1 g; **Dietary Fiber:** 0.7 g; **Sugars:** 1.5 g	
Cholesterol: 66 mg; **Sodium:** 689 mg; **Potassium:** 166 mg;	
Vitamin A: 5%; **Vitamin C:** 2%; **Calcium:** 11%; **Iron:** 10%	

Ingredients:

For the dough:

- 2 1/2 cups whole-wheat flour (use white type whole-wheat flour)
- 1 teaspoon granulated sugar
- 1 tablespoon olive oil
- 1 tablespoon honey
- 1 cup warm water (110F)
- 1 1/2 teaspoons kosher salt
- 2 1/4 teaspoons (1 packet 1/4 ounces) Active Dry Yeast

For the calzone filling:

- 1 pound Italian sausage, cooked, OR 1 pack uncured pepperoni, chopped (Applegate Turkey Pepperoni preferred)
- 1 1/2 cup mozzarella cheese, grated
- 1 whole egg, beaten
- 1/2 cup Parmesan cheese, grated
- 1/2 teaspoon Italian seasoning
- 1/2 teaspoon salt
- 1/4 cup fresh parsley, minced
- 1/4 teaspoon pepper
- 15 ounces ricotta cheese
- 2 whole eggs
- Marinara Sauce, for serving

Directions:

For the dough:
1. In the bowl of a stand mixer, combine the warm water with the yeast and the sugar; stir and let sit for about 10 minutes or till the yeast starts to bubble and foam.
2. With the dough hook, turn the mixer on LOW; slowly add the olive oil, the honey, salt, and, in 1 cup increments, the flour until everything is added. When the dough begins to form, increase the speed to MEDIUM; mix for 5 minutes or till the dough is combined.
3. Flour a work surface. Transfer the dough into the floured surface; knead for a couple of times, forming into a ball. Transfer into a well-greased bowl, loosely cover with a towel and let rise for about 30 minutes in a warm place.
4. At this point, make the calzones or freeze the dough for later.

For the calzone:
1. Preheat the oven to 400F.
2. In a medium-sized bowl, combine the ricotta with the parmesan cheese, mozzarella, parsley, egg, salt, Italian seasoning, and pepper. If using pre-cooked pepperoni or Italian sausage, stir in now. Set the mix aside.

171

3. Take an amount of dough, roll into about a 2-inch ball and then roll into ¼-inch thickness. Spoon 3 to 4 tablespoons of the ricotta mix onto 1/2 of the dough circle, leaving a little clear area around the edges. Make sure you do not overfill or they will split open while baking. Fold the other half of the dough over the filling, press the edges to seal, pressing with the back of a fork to seal well. With the fork tips, poke a few holes on top of each calzone.
4. Brush the surface with beaten egg; bake in a baking sheet lined with foil or parchment paper for about 10-13 minutes or till nicely golden brown. Serve warm with marinara sauce.

Freezing: Cook as directed and let cool completely. Put the calzones into airtight freezer containers or bags; freeze until ready to eat.

When ready to serve, wrap each frozen calzone with moist paper towel; microwave on DEFROST setting until they are warmed through.

Blueberry-Banana Buttermilk Bread

Prep Time: 1 hours; **Cook Time:** 20 minutes, plus 2 hours cooling		
Serving Size: 96 g; **Serves:** 10; **Calories:** 2oo		
Total Fat: 11.5 g **Saturated Fat:** 1.1 g; **Trans Fat:** 0 g		
Protein: 4.6 g; **Net Carbs:** 19.8 g		
Total Carbs: 24.2 g; **Dietary Fiber:** 4.4 g; **Sugars:** 4.2 g		
Cholesterol: 37 mg; **Sodium:** 228mg; **Potassium:** 244 mg;		
Vitamin A: 1%; **Vitamin C:** 7%; **Calcium:** 7%; **Iron:** 9%		

Ingredients:

- 1 cup bananas, ripe, mashed (about 3 medium)
- 1 cup almond flour
- 1 1/4 cups whole-wheat pastry flour
- 1 1/4 cups blueberries, fresh or frozen
- 1 1/2 teaspoons baking powder
- 1/2 teaspoon baking soda
- 1/2 teaspoon salt
- 1/4 cup canola oil
- 1/4 teaspoon ground nutmeg
- 2 large eggs
- 3/4 cup buttermilk, nonfat or low-fat
- 3/4 cup light brown sugar, packed (3/4 tablespoon molasses + 3/4 cup low carb sweetener)
- 3/4 teaspoon ground cinnamon

Directions:

1. Preheat the oven to 375F. Grease a 5x9-inch loaf pan with cooking spray.
2. Inside a large-sized bowl, whisk the buttermilk with the brown sugar substitute, eggs, and oil. Stir in the mashed bananas.
3. In a medium-sized bowl, whisk the flours with the baking powder, the baking soda, the cinnamon, the nutmeg, and salt.
4. Fold the dry ingredients into the wet ingredients; stir till just combined. Fold the blueberries in and then transfer the batter into the greased pan. Bake for about 50-60 minutes or till the top is golden and a skewer come out clean when inserted in the center. Let cool in pan for 10 minutes, turn onto a wire rack, and let cool for 2 hours. Slice and serve.

For muffins:
1. Preheat the oven to 400F. Grease a 12-cup, 1/2-cup muffin tin with cooking spray or line with paper liners. Divide the batter between the cups until each are full. Bake for about 20-25 minutes or till the tops are golden and a wooden skewer come out clean when inserted in the center. Cool in the muffin tin for 10 minutes, remove, transfer on a wire rack, and let cool for at least 15 minutes more, then serve.

Freezing: Wrap the loaf or the muffins and store for 2 days at most at room temperature or freeze for up to 3 months. For long-term freezing, wrap the loaf or slices or muffins with plastic wrap and then with foil.

Walnut Apricot Cereal Bars

Prep Time: 0 minutes; **Cook Time:** 35-40 minutes

Serving Size: 106 g; **Serves:** 16; **Calories:** 281

Total Fat: 12.1 g **Saturated Fat:** 1.1 g; **Trans Fat:** 0 g

Protein: 6.4 g; **Net Carbs:** 19.8 g

Total Carbs: 24.9 g; **Dietary Fiber:** 5.1 g; **Sugars:** 6.4g

Cholesterol: 12 mg; **Sodium:** 130 mg; **Potassium:** 248 mg;

Vitamin A: 8%; **Vitamin C:** 5%; **Calcium:** 3%; **Iron:** 18%

Ingredients:

- ☐ 3 cups rolled oats, old-fashioned
- ☐ 3 cups grain cereal, unsweetened puffed such as Kashi
- ☐ 2 tablespoons lemon zest, freshly grated
- ☐ 2 cups dried apricots, chopped
- ☐ 12 ounces silken tofu, drained (about 1 1/3 cups)
- ☐ 1/4 cup almond flour
- ☐ 1/2 teaspoon salt
- ☐ 1/2 cup walnuts, chopped (about 2 ounces)
- ☐ 1/2 cup canola oil
- ☐ 1 tablespoon vanilla extract
- ☐ 1 large egg
- ☐ 1 cup honey (3/4 cup low carb sweetener)

Directions:

1. Preheat oven to 350F. Grease a large-sized, preferably a 10 1/4 x 15 1/4-inch jellyroll-style pan with cooking spray.
2. Spread the walnuts and the oats into a rimmed baking sheet; bake in the oven for about 8-10 minutes or till fragrant and light golden. Transfer inside a large-sized bowl. Add the flour, salt, dried apricots, and the puffed cereal; stir to combine.
3. Put the tofu, oil, egg, honey, lemon zest, and vanilla into a food processor or in a blender; puree until smooth, scraping the sides as needed. Make a well in the center of the oat mix; fold the tofu mix in until combined. Evenly spread into the greased pan.
4. Bake for 35-40 minutes or till the center is firm and golden brown; let cool completely in pan. When completely cool, cut into bars using a sharp knife.

Freezing: Wrap each bar with plastic wrap and keep for up to 5 days at room temperature or freeze for up to 1 month. When ready to serve, thaw at room temperature. Alternatively, remove the plastic wrap, wrap with paper towel and defrost in the microwave according to microwave's instructions.

Chocolate Chip Oat Cookies

Prep Time: 30 minutes; **Cook Time:** 15 minutes per batch

Serving Size: 19 g; **Serves:** 30; **Calories:** 85
Total Fat: 5.3 g **Saturated Fat:** 2.3 g; **Trans Fat:** 0 g
Protein: 1.4 g; **Net Carbs:** 8.6 g
Total Carbs: 10.1 g; **Dietary Fiber:** 1.6 g; **Sugars:** 2.9 g
Cholesterol: 12 mg; **Sodium:** 79 mg; **Potassium:** 36 mg;
Vitamin A: 1%; **Vitamin C:** 0%; **Calcium:** 1%; **Iron:** 2%

Ingredients:

- 1 cup chocolate chips
- 1 cup whole-wheat flour
- 1 large egg
- 1 teaspoon vanilla extract
- 1/2 teaspoon baking soda
- 1/2 teaspoon salt
- 1/3 cup brown sugar (1 teaspoon molasses + 1/3 cup low carb sweetener)
- 1/3 cup granulated sugar (equal amount Swerve sweetener)
- 1/4 cup butter, softened
- 1/4 cup canola oil
- 3/4 cup rolled oats

Directions:

1. Preheat the oven 350F. Grease 2 baking sheets with cooking spray.
2. Put the oats into a food or a blender; grind until flour. Transfer into a medium-sized bowl. Stir in the flour, the baking soda, and the salt.
3. Inside a large-sized bowl, beat the butter using an electric mixer until fluffy. Add the oil, brown sugar substitute, granulated sugar substitute, egg, and vanilla; beat until creamy and smooth. With the mixer running on LOW speed, add the dry ingredients; beat until just combined. Stir the chocolate chips into the mix.
4. By heaping 1 teaspoonfuls, scoop the dough into the greased baking sheets, placing them at least 1 inch apart. One baking sheet at a time, bake for about 15 minutes or till the edges are firm and the tops are golden. Let cool in the baking sheets for 2 minutes, transfer onto wire racks, and let cool completely.

Notes: Keep the cookies in airtight containers for up to 3 days or freeze for up to 2 months. If stacking, place parchment paper between each stack.

Oat Waffles

Prep Time: 30 minutes; **Cook Time:** 4-5 minutes per batch	
Serving Size: 107 g; **Serves:** 8; **Calories:** 181	
Total Fat: 8.1 g **Saturated Fat:** 1.3 g; **Trans Fat:** 0 g	
Protein: 7.3 g; **Net Carbs:** 18.9 g	
Total Carbs: 21.9 g; **Dietary Fiber:** 3 g; **Sugars:** 3.9 g	
Cholesterol: 49 mg; **Sodium:** 238 mg; **Potassium:** 315 mg;	
Vitamin A: 2%; **Vitamin C:** 01%; **Calcium:** 15%; **Iron:** 8%	

Ingredients:

- ☐ 2/3 cup whole-wheat flour
- ☐ 2/3 cup almond flour
- ☐ 2 teaspoons vanilla extract
- ☐ 2 large eggs, lightly beaten
- ☐ 2 cups buttermilk
- ☐ 1/4 teaspoon salt
- ☐ 1/4 cup toasted wheat germ, or cornmeal
- ☐ 1/4 cup packed brown sugar (1/4 tablespoon molasses + 1/4 cup low carb sweetener)
- ☐ 1/2 teaspoon baking soda
- ☐ 1/2 cup rolled oats, old-fashioned
- ☐ 1 teaspoon ground cinnamon
- ☐ 1 tablespoon canola oil
- ☐ 1 1/2 teaspoons baking powder

Directions:

1. In a medium-sized bowl, mix the buttermilk with the oats; let stand for 15 minutes.
2. Inside a large-bowl, whisk the flours with the wheat germ/cornmeal, baking soda, baking powder, cinnamon, and salt.
3. Stir the eggs, oil, brown sugar substitute, and vanilla into the oat mix. Add the wet ingredients into the dry ingredients; with a rubber spatula, mix until just moistened.
4. Grease a waffle iron with cooking spray and preheat. Spoon just enough batter to cover 3/4 of the waffle iron surface, about 2/3 cup for an 8x8 waffle iron; cook for about 4-5 minutes or till the waffle is golden brown and crisp. Repeat the process with the remaining batter.

Freezing: Individually wrap the waffles with plastic wrap; refrigerate for up 2 days or freeze for up to 1 month. When ready to serve, just reheat in a toaster oven or toaster. . For long-term freezing, wrap the loaf or slices or muffins with plastic wrap and then with foil.

Goat Cheese Fig Muffins

Prep Time: 40 minutes; Cook Time: 13-15 minutes	
Serving Size: 95 g; Serves: 12; Calories: 269	
Total Fat: 19.8 g Saturated Fat: 5 g; Trans Fat: 0 g	
Protein: 7.2 g; Net Carbs: 17.4 g	
Total Carbs: 23.5 g; Dietary Fiber: 6.1 g; Sugars: 12.4 g	
Cholesterol: 48 mg; Sodium: 184 mg; Potassium: 404 mg;	
Vitamin A: 5%; Vitamin C: 1%; Calcium: 15%; Iron: 8%	

Ingredients:

- 3/4 cup goat cheese, soft, crumbled (or cream cheese, reduced-fat)
- 3 tablespoons granulated sugar (equal amount low carb sweetener)
- 2 tablespoons honey
- 2 large eggs
- 2 cups almond flour
- 1/4 teaspoon salt
- 1/3 cup extra-virgin olive oil
- 1/2 teaspoon baking soda
- 1 teaspoon lemon zest, freshly grated
- 1 large egg white
- 1 cup buttermilk, low-fat or nonfat
- 1 1/4 teaspoons vanilla extract, divided
- 1 1/4 cups chopped dried figs
- 1 1/2 teaspoons baking powder
- 3/4 cup packed dark or light brown sugar (mix 3/4 tablespoon molasses + 3/4 cup low carb sweetener)

Directions:

1. Preheat the oven to 425F. Line a 12-cup, 1/2-cup muffin tin with paper liners or grease with cooking spray.
2. In a small-sized bowl, combine the goat/cream cheese with the honey, 1/4 teaspoon vanilla, and lemon zest until well mixed; set aside.
3. Inside a large-sized bowl, whisk the flour with the baking soda, baking powder, and salt.
4. In a medium-sized bowl, lightly beat the eggs with the egg whites. Add the brown sugar substitute and the remaining 1 teaspoon; whisk for about 1 minute or until the sugar is dissolved. Gradually whisk in the buttermilk and then the oil until smooth.
5. Add the wet ingredients into the dry ingredients; stir till just combined, make sure not to overmix. Fold in the figs.
6. Spoon half of the batter into the prepared muffin tin. Add 1 generous teaspoon of the cheese filling into the center of each batter layer; cover with the remaining batter, making sure that the batter is not visible. Sprinkle the top with the sugar substitute.
7. Bake for about 13-15 minutes or till the edges begin to brown and the muffin tops spring back when pressed gently. Let cool in the muffin tin for 5 minutes, turn out onto a wire rack and let cool.

Notes: Wrap each muffin with plastic wrap; store for 2 days at most at room temperature or freezer for up to 1 month. When ready to serve, remove the plastic wrap, wrap with paper towel, and microwave for about 30-45 seconds on HIGH.

Sloppy Joes

Prep Time: 10 minutes; **Cook Time:** 35 minutes	
Serving Size: 231 g; **Serves:** 8; **Calories:** 222	
Total Fat: 4.6 g **Saturated Fat:** 1.3g; **Trans Fat:** 0 g	
Protein: 17.8 g; **Net Carbs:** 24.5 g	
Total Carbs: 28.6 g; **Dietary Fiber:** 4.1 g; **Sugars:** 9.1 g	
Cholesterol: 38 mg; **Sodium:** 443 mg; **Potassium:** 579 mg;	
Vitamin A: 12%; **Vitamin C:** 43%; **Calcium:** 6%; **Iron:**53%	

Ingredients:
- ☐ 2 cups of cremini mushrooms, chopped finely (around 4 ounces)
- ☐ 1/4 cup cider vinegar
- ☐ 12 ounces ground beef, 90% lean
- ☐ 2 tablespoons tapioca flour
- ☐ 1/4 cup chili sauce, I used Heinz
- ☐ 5 plum tomatoes, diced
- ☐ 1/4 cup ketchup
- ☐ 1/2 cup water
- ☐ 1 large onion, finely diced
- ☐ 8 hamburger buns, whole-wheat, toasted if preferred

Directions:
1. Inside a large-sized nonstick skillet, crumble the beef; cook on medium heat for about 1 minute or until it begins to sizzle. Add the mushrooms and the onions; cook for about 8-10 minutes, occasionally stirring, breaking the meat using wooden spoon, till the veggies are soft and moisture has cooked off.
2. Add the tomatoes and then the flour; stir the mix to combine.
3. Stir in the water, chili sauce, vinegar, and the ketchup; bring to simmer, frequently stirring. Reduce the heat to low simmer; cook, occasionally stirring, for about 8-10 minutes, or till the onion has become very tender and the sauce is thick. Serve warm in your preferred buns.

Notes: Make ahead of time, let cool, and then freeze for up to 1 month.

Date and Double Nut Tassies

Prep Time: 40 minutes; **Cook Time:** 15-17 minutes

Serving Size: 25 g; Serves: 24; Calories: 81		
Total Fat: 6.2 g Saturated Fat: 2 g; Trans Fat: 0 g		
Protein: 1.3 g; Net Carbs: 5.5 g		
Total Carbs: 6.9 g; Dietary Fiber: 1.4 g; Sugars: 3.4 g		
Cholesterol: 8 mg; Sodium: 29 mg; Potassium: 66 mg;		
Vitamin A: 2%; Vitamin C: 0%; Calcium: 1%; Iron: 2%		

Ingredients:
For the crust:
- 1/4 cup whole-wheat pastry flour
- 1/4 cup packed light brown sugar (mix 1/4 tablespoon molasses + 1/4 cup low carb sweetener)
- 1/2 cup walnuts, coarsely chopped
- 1 tablespoon cornstarch
- 2 tablespoons unsalted butter
- Pinch salt

For the filling:
- 4 tablespoons reduced-fat cream cheese
- 4 ounces dried dates, pitted (about 3/4 cup)
- 3/4 cup water
- 2 1/2 tablespoons unsalted butter
- 1/4 cup packed light brown sugar (mix 1/4 tablespoon molasses + 1/4 cup low carb sweetener)
- 1/2 cup pecans, chopped
- 1 1/4 teaspoons vanilla extract
- Confectioners' sugar, for dusting or whipped cream, for garnish

Directions:
1. Preheat the oven to 375F. Grease a 24-cup mini muffin tin with cooking spray.

For the crust;
1. Put the flour, walnuts, brown sugar substitute, 2 tablespoons butter, cornstarch, and salt into a mini food processor; pulse until the mix resembles coarse meal. Divide the crust mix between the muffin cups, about 1 1/4 teaspoons per cup; press evenly into the bottoms of the cups.

For the filling:
1. In a small-sized saucepan, combine the dates with the brown sugar substitute, water, and 2 1/2 tablespoons butter; bring to a boil on medium-high heat. Cook, frequently stirring, for about 8-12 minutes or till most of the liquid has evaporated. Let cool slightly, transfer the mix into a blender of a food processor; blend or process until the mix turns into a paste.
2. Add the cream cheese and then the vanilla; blend or process to combine. Transfer the mix medium-sized bowl. Stir in the pecans.
3. Divide the filling between the muffin cups, about 1 generous teaspoon per cup, pressing the filling down gently and smoothing the tops.
4. Bake for about 15-17 minutes or till the crust is golden brown and the filling is lightly cooked. Let cool in the muffin 10 for about 10 minutes. With a small spatula or with a butter knife, loose the edges and then transfer the

179

tassies onto a wire rack; let cool completely. Sprinkle the top with confectioner's sugar. If desired, serve with a dollop of whipped cream.

Notes: Store in airtight containers for up to 3 days or freeze for up to 3 months. For long-term freezing, wrap the loaf or slices or muffins with plastic wrap and then with foil.

Double Peanut Butter-Chocolate Chews

Prep Time: 30 minutes; **Cook Time:** 1 hour	
Serving Size: 22 g; **Serves:** 36; **Calories:** 96	
Total Fat: 7.4 g **Saturated Fat:** 1.5 g; **Trans Fat:** 0 g	
Protein: 2.6 g; **Net Carbs:** 4.8 g	
Total Carbs: 6.7 g; **Dietary Fiber:** 1.9 g; **Sugars:** 2.5 g	
Cholesterol: 10 mg; **Sodium:** 93 mg; **Potassium:** 42 mg;	
Vitamin A: 0%; **Vitamin C:** 0%; **Calcium:** 1%; **Iron:** 2%	

Ingredients:

- 1 cup peanut butter, natural, chunky
- 1 tablespoon vanilla extract
- 1 teaspoon baking soda
- 1/2 cup granulated sugar (equal amount Swerve sweetener)
- 1/2 cup packed dark brown sugar (mix 1/2 tablespoon molasses + 1/2 cup low carb sweetener)
- 1/2 teaspoon salt
- 1/3 cup cocoa powder, unsweetened
- 1/4 cup canola oil
- 1/4 cup rolled oats
- 1/4 cup semisweet chocolate chips
- 1/4 cup peanut butter chips, trans-fat-free
- 1/4 cup turbinado sugar (1/4 tablespoon molasses + 1/4 cup low carb sweetener)
- 2 large eggs
- 3 tablespoons yogurt, plain, low-fat
- 3/4 cup almond flour

Directions:

1. Preheat the oven to 350F.
2. Into the bowl of an electric mixer, beat the peanut butter with the granulated sugar substitute and the brown sugar substitute with the mixer speed on MEDIUM until the sugars are blended. Beat in the eggs, the yogurt, and the vanilla until combined.
3. In a medium-sized bowl, whisk the flour with the baking soda, oats, cocoa, and salt. With the mixer speed on LOW, gradually add the dry ingredients into the peanut butter mix until blended; the mix will be very sticky. Stir in the peanut butter and chocolate chips.
4. With a slightly rounded tablespoon measure or a small-sized cookie scoop, scoop dough into ungreased cookie sheets, placing them 2 inches apart.
5. Dip the bottom a glass in water and then in the turbinado sugar. With the sugared glass, slightly flatten the cookies, leaving a thin layer of sugar on top; as needed, re-wet the glass.
6. In batches, bake the cookies for about 8-10 minutes or till the tops appear cracked and cookies are set; do not over bake or the cookies will come out dry. Let cool for 2 minutes on the baking sheet; transfer onto a wire rack and let cool.

Notes: Make ahead of time; store into airtight containers and keep for up to 3 days or freeze for up to 3 months. For long-term freezing, wrap the loaf or slices or muffins with plastic wrap and then with foil.

Chocolate Chips Zucchini Bread

Prep Time: 2 hours; **Cook Time:** 15 minutes

Serving Size: 90 g; **Serves:** 12; **Calories:** 237

Total Fat: 9.3 g **Saturated Fat:** 2.3 g; **Trans Fat:** 0 g

Protein: 4.5 g; **Net Carbs:** 22.6 g

Total Carbs: 25.1 g; **Dietary Fiber:** 2.6 g; **Sugars:** 4.9 g

Cholesterol: 33 mg; **Sodium:** 124 mg; **Potassium:** 217 mg;

Vitamin A: 2%; **Vitamin C:** 5%; **Calcium:** 8%; **Iron:** 8%

Ingredients:

- ☐ 2 cups zucchini, shredded (about 2 small zucchini)
- ☐ 2 cups white whole-wheat flour
- ☐ 1/3 cup canola oil
- ☐ 1/2 teaspoon salt
- ☐ 1/2 cup chocolate chips
- ☐ 1 teaspoon vanilla extract
- ☐ 1 teaspoon ground cinnamon
- ☐ 2 large eggs
- ☐ 2 teaspoons baking powder
- ☐ 3/4 cup low-fat milk
- ☐ 3/4 cup sugar (equal amount Swerve sweetener)

Directions:

1. Preheat the oven to 350F. Grease a 5x9-inch loaf pan with cooking spray.
2. In a medium-sized bowl, whisk the milk with the eggs, oil, sugar substitute, and vanilla. Stir in the zucchini.
3. Inside a large-sized bowl, combine the flour with the baking powder, salt, and cinnamon.
4. Add the wet ingredients and the chocolate chips into the wet ingredients; stir till just combined. Transfer the batter into the greased pan.
5. Bake for about 50 minutes up to 1 hour or until golden brown and a wooden skewer come out clean when inserted in the center. Let the bread cool for10 minutes in the pa. Turn out on a wire rack and let cool for at least 1 hour. Slice in portions.

Notes: Make ahead of time; wrap and store for 2 days at most at room temperature or freeze for up to 3 months. For long-term freezing, wrap the loaf or slices or muffins with plastic wrap and then with foil.

Eggplant Parmesan

Prep Time: 2 hours, 30 minutes; **Cook Time:** 15 minutes	
Serving Size: 439 g; **Serves:** 8; **Calories:** 401	
Total Fat: 12.2 g **Saturated Fat:** 2.6 g; **Trans Fat:** 0 g	
Protein: 16.6 g; **Net Carbs:** 0 g	
Total Carbs: 58 g; **Dietary Fiber:** 13 g; **Sugars:** 17.8 g	
Cholesterol: 8 mg; **Sodium:** 1163 mg; **Potassium:** 395 mg;	
Vitamin A: 40%; **Vitamin C:** 29%; **Calcium:** 20%; **Iron:** 30%	

Ingredients:

- ☐ 2 eggplants (about 1 pound each), cut into 12 slices each
- ☐ 2 cans (28-ounce each) crushed tomatoes
- ☐ 2 1/2 cups whole-wheat breadcrumbs, fine dry
- ☐ 1 1/2 teaspoons kosher salt, divided
- ☐ 1 1/2 cups mozzarella cheese, part-skim, shredded, divided
- ☐ 3 tablespoons Italian seasoning, divided
- ☐ 3/4 cup liquid egg whites or 6 large egg whites
- ☐ 3/4 cup whole-wheat flour
- ☐ 4 tablespoons extra-virgin olive oil, divided
- ☐ 4 tablespoons Parmesan cheese, finely shredded divided
- ☐ Fresh basil, for garnish
- ☐ Olive oil cooking spray

Directions:

1. Put 2 layers paper towels on a cutting board or on a baking sheet. Put 1/2 of the slices of eggplants onto the paper towels; sprinkle with 3/4 teaspoon of salt. Cover with another 2 sheets paper towels; top with the remaining slices of eggplants and then sprinkle with the remaining 3/4 teaspoon of salt. Cover with 2 more sheets paper towel; let stand for 1 hour at room temperature.
2. Put the oven rack in the lower and the upper positions. Put a large-sized baking sheet onto each rack; preheat the oven to 425F.
3. Blot the slices of eggplant using more paper towels.
4. In a shallow dish, put the flour.
5. Put the egg whites in a different shallow dish.
6. In another shallow dish, combine the breadcrumbs with the 2 tablespoons Italian seasoning.
7. Dip each eggplant slice in the flour; shake off the excess. Dip in the egg; let excess drip off. Press into the breadcrumbs.
8. Remove the heated baking sheets from the oven; add 2 tablespoons of oil into, tilting them to coat. Put 1/2 of the breaded eggplant into1 baking sheet, placing them so that each slice do not touch. Put the other 1/2 breaded eggplant into the other baking sheet. Generously grease the tops of the breaded eggplant with cooking spray.
9. Bake for about 15 minutes; flip the slices over and bake for another 15 minutes or till golden brown.
10. In a medium sized bowl, combine the crushed tomatoes with the remaining 1 tablespoon of Italian seasoning.

To assemble:
1. Grease 2 pieces 8x8-inch baking dish with cooking spray.
2. Spread 1/2 cup tomato mix into each greased dish. Layer 6 eggplant slices over the tomato mix.

3. Spread with 1 cup tomato mix and then sprinkle with 1/4 cup of mozzarella cheese.
4. Top with a layer of 6 eggplant slices, 1 generous cup of tomato mix, 1/2 cup of mozzarella cheese, and then with 2 tablespoons of Parmesan cheese.
5. Bake for about 15 minutes or till the cheese is melted and the sauce is bubbling; if desired, garnish with basil.

Freezing: Let assembled, unbaked casseroles cool to room temperature. Tightly wrap each casserole with heavy-duty foil or with freezer paper and then freeze for up to 3 months. Grease the foil first with cooking spray to prevent them from sticking to the cheese.

When ready to cook, thaw for 2 days in the fridge. Remove the cover and bake at 400F for about 40-45 minutes.

Salmon Cakes with Lemon, Olives, and Dill

Prep Time: 30 minutes; **Cook Time:** 30 minutes		
Serving Size: 169 g; **Serves:** 8; **Calories:** 225		
Total Fat: 12.2 g **Saturated Fat:** 1.7 g; **Trans Fat:** 0 g		
Protein: 28 g; **Net Carbs:** 1.6 g		
Total Carbs: 2.5 g; **Dietary Fiber:** 0.9 g; **Sugars:** 0 g		
Cholesterol: 63 mg; **Sodium:** 287 mg; **Potassium:** 616 mg;		
Vitamin A: 6%; **Vitamin C:** 10%; **Calcium:** 9%; **Iron:** 11%		

Ingredients:
- 2 1/2 pounds wild salmon, skinned and then cut into 2-inch chunks
- 1/2 teaspoon salt
- 1/2 teaspoon freshly ground pepper
- 1/2 cup Kalamata olives, pitted
- 2 lemons, zested
- 3 tablespoons fresh dill or thyme, coarsely chopped
- 4 scallions, quartered
- 4 teaspoons extra-virgin olive oil, divided

Directions:
1. Put the olives, scallions, and dill/thyme into a food processor; pulse until chopped finely. Transfer the mix inside a large-sized bowl. Stir in the lemon zest, pepper, and salt.
2. Working in about 3-4 batches, pulse the salmon 2-3 times to chop finely; do not puree.
3. Transfer the chopped salmon into the olive mix; mix gently until combined.
4. Alternatively, you can finely chop the olives, scallions, herbs, and salmon by hands.
5. Divide the salmon mix into 8 portions, forming into 3-inch diameter, 3/4-inch thick patties. Chill for at least 20 minutes in the fridge up to 2 hours.
6. Inside a large-sized skillet, heat 2 teaspoons oil on medium heat. Put 4 salmon cakes into the skillet; cook for about 6-8 minutes total or until cooked through or both sides are browned. Repeat with the remaining oil and the remaining 4 salmon cakes.

Freezing: When cooked, let the salmon cakes cool completely. Individually wrap each with plastic wrap and then with foil; freeze for up to 3 months. When ready to serve, remove the plastic and the foil wraps. Reheat in a 450F oven for 20 minutes. Alternatively, you can wrap each with paper towel and microwave for about 2-3 minutes.

Conclusion

Ihope this book was able to help you to get started on successful meal prepping Journey. You now have the building blocks to go out and make healthy

Finally, if you enjoyed this book I'd like to ask you to leave a review for this book on Amazon, it would be greatly appreciated!

I am constantly looking for way to improve my content to give readers the best value so If you didn't like the book I would like to also hear from you:

Twitter: @JeremyStoneEat

Thank you and good luck,

Jeremy

http://www.shortcuttoketosis.com/

59777452R00104

Made in the USA
Lexington, KY
15 January 2017